Who Are My People?

CONTENDING MODERNITIES

Series editors: Ebrahim Moosa, Atalia Omer, and Scott Appleby

As a collaboration between the Contending Modernities initiative and the University of Notre Dame Press, the Contending Modernities series seeks, through publications engaging multiple disciplines, to generate new knowledge and greater understanding of the ways in which religious traditions and secular actors encounter and engage each other in the modern world. Books in this series may include monographs, co-authored volumes, and tightly themed edited collections.

The series will include works that frame such encounters through the lens of "modernity." The range of themes treated in the series might include war, peace, human rights, nationalism, refugees and migrants, development practice, pluralism, religious literacy, political theology, ethics, multi- and intercultural dynamics, sexual politics, gender justice, and postcolonial and decolonial studies.

WHO ARE MY PEOPLE?

Love, Violence, and Christianity
in Sub-Saharan Africa

EMMANUEL KATONGOLE

University of Notre Dame Press
Notre Dame, Indiana

This book is made possible in part by support from
the Institute for Scholarship in the Liberal Arts,
College of Arts and Letters, University of Notre Dame.

Published in the United States of America

Paperback edition published in 2023

Library of Congress Control Number: 2021948631

ISBN: 978-0-268-20256-9 (Hardback)
ISBN: 978-0-268-20257-6 (Paperback)
ISBN: 978-0-268-20258-3 (WebPDF)
ISBN: 978-0-268-20255-2 (Epub)

CONTENTS

Acknowledgments   ix

Introduction   1

PART I.   WHO ARE MY PEOPLE? PHILOSOPHICAL AND
THEOLOGICAL REFLECTIONS

1   On Being an African   11

2   On Being an African Christian: The Journey of   33
Christian Identity

PART II.   LOVE'S INVENTION IN THE MIDST OF AFRICA'S
VIOLENT MODERNITY

3   Ethnic Violence and the Reinvention of Identity   67

4   Religious Violence and the Reinvention of Politics   99

5   Ecological Violence and the Reinvention of Land   131

Conclusion: The Logic of the Cross   171

Afterword: A New We—on Being Some Kind of Catholic: 181
A Sermon

Notes   189

Bibliography   203

Index   213

ACKNOWLEDGMENTS

While writing can be a lonely project, a book is never the product of a single individual. In the process of writing *Who Are My People?* I have benefited from the generosity and support of many people and institutions. They are too many to name here, but allow me to single out a few. One individual about whom I can genuinely say that without him this book would not have been written is Scott Appleby, the dean of the Keough School of Global Affairs at Notre Dame. When Scott hired me at Notre Dame (2012), it was through the Contending Modernities Project, which Scott had established as a research cluster within the Kroc Institute for International Peace Studies, of which he was the director. Scott also invited me to be the convener of the Africa Working Group on Authority, Community, and Identity within the Contending Modernities Project. I thank him for encouraging me to write this book in the first place, for his ongoing interest in the topic, for his generous support for the project with funding from the Contending Modernities Project, and for his feedback and helpful recommendations on the draft of the manuscript. Scott is not only my dean but a friend, and I am grateful for his and Barbara's warm friendship. I thank all my colleagues at the Kroc Institute and my colleagues in the Department of Theology at Notre Dame for their collegial support. I am especially grateful to Asher Kaufman and to Tim Matovina for their exemplary leadership and support, which has allowed me to claim both the Kroc Institute and the Theology Department as "home." I owe a debt of gratitude to my colleagues at the Contending Modernities Project: Mun'im Sirry, Moosa Ebrahim, Atalia Omer, Kyle Lemberet, and especially Dania Maria Straughan, the program manager, for her support for me during the research and in the process of writing, as well as for helping me to coordinate the Africa Working Group. Before Dania, James Adams and Paola Bernardini were instrumental in setting up and coordinating the working group. I am grateful to them. I am especially grateful to the members of the Africa Working Group, Cecila Lynch, Elias Bongmba, Ludovic Lado, and Ebenezer Obadare, for their encouragement, support, and numerous conversations. From them and with them, I have learned a lot about the changing patterns of authority, community, and identity in Africa that are at the heart of the argument of *Who Are My People?*

The argument and outline of the book were first worked out through the 2017 Annual Martyn Lloyd-Jones Memorial Lectures at Cambridge University in the United Kingdom. I am grateful to the Reverend Jesse Link, then director of the Cambridge Center for Christianity World-Wide, for the honor and invitation to deliver the lectures. I am also grateful for the helpful feedback and recommendations from various audiences with whom I have shared sections of the book: at the Kellogg Institute Faculty Workshop, the Kroc Institute PRES, the African Studies Association Annual Convention, various graduate seminars at Notre Dame, the African Theological Advance Project, the Lund Workshop on Christianity as Politics in Africa, and the Department of Literature, History of Ideas and Religion at the University of Gothenburg. I am grateful for the organizers and for all my hosts at these different programs and institutions, most especially to Arne Rasmusson for the weeklong visiting professorship at the University of Gothenburg.

Most of the research and writing of the first draft of the book was realized during a year of sabbatical leave that was made possible by the Association of Theological Schools (ATS) and the Henry Luce Foundation. I am grateful to Stephen Graham and Jonathan Vanantwerpen and their staff at ATS and at Luce respectively for the sabbatical. I am also grateful to my colleagues in this final class of Henry Luce III Fellows in Theology for their interest in my project and for the lively conversations and discussions. Besides Contending Modernities, other units at Notre Dame supported this project. I am grateful to the Kellogg Institute for a grant that enabled me to travel to and conduct research in Uganda, Rwanda, Kenya, Benin, and the Central African Republic.

Different colleagues and graduate students have read and commented on drafts of the chapters and have given me helpful feedback. To them I am grateful. A special debt of gratitude to Stan Ilo, Jay Carney, Atalia Omer, Ebrahim Moosa, the members of the Contending Modernities Africa Working Group, and the reviewers solicited by the University of Notre Dame Press. I am grateful to those who coordinated my travel to and within the countries where I did the research for the book and those who coordinated the various interviews. I am especially grateful to Soh Keugne Nouthak Jules Martial, S.J., and Barwendé Médard Sané, S.J., in the Central African Republic, and to Blandine at the Songhai Center in Benin. I am grateful to all those who agreed to be interviewed, and most especially to those whose life and work I profile in this book: Maggy Barankitse, Godfrey Nzamujo, Jean Baptiste Mvukiyehe, Father Anthony, Bernard Kinvi, Imam Omar Kobine Layama, and others. Thank you for the many hours of conversation, and most importantly for the witness you provide about the possibility of a different modernity in Africa. To research assistants Marie-Claire Klassen, Josephine, and Nnadozie I am grateful. Thanks also to Amanda Rooker and Katherine at SplitSeed for your editorial support. I am grateful to the team at the University of Notre Dame Press for all their labor in turning the manuscript into a book. Finally, I am grateful to my family and friends, here in the US, in Uganda, and around the world. Your love and friendship not only keep me grounded, they have brought me to a new sense of who my people are. On Epiphany Sunday, January 2019, my mother passed from this life. I miss her a lot, but I know that she lives on and continues to cover me with her motherly love, protection, and prayers. To her and her indomitable spirit this book is dedicated.

Emmanuel Katongole
Notre Dame
November 1, 2020
All Saints Day

Introduction

Who Are My People? has been slow in coming. The questions that sparked it and the issues of identity it addresses were first raised in the wake of the 1994 Rwanda Genocide. In the spring of 1994, as the genocide was under way, a fellow graduate student at KU Leuven in Belgium asked me, "Why do you Africans kill your own people?" Around the same time, a continent away in Rwanda, Cardinal Etchegaray asked the Rwandan Christian leaders, "Is the blood of tribalism deeper than the waters of baptism?"[1] *Who Are My People?* grapples with these two questions and the complex philosophical, theological, and practical assumptions behind them. Even though I am addressing directly for the first time questions that have been with me since 1994, readers familiar with my work might recognize some stories and arguments that I have rehearsed in my previous work. However, the overall argument I make in this book is new, and this is the first time that I explicitly engage the question of the relationship between identity, Christianity, and violence in Africa. This also means that even though the questions that sparked this investigation arose in relation to the 1994 Rwanda Genocide, this is not a book about Rwanda.

Who Are My People? is first and foremost about identity, more specifically about what it means to be an "African" and a "Christian." I do not engage this question in the abstract but grapple with my own identity as an African and as a Christian. The goal is to explore the journey that this complex identity has made possible, the challenges that I find myself constantly negotiating, and the resources I have found helpful in conceptualizing and living through that complex identity. At the risk of prematurely letting the cat out of the bag, these resources have been mostly of two kinds. The first kind has been scholarly and intellectual. In working through the various theoretical questions connected to what it means to be an "African" and an "African Christian" I have found myself drawing on and engaging other scholars, both philosophers and theologians, whose work I have found illuminating. Through my engagement with them and their theoretical frameworks, I have come to a better understanding not only of 1994 Rwanda but of other manifestations of violence on the African continent. Moreover, engaging different scholars has provided some useful handles for understanding and articulating the complex issue of identity, as it has offered images and metaphors that help to capture the sense of journey that lies at the heart of any conception of identity, African Christian identity in particular.

The second set of resources has been stories. While I of course do not assume a clear dichotomy between theoretical work and stories, in engaging the complex issues raised by the two questions that sparked this investigation, I have found myself being drawn to and engaging a variety of stories: the "story" of modernity in Africa, the stories of victims and perpetrators of violence, and the stories of communities and individuals who are able to resist violence and thus "testify" to a different— nonviolent—way of living within the reality of modern Africa. I am particularly interested in this latter group of stories—about those who resist violence—for it is especially these individuals and communities that have led me to *see* and have confidence in the possibility of a different modernity in Africa. What is particularly significant is that the "seeing" has not been merely academic, merely a philosophical grasping or mental elucidation. It is at the same time a constant invitation to discover and live into a new sense of community, to risk new forms of "belonging" that are not premised on a static sense of identity. It is an ongoing journey and practical commitments that assume and "invent" an ever-expanding sense of "my people." In the end, this is what *Who Are My People?* is about.

On a theoretical level, *Who Are My People?* is a book about the difference Christianity makes in the context of violence in Africa. At the heart of the two questions that sparked this investigation is the reality of prevalent violence on the African continent, a continent that has also been hailed as the new center of Christian faith. *Who Are My People?* explores the complex relationship between identity, violence, and Christianity in Africa. As I have wrestled with the contradictions in this relationship, what has emerged is a clear conviction that a crisis, what I describe as "a crisis of belonging," lies at the heart of modern Africa. The recurrent forms of violence, of which the 1994 Rwanda Genocide is an example and a metaphor,[2] reflect this ongoing crisis in postcolonial Africa. In *Who Are My People?*, I trace the crisis of belonging through three key markers of modern African identity: ethnicity, religion, and land. On the surface, "ethnicity," "religion," and "land/village" might seem to be associated with a traditional and one might say "tribal" outlook, and a number of enthusiasts of modernization continue to see recurrent patterns of violence, religious warfare, and land conflicts in Africa as confirming the persistence of atavist, primitive, tribal, and ethnic forms of belonging in Africa. The way forward, according to those who subscribe to this view, are processes and institutions that help Africa become more modern.[3] My contention in *Who Are My People?* is that Africa is already very modern. Ethnicity, religion, and land operate in a unique and very modern way in Africa today. The issue has to do with understanding the unique modernity that these markers of identity are now inscribed in and help to advance. Accordingly, while much of the violence in Africa may be easily labeled "ethnic" or "religious" or "tribal," what is at stake quite often is a set of modern goals and ambitions that have to do with belonging and access to the social, political, economic, and cultural institutions of modern Africa. Understood from this ongoing crisis of belonging, ethnic violence, religious warfare, and land conflicts in Africa constitute, not three separate forms of violence, but modalities—a better word might be "echoes"—of the same crisis of belonging. Since my primary interest is theological, the question that drives my investigation in *Who Are My People?* is: Can Christian theology illumine Africa's crisis of belonging? Can Christianity in Africa, Christian identity in particular, offer resources with which to navigate in nonviolent ways this uniquely modern crisis of belonging in Africa, or does it simply radiate and amplify the crisis, as often seems to be the case? I argue that Christian theology, to be helpful, needs to point to stories and provide images and metaphors that illumine Christian identity as a journey that fosters new forms of community. Such forms of community defy static notions of identity and engender nonviolent agency and new economic and ecological possibilities in modern Africa.

Who Are My People? is also about competing notions of identity and community in Africa. Since I joined the University of Notre Dame in 2013, I have been part of its Contending Modernities Research Project. An interdisciplinary research effort, Contending Modernities seeks to generate knowledge on how religious and secular forces interact in the modern world. As part of this project, I was invited to convene and lead a research team to investigate ways in which secular and religious forces at times compete and collide, and at other times collaborate and implicate each other, in shaping notions of authority, community, and identity in Africa. When considered in this context, *Who Are My People?* confirms that in Africa (as elsewhere) the "secular" and the "religious" are not two separate spheres but "stories" that are shaped by and in turn help to shape ("invent") different visions of identity and different forms of community. The overall argument I provide in *Who Are My People?* is that the ongoing crisis of identity in modern Africa reflects and is driven by a story or set of stories that shape a unique modernity on the continent, within which violence is a recurrent and recognizable pattern.

Finally, *Who Are My People?* is about the "invention" of love in Africa. A key assumption behind the book is that Christianity is, in its essence, a story: the story of God's love manifested in God's creation, God's providence, and God's self-sacrificing love on the cross. The power of this story lies not only in resisting violence and healing its wounds but in shaping a new sense of self, a new sense of community ("my people"), and a new social order infused with love. The stories of the individuals and communities I explore in this book confirm that this invention of love is not simply a utopian dream or a *mere spiritual* idea; it is a concrete social reality in the world. In the end, this invention of love is the antidote to Africa's violent modernity. This is the argument of *Who Are My People?*

My investigation of African violence, identity, and the antidote of love is developed in five chapters spread over two parts. Part One, the shorter and more theoretical, has two chapters that deal directly with the philosophical and theological issues triggered by the two questions that were raised for me in the wake of the Rwanda Genocide. Chapter 1 ("On Being an African") recounts my journey of philosophical inquiry into the issue of African identity. The question in this chapter, "Why do you Africans always kill your own people?," led me to the work of Valery Mudimbe, Anthony Appiah, and Ali Mazrui in an attempt to understand the complex issue of African identity—what it means to be "African." The combined insights from these scholars confirm a crisis—"the crisis of African emergence into modernity"[4]—which gives rise not only to a unique view of what "Africa" is and who "Africans" are but also to an "invention" of a continent marked by major paradoxes and contradictions. African identity, therefore, is not a reflection of a metaphysical essence or some biological, geographical, or cultural oneness. Rather, it is the result of the way that Africa and Africans have been, and continue to be, imagined through contact with other civilizations, especially modern Europe. In this connection one can speak, following Mudimbe and Mazrui, of the "invention" of Africa.

Chapter 2 ("On Being an African Christian") deals with the question of African Christian identity and its relation to other identities. Cardinal Etchegaray's haunting question, "Is the blood of tribalism deeper than waters of baptism?," leads me to engage various African scholars to discover ways in which the issue of African Christian identity in general, of what it means to be both an "African" and a "Christian" in particular, has been treated within African theology. I discover that theologians have tended to view Christian identity either as a static "spiritual" essence that "transcends" the realities (politics, economics) of everyday life or as an identity that builds on one's "natural" (African, ethnic) identity. I argue that both these approaches fall short of an adequate understanding of Christian identity as a journey. I reflect on my own journey and use the work of Miroslav Volf, Virgilio Elizondo, and Andrew Walls to suggest images that illustrate African Christian identity as a journey whose goal is the formation of a new people (a "new we") in the world.

In Part Two, the discussion of "Love's Invention" is distributed over three chapters. In each of the chapters, I examine a form of violence within the story of modern Africa. I also explore stories of Christian individuals and communities whose lives and agency do not fully "fit" within the larger narrative of a violent modern Africa. These people and communities not only resist the violence but are determined to heal its wounds and the "burden of history" shaped by Africa's unique modernity. In doing so, they invent new forms of identity, new communities, and a new relationship with the land. Such invention, I argue, is made possible by the story of God's love, within which they locate their lives and agency. Thus, in chapter 3 ("Ethnic Violence and the Reinvention of Identity"), against the background of the story of the "invention" of tribe and ethnicity that made the 1994 genocide thinkable, the stories of the students of Nyange and the community of Ruhango offer examples of the kind of love necessary to resist violence, heal its wounds, and ultimately heal "the burden of ethnicity." The story of Maggy Barankitse's work at the Oasis of Peace Center in Kigali confirms that healing this burden is at the same time an invitation into a "new we," made possible by God's self-sacrificing love, which is extended to all, especially the wounded victims of Africa's endless succession of regimes of violence.

Chapter 4 ("Religious Violence and the Reinvention of Politics") examines the 2013 "religious war" between Muslims and Christians in the Central African Republic (CAR) and argues that this violence is intelligible only within the story that created and drives CAR and its politics. Fr. Bernard Kinvi's practice of welcoming refugees (both Christians and Muslims) at the mission hospital in Bossemptele during the war points to an altogether different politics than that which drives CAR. Kinvi's politics, shaped by his vocation as a Camillian priest, are based on the same story of God's self-sacrificing love.

Chapter 5 ("Ecological Violence and the Reinvention of Land") examines the manifestations of Africa's ecological crisis and depicts them as instances of "slow violence."[5] The depth of Africa's ecological violence, the chapter argues, becomes intelligible only within the context of a modern outlook that rejects a connection with, and belonging to, the land (African native spirituality) as "primitive" and "backward" and promotes an artificial model of development economics focused on progress and development. The latter, however, has resulted not only in environmental degradation but in the ensnaring of millions of Africans within the "trap of poverty." The story of Godfrey Nzamujo and the Songhai

Center in Benin offers a model of integral development that can reduce poverty, protect creation, and restore human dignity in Africa. The secret behind Songhai's promise is its spirituality, which is grounded in a return to the deep connection and belonging to the land, and which Nzamujo has discovered through his Dominican spirituality.

A note about the research behind *Who Are My People?* In the process of writing this book I have read and engaged a number of scholars and theoretical frameworks (more evidently, but not exclusively, in Part One). I have also carried out extensive interviews and structured conversations in Uganda, Rwanda, Kenya, CAR, and Benin. The decision to engage in ethnographic research was motivated by a number of objectives. The first was to advance *Who Are My People?* as an interdisciplinary inquiry. As mentioned, this book is part of the Contending Modernities Project, through which I have been fortunate to collaborate with colleagues across multiple disciplines, including social scientists, around the issues of authority, community, and identity. Encouraged by these colleagues, as well as those at the Kroc Institute for International Peace Studies, many of whom employ social science research methodologies, I experimented with ethnographic inquiry. I did so because I wanted *Who Are My People?* to be, not a merely speculative argument, but an argument supported by empirical evidence.

Second, I wanted to refine and advance a methodology I had been developing, following Lawrence-Lightfoot, of theological portraiture as a distinct method of inquiry and storytelling.[6] Although theological portraiture shares a number of features with other qualitative research methods, such as ethnography, case study, and narrative, what makes it distinctive is its "blending of aesthetics and empiricism in an effort to capture the complexity, dynamics, and subtlety of human experience and organizational life."[7] Another distinctive element is that the portraitist is not simply *listening to a story* but *listening for a story*, being actively engaged in searching out for, and identifying the patterns of, an underlying story.[8] When I interviewed and conversed with select activists, I needed to *listen to* their stories to capture their intricacies, but I was also *listening for* a story, tracing the extent to which their lives and agency were grounded in and reflected a different account of belonging. The hope was that out of the interviews and conversations I would be able to build rich portraits that would testify to the possibility of nonviolent ways of living in modern Africa. I leave it to the reader to decide how successful my efforts have been. But I hope that the conversational and journalistic style and the portraits I provide make my argument and the book in general not only accessible but also engaging, and not only informative but also inspiring.

PART I

WHO ARE MY PEOPLE?
Philosophical and Theological Reflections

CHAPTER 1

On Being an African

Europe's supreme gift was the gift of African identity, bequeathed without grace or design—but a reality all the same.
                                                                    —Ali Mazrui

When the genocide broke out in Rwanda in the spring of 1994, I had been living in Belgium for almost three years. Having finished my master's in philosophical ethics, I was just starting my PhD research on moral rationality at the KU Leuven Hoger Instituut voor Wijsbegeerteat (Higher Institute of Philosophy). I was living at the Heilig Geest College, formerly a seminary for Flemish seminarians, which had been turned into a residence hall and housed a number of foreign priests, mostly from Africa, India, and the Philippines. The fact that Rwanda was a former Belgian colony and that ten Belgian UN soldiers had been killed at the start of the genocide meant that the event received extensive coverage in the Belgian press. At the Heilig Geest College we had one television set in the common room, where a number of us foreign priests and a few Belgian students gathered to watch the news. As the genocide unfolded, we watched in silent disbelief as bodies of Rwandan children, women, and men floated in rivers, piled up in churches, and decomposed by the roadside.

It was not just the speed and efficiency of the killing (in less than a hundred days, close to a million people were killed, mostly using machetes, sticks, and rudimentary weapons) that baffled us into silence, but

11

also its intimacy. Neighbors killed neighbors, family members killed family members, priests and the religious killed members of their congregations and the other way round. There was very little to say; we could only watch in stunned silence as the brutality and inhumanity of the genocide raised questions about the sacredness of human life and even what it meant to be human. The genocide also raised doubts about global human community and solidarity, as we saw scenes of hundreds of Rwandans seeking protection at various Western embassies and compounds, only to be abandoned to the Interahamwe militias as foreign governments evacuated their nationals. Barely fifty years after 147 states had vowed "never again" and signed the Genocide Convention, the world turned a blind eye on Rwanda. The reason, it would become increasingly clear, was that Rwanda was an African country of little strategic interest to Western governments. Are there any bonds of community and society that transcend national interests, I wondered?

But the genocide also raised a number of questions about Africa: about ethnicity and community in Africa, about recurrent patterns of violence across the continent, about the so-called African traditional values of communality and solidarity, and ultimately, about what it means to be an African. Kurian, an Indian priest friend enrolled in the same PhD program as I was, turned to me one evening as we were heading out of the common room after watching the news from Rwanda and asked, "Why do your people always kill each other like this?" I was not sure whether "your people" in Kurian's question referred to Rwandans, Hutus, or Africans. Kurian might have sensed my hesitation, and so he clarified, "I mean, why do you Africans always kill your own people?"

I was deeply troubled by the question. As if the images of the genocide were not enough, here was another example of Afro-pessimism, I thought to myself, this time coming not from the usual suspects, Western racists and bigots, but from an Indian! What did he know about Africa? Where in Africa had he been? On what basis could he generalize from a case of genocide happening in one country to "Africans"? He probably thinks Africa is one village, or one country. I wanted to fight back, but all I could muster at that time was a more measured response. "Not all of Africa is having genocide," I told Kurian. But the question continued to haunt me in ways that, looking back, I see have driven my scholarship. For I now realize that most of my work has been an attempt to understand the nature and recurrent patterns of violence in modern Africa.[1] This attempt culminated in *The Sacrifice of Africa*, in which I traced the violence in Africa to what I called the imaginative landscape of Western modernity on the continent. I argued that the prevailing forms of violence in Africa are not merely hangovers from Africa's primitive or premodern past (reflecting ancient hatreds between tribes) but a modern phenomenon that has partly to do with the stories that shape modern Africa, and thus the stories with which modern Africans live. These stories are embedded within and help to sustain the modern institutions of politics, education, and economics in Africa. As Patrick Chabal and Jean-Pascal Daloz argue, violence, disorder, and corruption are not the exception.[2] They are the way modern Africa works. What I sought to make clear in *The Sacrifice of Africa*, drawing on the work of scholars like Benedict Anderson and William Cavanaugh, is that this "imagining" of Africa has greatly to do with the stories that justified and informed Europe's modern (that is colonial) project on the African continent.[3] I argue that even though colonialism has officially ended in Africa, the nation-state (the successor political institution as well as its related economic and social institutions in modern Africa) still operates out of the same imaginary that there is "nothing good out of Africa." Wired within the architectural foundations of modern Africa, this story supports the ongoing devaluation and sacrificing of African lives by fellow Africans. For this reason I claim in *The Sacrifice of Africa* that what is required, even more than the usual attempts to stem violence in Africa, is a fresh social imagination of Africa and of Africans. We need another imaginary, and for this, another and better story.

However, beyond the immediate questions of the 1994 violence, Kurian's question helped to bring into sharper focus some of the questions I was already having about African identity. What does it mean to be African? What is it that I share with other Africans that makes them "my people" more than any history, friendship, or relationship with Europeans or Americans could ever make them "my people"? Is it the color of my skin, history, geography, or culture that makes me naturally, and thus without effort, allied to other "Africans" more than to a Belgian or Norwegian? What does it mean to belong to a group of people called

Africans? On one level, these were philosophical questions, the kind of questions that only a scholar would raise. On another level, however, they were existential questions, for being "African" was not only a speculative question for me but a fact of everyday life. When people saw me on the streets or in the classroom at Leuven, they saw me, treated me, and related to me as an African.

Related to my being "African" were further questions of identity connected to the association of "Africa" with "tribes." Whenever I would introduce myself as from Uganda, people would sooner or later ask, "What is your tribe?" For more than personal reasons, I always had problems with the word *tribe*.[4] Some of these objections were confirmed by the Rwanda Genocide. The standard way the genocide was explained was in terms of "age-old animosities" between Hutu and Tutsi tribes, which had now exploded into "ethnic" violence. But whatever notion of a tribe one has, Hutus and Tutsis did not seem to fit within the usual notion of "tribe." They spoke the same language; shared the same culture, history, and religion; and were closely intermarried. In fact, as the missionary Louis de Lacger said of Rwandans in the 1950s, "There are few people in Europe among whom one finds these three factors of national cohesion: one language, one faith, one law."[5] What then is a tribe and what is tribal identity, I found myself asking afresh. Again, the question was not simply speculative. I had a personal interest in it. My parents had migrated from Rwanda in the late 1940s and settled in Uganda, where I was born. Whenever I told this story, some of my friends would say, "But that means you are *really* Rwandan." All they wanted to know was whether I was Hutu or Tutsi. But since one of my parents was Hutu and the other Tutsi, I was always left wondering, "What is my tribe? Am I Hutu or Tutsi?" I did not speak Kinyarwanda and had been to Rwanda only once, when I was a child. What was it then that made me *really* Rwandan, and Ugandan only superficially, I wondered. Who am I, and who are my people, anyway?

As I struggled with this identity crisis and sought answers, I took interest in the work of other African scholars who had also pondered the question of "Africa" and "African identity." Three scholars whose work I found particularly helpful in sorting through the jumble of ideas of what it means to be African are Valentin Mudimbe, Ali Mazrui, and Anthony

Appiah. By briefly sketching what I found illuminating about the work of each of these scholars in my attempt to grapple with the question of "African" identity, I will provide an outline of the processes and assumptions that have led to a particular vision of "Africa" and "Africans" in modern history. My interest here is to offer the reader, not a comprehensive discussion and assessment of these authors' works, which obviously lies outside the scope of this book, but a sense of the scholarly journey that led me to the realization that identities are not things or entities grounded in an enduring essence. Identities have to do more with imagination. Accordingly, "African" identity (not unlike "tribal" or "ethnic" identity) is not a reflection of some metaphysical essence or some biological, geographical, or cultural oneness. Rather, it is the way that Africa and Africans have been *imagined* (by others and by themselves), and of the shared history shaped by this imagining. Moreover, since "African" identity is not a static thing or essence, there are many ways of being an African, largely related to who one is and where, when, and how one finds oneself located in the story of Africa. In the end, then, what we need is not so much a definition of "African" identity as stories that depict helpful and not-so-helpful, violent and nonviolent ways of negotiating the limits and possibilities of any identity, in this case "African" identity.

Mudimbe on the Idea of "Africa"

It was the Congolese-born philosopher, novelist, and literary critic Valentin Mudimbe who first helped me see that "Africa" was not so much a place as a concept, not so much a geographic designation as an idea. I discovered Mudimbe around the time of the Rwanda Genocide, having first encountered his work in a PhD seminar on phenomenology. He is widely considered the Edward Said of African studies, and his *The Invention of Africa* is as significant to the field of African studies as Said's *Orientalism* has been to postcolonial studies. Even though, with his background in classic literature and French poststructuralism, Mudimbe's writing is not always easy to follow, I found his central argument and insights illuminating.

Mudimbe's central concerns are conceptual and methodological, or, more fundamentally, epistemological. He is interested in the way "Africa" is represented in a variety of texts and discourses, and he seeks to explore the epistemological context that makes possible a particular discourse on Africa at a given time and place. Until relatively recently, Mudimbe notes, these discourses originated outside Africa, primarily in Europe. These representations have been integral to the history of Europe's expansion and quest for imperial power: that is, they are associated with the slave trade and institutions of slavery in the Americas, with colonial conquest, and with Christian missionary activity. Thus for Mudimbe the representations of African cultures and societies found in the writings of various early explorers, missionaries, merchants, travelers, and European armchair commentators are dominated by the need to present Africa in a particular way so as to bolster the European colonial adventure in Africa, which Mudimbe describes as a tripartite project of conversion. The three parties to this project were first the missionaries, who claimed that Christianity would bring "true light" to local tradition. Second was the colonial administration, whose aim was to convert "savage spaces" into "civilized" ones. The third partner was the newly founded discipline of anthropology, designed to codify local human behavior and institutions in the colonies.

It is in this sense that Mudimbe speaks of the "invention" of Africa—imagining Africa as the other of Europe. This imagination plays a double role in the European project. First, the "discovery" of a dark, pagan, and barbaric Africa confirms Europe's own identity as enlightened, Christian, and civilized. Hegel's view of an Africa without a history is most often mentioned in the literature, but the phenomenon was much more general.[6]

Second, to confirm the European sense of mission, "The West," Mudimbe notes, "created the 'pagan' in order to 'Christianize,' 'underdevelopment' in order to 'develop,' the 'primitive' in order to engage in 'anthropology' and 'civilize.'"[7] This is also what makes "Africa" more of an "idea" than a place.[8] One gets this sense of the "idea" of Africa when asking a European if they have been to Africa and receiving a reply like "I have been to Egypt, but have never been to real Africa." The first time I visited South Africa, I was surprised when I encountered many South

Africans talking about going to, or never having been to, Africa (that is, north of the Limpopo River). Some of these were the same people who on other occasions would insist they were "Africans"! In both instances the implication was that real Africa, "Africa proper," as Hegel had put it, was a "dark" and primitive continent "lying beyond the day of self-conscious history."[9]

This is neither the time nor the occasion to critically engage Mudimbe's work,[10] but one clear takeaway from it is that "Africa" emerges in the post-Enlightenment European imagination and discourse as disabled, deficient, and lacking—lacking religion, history, civilization, development, democracy, human rights, and ethics. Achille Mbembe was later to make the same observation when he noted that the African human experience constantly appears in the discourse of our time as understandable only through a negative interpretation: "Africa is never seen as possessing things and attributes properly part of 'human nature.' Or, when it is, its things and attributes are generally of lesser value, little importance, and poor quality. It is this elementariness and primitiveness that makes Africa the world par excellence of all that is incomplete, mutilated, and unfinished, its history reduced to a series of setbacks of nature in its quest for humankind."[11]

Edward Said would make a similar point about the Orient in *Orientalism*.[12] But while Said would insist that the Orient does not exist and has never existed outside the imagination of the West, Mudimbe, even without saying so explicitly, seems to suggest that the invention of Africa is a self-fulfilling prophecy. The imagination of a dark, primitive, and underdeveloped Africa succeeds in inventing the very continent that is imagined.

Stanley Hauerwas, the American theologian and ethicist, whose work I was investigating for my PhD dissertation, had already helped me to see how stories shape not only personal identity but also the world in which we live. To understand the characters or identities formed within a given politics, Hauerwas had argued, it is important to understand the stories that shape that politics, especially what is assumed "in the beginning."[13] Later, I was to confirm this conclusion in relation to Rwanda by examining the Hamitic mythology that had been used to colonize and evangelize Rwanda (defining Hutu as "natives" and Tutsi as "foreigners").

As the Hamitic story of separate origins was used to describe people who spoke the same language, lived on the same hills, and had the same culture, it succeeded in forming a political community (modern Rwanda) where Tutsi and Hutu actually became separate communities, united in their hatred of each other.[14] But that was to come later. At this stage of my intellectual development, during my graduate studies, the full implications of Mudimbe's work would only gradually become clear. The work of Ali Mazrui was helpful in this development, as it confirmed that while modern Europeans were not the first ones to know and relate to Africa, there was something unique about the modern encounter between Europe and Africa, an encounter that would not only result in the "invention" of modern Africa but shape the processes, contradictions, and institutions that constitute what we can call Africa's unique modernity.

Mazrui on the Ongoing Invention of Africa

Once described by Kofi Annan, the former UN secretary-general, as "Africa's gift to the world," Ali Mazrui was named in 2005 by *Foreign Policy* and *The Prospect* as one of the world's top one hundred public intellectuals.[15] I had been a great admirer of Ali Mazrui ever since I first watched his popular BBC series *The Africans: A Triple Heritage* in 1990. In the series, Mazrui comments on the history, geography, and culture of Africa, discusses native, Arab, and Western influences on the continent, and provides penetrating insights and anecdotes on African politics, sports, and religion as well as other aspects of life on the continent. I had since read and used some of his work in my courses and was very much looking forward to meeting him in person, but that was not to happen. In the process of my putting together a research team on the issues of authority, community, and identity in Africa in the Contending Modernities Project, he and I corresponded, and I invited him to speak at Notre Dame. At that time, he was at the State University of New York. He agreed and came to speak at Notre Dame in 2013. However, the day before he came to campus, a medical emergency took me to hospital, so I missed both his visit and talk. He passed the following year.

In 2005, Mazrui wrote a very influential essay, "The Reinvention of Africa," which provides helpful insight on the ongoing imagination of Africa. In the essay, commenting on the work of Mudimbe, Mazrui notes that "Africa" (how Africa has been defined) is the product of its interaction with other civilizations, not simply Europe. These interactions are partly reflected in the name "Africa."

> Some have traced the name to Berber origins; others have traced it to a Graeco-Roman ancestry. The ancient Romans referred to their colonial province in present-day Tunisia and eastern Algeria as "Africa," possibly because the name came from a Latin or Greek word for that region or its people, or perhaps because it came from one of the local languages of that region—either Berber or Phoenician. Here are the origins of the invention of Africa. Did the Romans call the continent after the Latin word *Aprica* (meaning "sunny")? Or were the Romans and the Greeks using the Greek word *Aphrike* (meaning "without cold")? Or did the name come from the Semites (Phoenicians) referring to the productivity of what is today Tunisia—a term that means "Ears of Corn"? Later the Arab immigrants Arabized the name into *Ifriqiya*.[16]

According to Mazrui's 2005 essay, the history of the external conceptualization of Africa has had five phases. The first phase regarded North Africa as an extension of Europe and the rest of Africa as an empire of barbarism and darkness. The second phase was defined by the interaction with the Semitic people and with classical Greece and Rome. This was the era when Christianity as a Semitic religion spread across North Africa and into Ethiopia. The third phase involved the birth of Islam on the Arab peninsula and its expansion into Africa. At this stage, which lasted for several centuries, much of West Africa was the product of two civilizations—indigenous African culture and Islam. This duality included the great empires of Mali (ca. 1230 to 1670) and Songhai (ca. 1325 to 1591), with Timbuktu as the most historically significant city produced by the two empires. The fourth historical phase involved the Western impact in the late eighteenth and nineteenth centuries, which coincided with European colonialism—a crucially significant phase whose effect was the making of modern Africa as a product of a dialogue between three civilizations: African, Islamic, and Western. The convergence is what constitutes Africa's "triple heritage," which was the subject of Mazrui's 1986 BBC television series, *The Africans: A Triple Heritage*. The fifth phase of the historical conceptualization of Africa was the realization that the continent was the birthplace of the human species. Africa thus became the Garden of Eden and a major stream in world civilization. A transition occurred from Africa's triple heritage to the paradigm of Afrocentricity—and from the Dark Continent to the Garden of Eden. "This final paradigm," in Mazrui's opinion, "globalizes Africa itself."[17]

In identifying these phases, Mazrui not only confirms Mudimbe's insight of the "idea" of Africa but shows that "Africa" is not a static notion or concept but an ongoing reality that is invented and continues to be reinvented in the context of Africa's relation to other civilizations. Therefore, "Africa" or being "African" does not mean the same thing at every phase of Africa's conceptualization. In this connection, Mazrui notes that one of the paradoxes of history is that it took Africa's contact with the Arab world to make Africans realize that they were black, even though for Arabs this was merely a description, not a judgment about their status. The fact that Islamization in Africa awakened black consciousness without promoting black inferiority can best be illustrated by the reputation of classical Timbuktu, which was recognized as black and still saluted as a civilized achievement. This would, however, change with the European contact of the late eighteenth and nineteenth centuries. This "modern" European contact Africanized Africa in at least three unique ways.

First, European cartography and mapmaking turned Africa into the continent as we know it today. Europeans may not have invented the name "Africa," but they played a decisive role in applying it to the continental landmarks that we recognize today.[18]

Second, according to Mazrui, European racism convinced at least sub-Saharan Africa that one of the most relevant criteria of their Africanity was their skin color. Moreover, to Europeans *black* was not merely descriptive; it was also a judgment. Thus, while contact with Arabs alerted the people of sub-Saharan Africa that they were black, Europe associated their "blackness" with inferiority.

Third, closely related to racism, Mazrui notes, was the experience of European imperialism and colonization on the continent. The humiliation and degradation of black Africans across the centuries contributed to their mutual recognition of each other as "fellow Africans."[19]

Thus the process of the Africanization of Africa through contact with modern Europe was to give rise to a sense of shared "African identity." Mazrui notes: "It is one of the great ironies of modern African history that it took European colonialism to inform Africans that they were Africans. . . . Europe's greatest service to the people of Africa was not Western civilization . . . or even Christianity. Europe's supreme gift was the gift of African identity, bequeathed without grace or design—but a reality all the same."[20] There was another gift, namely the gift of a continent that is mired in various contradictions, which Mazrui depicts as the "paradoxes" of Africa's postcolonial condition in his 1979 BBC Reith Lectures, later published as *The African Condition: A Political Diagnosis*. He identifies six paradoxes or contradictions. The first is the "paradox of habitation," which describes Africa as a continent that has been identified as the "cradle of mankind" but one that remains the least inhabitable. There is also the "paradox of humiliation," which highlights how Africa is a product of a humiliating history of enslavement, colonization, and racial discrimination. The third paradox is the "paradox of acculturation," cascading from the imposition of foreign cultural, political, economic, and social forms that disturbed and reproduced Africanity as a conflicting set of identities. The fourth is the "paradox of fragmentation," rooted in capitalist economic exploitation that reproduced Africa as a site of underdevelopment, maldistribution, and economic disarticulation. The fifth is the "paradox of retardation," manifesting itself in the form of Africa's failure to act as a unit as a result of internal fissuring from national, ethnic, ideological, and religious cleavages. The last is the "paradox of location," which speaks to how a continent that is centrally located is at the same time the most marginal in global power politics.[21]

For Mazrui these paradoxes are related to—or rather are—the way modernity is experienced in Africa. They constitute Africa's unique modernity, a unique social history and African identity shaped by contact with European modernity. The Nigerian playwright Wole Soyinka has similarly commented on this unique African modernity. Soyinka notes that the African continent does not exist in isolation but is an intimate part of the history of others. In this connection, Africa has always been "known about, speculated over, explored both in actuality and fantasy, even mapped—Greeks, Jews, Arabs, Phoenicians etc. took their turns."[22] And even though he does not say so as explicitly as Mudimbe or Mazrui, for Soyinka what is different about the eighteenth- and nineteenth-century European contact with Africa is the unique way in which Europe "fictionalized" the continent as the object of European colonial adventure and commercial interest, thus turning Africa into a "monumental fiction of European creativity"[23]—an imagination that has largely remained in place until today. This, for Soyinka, constitutes what he calls the "crisis of African emergence into modernity."[24] It is most evident in Africa's postcolonial leadership as "largely a crisis of leadership alienation." By this Soyinka means that even as Africa's postcolonial political leaders seek to inaugurate a new era in Africa's independence, or "liberation," they do so "with the same mentality of domination and/or exploitation" as the West, thereby perpetuating the same agenda as their colonial predecessors.[25] It is this phenomenon that I describe in *The Sacrifice of Africa* as the looming shadow of King Leopold's Ghost that continues to define and shape Africa's imaginative landscape. However, by pointing to leadership alienation as one manifestation of the crisis of Africa's unique modernity, Soyinka draws attention to the contradictions at the heart of postcolonial African society—the postcolony, as Mbembe would call it. In the postcolony, the ruling power is no longer an alien (European) colonial master race subjugating "primitive" and backward peoples but a "son of the soil" who nevertheless continues to carry the "white man's burden"—and thus often views himself as a divinely appointed shepherd among a mindless flock. In his desperate attempt to hold onto power, he "fictionalizes" the population as not "ready for democracy" or the country as still lacking a capable replacement for him.

Here Mazrui and Soyinka converge regarding the African postcolonial condition as one characterized by "paradoxes" or contradictions that arise out of Africa's contact with European modernity. And even though Mazrui does not offer much in terms of suggestions for a way forward out of these paradoxes within Africa's postcolonial condition (neither does Soyinka) his work proved particularly helpful in my attempt to understand Africa's unique modernity and the paradox of violence that arises from within it.[26] In this connection, the Rwanda Genocide is particularly telling and does indeed serve as a "metaphor" (as Mamdani rightly notes) for the paradox of violence. For the kind of violence that we witnessed during the Rwanda Genocide—neighbors killing neighbors, family members killing other family members—does not make sense, especially in a country and a people (Rwandans, Africans) so often known for their sense of communal and family solidarity, for hospitality and generosity even to strangers. How could this be possible? What is going on? In light of Mazrui's work, I began to see how the Rwanda Genocide and other outbursts of "ethnic" violence in Africa become thinkable within the context of a larger set of contradictions and paradoxes that constitute Africa's modern condition. Such violent outbursts do not make sense outside the crisis occasioned by the European "discovery" and thus "invention" of Africa as a modern "dark continent."

If Mudimbe's *The Invention of Africa* helped me to begin to understand Africa as an "imagined" reality, Mazrui confirmed that Europe's interaction with Africa was to invent Africa in a unique way—to bequeath not only the "gift" of a shared sense of "African identity" but a continent that is in many ways still reeling from the "crisis of African emergence into modernity." It is this modernity into which Africa is received (and that Africa receives) as at once a gift and burden, a promise and an impossibility (for the continent is perpetually modernizing, yet stuck in "darkness" and in its "primitive" destiny). Thus, from the start, the European modernity into which Africa is received will define Africa as at once a victim (humiliated by enslavement and colonialism), a victor (triumphant in its historical achievements), and a villain (home of unbridled corruption, greed, and violence). How do we proceed in the face of these paradoxes and contradictions of modern Africa? As noted, Mazrui does not provide much guidance. But of course, there can be no return to a premodern glorious past of Africa's independence. No such thing ever existed, even if a return were available. For as Mazrui rightly notes, Africa has always historically been defined through its interaction with other civilizations. But by the same token, since there is no such thing as an ahistorical "Africa" or an enduring "African identity," an appeal to recover African identity as the foundation of a new modernity in Africa

cannot provide much hope in the midst of the paradoxes and contradictions that beset the continent. In fact, appealing to an African identity
might turn out to be misleading and disabling, as Anthony Appiah
makes clear.

Appiah on the Pitfalls and Usefulness of African Identity

Around the time I read Mudimbe's *The Invention of Africa* in the spring
of 1994, I also chanced upon Anthony Appiah's 1992 collection of essays,
In My Father's House, in which Appiah critically examines the discussion
of African intellectuals on what it means to be African. Among other
things, Appiah arrives at the conclusion that African identity is not a
stable metaphysical essence or "oneness" but rather a way of locating
oneself or being located in the world. It is not the only way, but it reflects
a shared history of subjugation of peoples from the African continent.
Given this conclusion, Appiah takes issue with how the notion of African
identity has been historically used as a rallying call in ways that assume
either a racial unity, a biological essence, or a cultural oneness. First, Appiah notes, the "myth" of racial unity as the basis of African identity,
which in many ways has defined the debates on African identity, must
be rejected. For generations who theorized the decolonization of Africa
(Nkurumah and others), "race" was a central organizing principle. This
principle (of the essential unity of the Negro race) was inherited from
the African American fathers of pan-Africanism (Crumwell, Du Bois,
Blyden), who took for granted the distinction between black and white
races. However, Appiah notes, the notion of race as a defining factor of
African identity is both misleading and disabling. In the first place, by
accepting the black/white distinction initially employed by the colonizers, the pan-Africanists subordinated themselves to (and thus perpetuated) the discourse providing the ideology for their domination.
Even though they sought to redefine "Negro identity" from a negative
to a positive designation, a move that was necessary in the dialectics of
the struggle against white domination, this effort simply perpetuated
it.[27] That is why, for Appiah, if we are to define African identity today we
must discard the biological notion of race as well as the dichotomy of

"we/blacks" and "they/whites." Not only does the dichotomy entail a scientifically untenable notion of race, it is based on an erroneous essentialism that assumes some deep similarity at the core of every identity that binds the people of that identity together.[28] Such a view creates an illusion that black (and white and yellow) people are fundamentally allied by nature and, thus, without effort. In this way, it leaves us totally unprepared to understand, let alone "handle[,] the 'intraracial' conflicts that arise from the very different situations of black (and white and yellow) people in different parts of the economy and of the world."[29] Overall, I found Appiah's argument convincing and his *In My Father's House* quite helpful in my attempt to philosophically understand the issue of identity in general and African identity in particular, and more specifically in my attempt to come to terms with my "Africanness" in the wake of the Rwanda Genocide. Appiah advanced my thinking in four crucial ways.

First, reading *In My Father's House* in the wake of the Rwanda Genocide, I could immediately relate Appiah's critique of racial unity as the foundation of African identity to the issue of "tribe" and "ethnicity" in Africa. I could see that through a similar process "tribal" identity became an unquestionable building block for the African nation-state. For the colonialists, Africans lived in "tribes." But *tribe* also named whatever was primitive, backward, unmodern, in a word, all that modernity came to "civilize." When the architects of African independence accepted the notion of "tribe," which had initially been employed by the colonizers, and redefined it in positive terms (the redefinition would later see the rejection of language of "tribal identity" in favor of "ethnic identity"), they took a necessary step in the dialectics of the struggle against European colonialism, but at the same time they also unwittingly subordinated themselves to the same politics of "difference" that was the basis of Africa's subjugation.

What Appiah was helping me see was that the idea of "tribal" or "ethnic" unity, like the idea of "racial" unity, is a myth that does not reflect the reality of the multiple identities that Africans bear. For as Appiah notes, given the "circulation of cultures," there can be no such thing as a pure Igbo, Western, or African culture, no such thing as "a fully autochthonous *echt*-African culture" or identity. "We are already contaminated by each other."[30] We find ourselves always caught up in many entanglements and identities, so that it is a "lie" to reduce these to one identity that is *really* me! Appiah's own polyglot identity is a telling case: he was born in London of an Asante father and an English mother, was raised in Ghana and educated in Britain, and is now teaching (living) in the United States. But Appiah was also helping me see that because the categories of difference often cut across our economic (and political) interests, the myth of racial or tribal unity often serves an ideological goal: to blind us to these economic and political interests. In this way, the appeal to "racial" or "tribal" unity prevents oppositional attitudes from generating a "coherent alternative view, which would provide a basis for political action."[31] As Appiah notes, "The inscription of difference in Africa today plays into the hands of the very exploiters whose shackles we are trying to escape. 'Race' in Europe and 'tribe' in Africa are central to the way in which the objective interests of the worst-off are distorted."[32]

Another crucial insight that emerged from Appiah's *In My Father's House* was that even though Appiah rejected the myth of a biological, metaphysical, or mythic unity or even a singular worldview as the basis of identity, he did not dismiss the notion of identity. As he would later note in *Lies That Bind*, "There is no dispensing with identities but we need to understand them better if we are to reconfigure them."[33] Identities are historical-political actualities and are thus fluid and always in an ongoing process of interpretation and reinterpretation.[34] Accordingly, he notes in *In My Father's House*, the idea of African identity is a fact. Being African already has "a certain context and a certain meaning. . . . We share a continent and its ecological problems, we share a relation of dependency to the world economy, we share the problem of racism in the way the industrialized world thinks of us."[35] However, this identity is based, not on a shared essence, a "common stock of cultural knowledge," or a "central body of ideas" shared by Africans, but on common history, problems, and interests.[36] Moreover, being African is not a static identity; like all identities, it is fluid and dynamic and is thus capable of being constantly shaped and reformed in the context of present realities and future ideals and aspirations. It is in this respect that the idea of "African identity" can prove useful. For given the shared history of colonialism and the common problems resulting from the history of colonial subjugation

and marginalization, the idea of "African" identity can be a useful organizing concept to mobilize continental and global alliances in the emancipatory struggles of African peoples. "A Pan-African identity, which
allows African-Americans, Afro-Caribbeans, and Afro-Latins to ally with
continental Africans, drawing on the cultural resources of the Black
Atlantic World, may serve *useful* purposes."

What is evident in the foregoing remarks is Appiah's rejection of an
essentialist view of African identity in favor of a pragmatic conception of
identity. Later in *Lies That Bind* he will note: "Identities . . . divide us and
set us against one another," but they can also unite us.[37] The idea of
"Africa" can be used to foster solidarity in the pursuit of justice and liberation for the excluded and marginalized. At the same time, Appiah
warns, African identity, like other identities, is not exclusive—it is for its
bearers one among many. Accordingly, while African solidarity can surely
be a vital and enabling rallying cry, "In this world of genders, ethnicities,
and classes, of families, religions, and nations, it is as well to remember
that there are times when 'Africa' is not the banner we need."[38] I found
this observation refreshing, as it could articulate much of the uneasiness
I was feeling at that time about the "fixity" of my being "African" in
Belgium. For to a number of people that I met at KU Leuven, including
some of my professors and even fellow students, the only thing that
mattered was that I was "African." It was as if I did not have any other
story, any other identities, any other interesting projects to pursue, except to be "African." The label "African," it seemed, had named all that
they needed to know about me!

Appiah's *In My Father's House* was also invaluable to me in terms of
pointing to the need for "testifying" and the primary role of stories in
making the case for or against the usefulness of African identity. All identities are relative, Appiah notes, and thus "We must argue for and against
them case by case."[39] The arguing is not so much a theoretical exercise
as a practical and ethical imperative. He notes, "It is also important to
testify . . . to the practical reality of the kind of intercultural project
whose theoretical ramifications I explore . . . to show how easy it is,
without theory, without much conscious thought, to live in human families that extend across the boundaries that are currently held to divide
our race."[40] In *In My Father's House* Appiah constantly returns to the story

of his father and his multiple identities—as an Asante, a Ghanaian, an African, a Christian, and a Methodist—"to learn from his capacity to make use of these many identities without, so far as I could tell, any significant conflict."[41] Appiah's reference to the story of how his father was able to negotiate his many identities and their obligations without feeling the need to resort to violence struck a deep chord in me. I had encountered a similar emphasis on narrative and story in the work of Stanley Hauerwas. In fact, as already noted, through Hauerwas's work I had already come to appreciate the role that stories play in shaping individual and communal identities. From Hauerwas I had also learned that two key criteria for assessing the truthfulness of a story had to do with the sorts of characters it was capable of shaping and whether the story offered sufficient skills and resources for individuals to negotiate the contradictions of their lives without resorting to violence. But of course this could not be known a priori, but only through stories. For Hauerwas, therefore, a narrative methodology was essential as the only way that characters formed by a story, as well as the limits and possibilities of the story for negotiating everyday challenges, could be displayed. Stories for Hauerwas provided both the argument and the evidence that a different world is possible.

Appiah's *In My Father's House* was pointing in the same direction, thus confirming that the issue of "African identity" (what it means to be "African") is an issue that can be settled, not through philosophical speculation, but only narratively, by displaying the various ways in which "African identity" has been invoked in a number of contexts and the various purposes for which the notions of "Africa," "Africanness," and "African identity" have been deployed. Not only had Appiah succeeded in doing this, thus dispelling the myth of a stable, essentialized notion of African identity, he had also confirmed that there are many ways of being an African—many ways of bearing African identity. Stories are what we need if we are to see the possibility of living in "human families that extend beyond the boundaries that are currently held to divide our race."[42]

Finally, Appiah's *In My Father's House* confirmed a restlessness I was already beginning to feel about theoretical speculation and the life of the academy in general. Here I was one of the very few African students to be admitted into KU Leuven's doctoral programs in philosophy, with the hope of perhaps one day holding a chair in philosophy at a university in my home country or somewhere else. I should have been happy and proud of myself. But I was not. Instead, even before the 1994 Rwanda Genocide, I was feeling restless. What was the use of all this philosophical speculation? What did it amount to? With the Rwanda Genocide, I turned to seeking to understand the reality of Africa and how such violence as the genocide could ever make sense. Kurian's question had set me on a journey of philosophical exploration on the status of "Africa" and the nature of "African identity." And the works of Mudimbe and Mazrui had thrown light on the complex processes of the ongoing imagination of "Africa." But in pointing to the need to "testify" to the possibility of inter- and cross-cultural peaceful coexistence, Appiah was also pointing to the limits of theoretical speculation and highlighting the need for practical commitment and interventions that engage "the dialects of need."[43] This of course does not mean that for Appiah theoretical, philosophical speculation is totally irrelevant and therefore cannot contribute to the advancement of cross-cultural understanding and solidarity. He notes, "What we in the academy *can* contribute—even if slowly and marginally—is a disruption of the discourse of 'racial' and 'tribal' differences." No doubt, this task is important, for "'Race' in Europe and 'tribe' in Africa are central to the way in which the objective interests of the worst-off are distorted" (179). In the end, however, the possibility of a different Africa calls for practical forms of engagement that meet Africa's dialectics of need. "Every time I read another report in the newspapers of African disaster—a famine in Ethiopia, a war in Namibia, ethnic conflict in Burundi—I wonder how much good it does to correct the theories with which these evils are bound up; the solution is food, or mediation, or some other more material, more practical step."[44]

When I first read this statement in 1994 it was Appiah's observation about the limits of the academy and theory that struck me. Looking back, however, I realize that the need to engage the material realities of Africa—"food, mediation, or some other material [needs]"—has been far more determinative in my journey than I would have imagined then. Appiah had noted, "We cannot change the world simply by evidence and reasoning, but we surely cannot change it without them either."[45] So I now find myself, as a scholar, trying to disrupt the discourse of "racial" and "tribal" identity, and as a practitioner, engaged in Africa's dialects of need: food, mediation, ecology, and economy. In all this, I am trying to come to terms with the issue of my African identity: not simply what it means to be an African (in the abstract) but what it means to be this particular African, with the hope that my story as well as the stories of others I tell in this book can testify to the possibility of living in families and communities that extend across the boundaries that are currently held to divide us.

Conclusion: On a Theological Doorstep

If the violence of the 1994 Rwanda Genocide and Kurian's question had set me on a theoretical exploration on the status of "Africa" and the nature of African identity, with Appiah's *In My Father's House*, that exploration had led me to a practical and ethical conclusion: African identity reflects shared historical, cultural experiences and emergent forms of international organizations in the modern postcolonial world. But like any identity, it is not the only way that its bearers view themselves. Moreover, there are good and bad ways, violent and nonviolent ways, useful and not-so-useful ways of living in this unique modernity. Kurian's question "Why do you Africans always kill your own people?" requires more than theoretical arguments to account for the reality of Africa and its violent contradictions and outbursts (necessary as these are): it calls for stories that testify to the possibility and reality of a different "Africa" and for concrete practical and material engagements that reimagine, and thus invent, a different modernity in Africa.

Appiah's reflections also landed me on a theological doorstep. To be sure, it was the hint of this theological opening that first drew me to Appiah's *In My Father's House*. For as he himself notes, the title refers first not to Appiah's father but to God. He elaborates, "Thus for me the phrase 'in my father's house' must be completed 'there are many mansions'—and the biblical understanding that, when Christ utters those words at the Last Supper, he meant that there is room enough for all in heaven, *his* Father's House."[46] Even though Appiah does not explore the full implications of this theological opening, I was increasingly fascinated by it and sought to explore its concrete practical and social possibilities for the here and now. At the time I was working on a PhD in philosophy on issues of moral rationality, the Rwanda Genocide was, even without my full awareness, beginning to shift my intellectual orientation in a decisive theological direction. Part of this shift was no doubt connected to my identity as a Catholic priest, and as a priest I am always naturally drawn to the theological and ecclesial implications of whatever engagements I find myself part of. But the other reason was that I was studying the work of theologian Stanley Hauerwas and had found his argument for the need for a distinctive theological voice quite persuasive. At any rate, with the Rwanda Genocide happening in a country that was predominantly Christian, and with the widespread participation of Christians in the genocide, I found myself constantly wondering about the issue of Christian identity in Africa. What difference if any, does being a Christian make to the way that one understands one's own identity? And how does this understanding of oneself as a Christian relate to one's being an African, or a member of a particular tribe or ethnicity, Hutu, Tutsi, Ganda, Igbo? Why did the fact that the majority of Rwandans were Christians make no difference to the Christians who readily killed their Tutsi brothers and sisters? To these and similar questions of African Christian identity we now turn—again, not in an abstract way, but in a way that highlights what my own journey as a Ugandan Catholic priest living in America, as a philosopher turned theologian, and as a scholar-practitioner has taught me about Christian identity in general and African Christian identity in particular.

CHAPTER TWO

On Being an African Christian

The Journey of Christian Identity

The issue of identity lies at the heart of the process by which the Christian theological enterprise is actually carried forward.

—Kwame Bediako, *Christianity in Africa*

Are you saying that the blood of tribalism is deeper than the waters of baptism?

—Cardinal Etchegaray

As I watched the events of 1994 unfold, I kept wondering about my family and what would have happened to me had I grown up in Rwanda. Would I have been a victim, a perpetrator, or a bystander during the genocide? I thought about my parents and the journey that had brought them from Rwanda to settle in Uganda in the late 1940s. They had been born and raised in Rwanda, my mother in the village of Nkulungwe near Ruhengeri in Musanze District in the Northern Province of Rwanda, and my father, just two villages away. When I was four, my parents took us (my two brothers and me) to visit our grandparents in Rwanda. I have memories of my maternal grandfather's house on a hilltop, overlooking a small lake (Mukungwa), and of us kids running down to get water from the lake. There were always people coming and going at the house. I later learned that my grandfather was the chief in the village—and that it was he who, when I was born, had insisted that I be named "Katongole" (little chief).

My father's family was not as well off. Dad was one of thirteen children, and his father (my grandfather) died when he was a young boy. Soon afterwards Dad had gone to seek work at my maternal grandfather's house and had ended up looking after the chief's cows. My father stayed and grew up in the same compound as my mother. Later, he heard about opportunities in Uganda, where the British had introduced coffee and had set up coffee plantations. He jumped at the opportunity, not only as a way to earn money for the dowry to marry my mother (he'd had the audacity to ask for the hand of his boss's eldest daughter!), but also to escape conscription into forced labor (the Belgians were rounding up young able-bodied men and sending them to work in the rubber plantations in Congo). He worked in Uganda for two years, got enough money for the dowry, returned to marry my mother, and brought her back to Uganda. They settled there at Malube in Buganda, where he had acquired a small piece of land. This is where my siblings and I were born and raised.

Growing up, we never had much contact with Rwanda. My parents were planning another family trip in 1972 when my father was taken ill and unexpectedly died. I was twelve then and never got another chance to visit Rwanda—that is, not until more recently, after the genocide. On coming into Uganda as a married couple, my parents settled in their new home, became active in the local community (my dad became a member of the coffee cooperative, served as chairperson of the teacher-parent association for five years, and hosted either the annual village Christmas or Easter party at our house). They tried to learn the local language and did not seem to be as bothered or as embarrassed as we children were that they spoke Luganda with a Rwandan accent. Unfortunately, we children never learned to speak Kinyarwanda. I do not remember my parents ever talking much about Rwanda. Now and then there would be conversations between the two of them, or with a visiting relative, but we grew up not knowing much about the problems of Rwanda and certainly little about the Hutu and Tutsi divisions.[1] When the 1990 violence broke out and the Tutsi-Hutu division was so much in the news, I asked my mother whether we were Hutu or Tutsi. That was when she told me that her father was Hutu (and I guess that made her Hutu) but that Dad was from one of the poor Tutsi families in the Ruhengeri region, which was predominantly Hutu. I wanted to find out more about Dad's family and the relationship between the local Hutu and Tutsi as she remembered them growing up. She did not have much to say except that Dad's family was very poor and that "the issues of *Ubwoko* [ethnicity] in Rwanda are very complicated!"

One of the many things I remember growing up is the zeal and dedication of my parents to their Catholic faith. Mother had been born in a devout Catholic family. Dad became a Christian only in order to marry my mother, a condition that my mother's father had insisted on. However, after he became a Catholic, my father practiced the Christian faith with the zeal of a new convert. Every Sunday, he and mother walked seven miles to attend mass at the local parish church of Katende; morning and evening devotions were a daily routine at home; and whenever a priest would come to our mission, Dad made sure he introduced us to him. For Anthony, my father, Christianity and the church not only mattered but were part of our daily life. Dad cared about education and made sure we took our studies seriously. All seven of us children went to the nearby Catholic-founded school, although by the time I enrolled, my eldest sister and brother had graduated. Given Dad's love for church and education and overall the Catholic upbringing it is perhaps not surprising that when I was in grade 4, when our teacher asked us what we wanted to do, I mentioned that I wanted to study to be a priest—an idea that both my father and mother greatly welcomed. But this dream as well as our father's dream for us children to stay in school was thrown in jeopardy when Dad abruptly died at forty-five. I was in grade 5. Since we did not have an extended family to depend on, mother was left as the sole provider for our family. But my parents had made some friends, who came to our family's assistance and supported mother with our education. One of these friends was Elias, a Muslim man who taught at the Catholic school we attended and was actually my P.5 social science teacher. He offered to pay for my school fees through the rest of grade school into high school. He also supported me through my seminary training. After ordination, I worked briefly in a parish before I was assigned to teach in the Catholic seminary for three years, before eventually going to Belgium in the fall of 1991 to study philosophy at KU Leuven.

As I watched the events of 1994 unfold in Rwanda from Belgium, I wondered about the presence of the church in Rwanda and the fact that Christianity did not seem to make a significant difference during the genocide. Not only did Christians kill other Christians, often in the same churches where they had worshipped together, but the genocide had started during Easter week, the most sacred of Christian holidays. At that time, Cardinal Etchegaray was the president of the Pontifical Council for Justice and Peace in Rome. When the pope dispatched him to Rwanda during the genocide, Cardinal Etchegaray challenged the gathered Rwandan church about the significance of being a Christian. "Are you saying that the blood of tribalism is deeper than the waters of baptism?" he asked. It is reported that one of the gathered leaders answered in the affirmative.[2] As soon as I returned to Uganda after my studies in Belgium, I made a "pilgrimage" to Rwanda in 1998, visiting various genocide memorials and hearing eyewitness accounts of what had happened. Cardinal Etchegaray's question particularly haunted me as I stood in churches and at church compounds that had turned into killing fields during the genocide. "Is the blood of tribalism deeper than the waters of baptism?" The question continues to haunt me and raises significant theological and missiological questions beyond Rwanda. What is the relation between Christian identity and African identity, and more specifically what is the relationship between being a Christian and one's tribal or ethnic identity? What difference does being a Christian make to one's ethnicity? What role does ethnicity play in Christian self-understanding? While these questions became pressing for me in the wake of the Rwanda Genocide, they are not new questions for African theological exploration. For indeed, as Kwame Bediako rightly notes, "The issue of identity lies at the heart of the process by which the Christian theological enterprise is actually carried forward."[3] However, while the questions of African Christian identity may not be new, the Rwanda Genocide provides an opportunity, even urgency, to reexamine these questions with a view of offering fresh insights and a more adequate understanding of African Christian identity in light of what we have learned from the 1994 Rwanda Genocide.

That is why rethinking the question of Christian identity in Africa in the wake of 1994 must begin with an assessment of the dominant ways in which the nature of African Christian identity has been understood. In conceptualizing the nature of Christian identity and its relation to African identity, African theology has tended to follow one of two dominant trajectories. One trajectory views Christian identity as a spiritual identity that stands above any other identities (African or otherwise) and is thus able to guarantee one's freedom in Christ. The other approach understands Christian identity as a reality that builds on one's "African" identity. Both approaches, however, miss an adequate understanding of Christian identity as an ongoing journey, whose ultimate goal is the creation of a new sense of self and a new sense of belonging that extends beyond the boundaries of race, nation, tribe, and religion. It is this journey into a "new we" that is the goal of Christian life, and it offers Christians resources and skills to negotiate the various social, political, and material conditions of their existence. To the extent that this inherent social, material, and political nature of Christian identity is lacking within the dominant streams of African theological exploration, Christians are not offered resources to fully understand not only the gifts but also the limits of "ethnic" identity. Such understanding is crucial if Christianity is to offer some measure of relief from, and an interruption of, the recalcitrant forms of ethnic violence on the African continent. A brief overview of some representative voices in the dominant trends of theological exploration on the nature of African Christian identity easily confirms why Christianity, its statistical growth and vibrancy on the African continent notwithstanding, has often found itself helpless in the face of the kind of violence that was unleashed during the 1994 Rwanda Genocide.

The Pitfalls of a "Spiritual Identity"

The late Kwame Bediako, founder and director of the Akrofi Christaller Memorial Center for Mission and Applied Theology in Akropong, Ghana, is admittedly one of the most outstanding theologians and teachers that Africa has produced.[4] The theme of Christian identity lies at the heart of Bediako's extensive and widely influential theological contribution. For Bediako, the interaction between Christianity and the religious heritage of Africa makes identity not only a pertinent theological question but the driving force behind African theological exploration. He notes,

> As it emerged in the post-missionary context of African Christianity in the 1950s and 1960s, the question of identity entailed . . . confronting constantly the problem of how "old" and "new" in African religious consciousness could become integrated in a unified vision of what it meant to be Christian and African. . . . African theology, therefore, by becoming something of a dialogue between the African Christian scholar and the perennial religions and spiritualities of Africa was thereby a struggle for an appropriate Christian discourse which would account for and hold together the total religious experience of Africans in a coherent and meaningful pattern. Identity itself thus became a theological concern and the formulation of theological questions were [*sic*] linked as the inevitable by-product of a process of Christian self-definition.[5]

This statement captures the heart of Bediako's theological contribution, which he works out in his numerous essays and books, most explicitly in *Theology and Identity: The Impact of Culture upon Christian Thought in the Second Century and in Modern Africa.*[6] The basic outline of Bediako's argument goes like this: The problem of Christian identity in Africa is the problem of the integration of old and new. A similar concern characterized Christianity in the second century, following the encounter between Christianity and the pagan world of Greco-Roman heritage. Thus, notes Bediako, African theologians in the formative stages—Bolaji Idowu, Mbiti, Mulago, and Byang Kato—are engaged in a similar attempt to bridge the old and new, just as Tatian, Tertullian, Justin, and Clement of Alexandria were.[7]

What makes this effort more urgent in the African context is the crisis created by the impact of the West, which tended to disregard and denigrate the African past, with the result that the African Christian had either to begin with a blank slate or to turn against his or her heritage. Bediako's goal is to seek a unified vision of Christian life, one that allows the African Christian to be both truly Christian and truly African.

Bediako discovers the continuity in the religious consciousness of God in Africa, thus rejecting Byang's discontinuity stance in favor of theologians Idowu, Mbiti, and Mulago. Quoting Mbiti, he notes, "God the Father of our Lord Jesus Christ is the same God who for thousands of years has been known and worshipped in various ways within the religious life of African peoples, and who, therefore, was not a stranger in Africa prior to the coming of the missionaries. . . . Missionaries did not bring God to Africa, God brought them."[8] Thus, like Mbiti—and like Clement and Justin in relation to pre-Christian cultures of the first and second centuries—Bediako considers African cultures and religions as "preparation," or "preparatio evangelica."[9]

While Bediako's focus on Africa's past religious experience had the desired effect of providing the continuity he sought (and thus allowing the African Christian to be both truly African and truly Christian), it also had the unfortunate effect of turning the identity question into a *religious* and *spiritual* question. For Bediako, African Christian identity became a spiritual identity, which stood above the everyday material realities of politics and economics. True, Bediako was still aware that the African Christian, now firm in his spiritual identity, could draw implications from that identity for how to engage in politics and economics. He could do so precisely because Christian identity operated on an *altogether different plane*. Drawing on the theologian and church historian Adolf von Harnack, he noted that for St. Paul "The basis of Christian self-definition was essentially to be a *religious* one, not national, nor cultural, nor social."[10] For Bediako, therefore, the Gospel introduced into history a new overarching identity that transcended all social identities, whether based on gender, race, nation, or culture. Here Bediako came to a similar conclusion as Mbiti before him regarding African Christian identity. Identity in Christ, Mbiti notes, "makes nonsense of all other identities in that it claims the whole person and the whole cosmos as the property of Christ. Then, deriving from this Christocentric identity, the person is free to become whatever else he wishes, to be identified as an African, nationalist, neutralist, trade unionist or even beggar. That is the height to which Christianity in Africa must soar."[11]

In the end, however, the fact that identity in Christ soars above everything else in order to guarantee one's "freedom" in Christ turns this identity into an unreal sublime, as Maluleke rightly points out in his assessment of Bediako's project: "The African Christian's identity crisis, like that of African Christian theology, is not merely one of consciousness— psychological schizophrenia born of vexed, confused and 'messed up' souls. Beyond the religious realm, there is a 'material basis' for the African Christian identity problem connectable to colonialism, post independence oppression, and material dispossession. . . . Insensitivity to the 'material basis' of the African Christian's identity problem has the potential to reduce [the] quest for the 'true character of African Christian identity' into a superficial, albeit well-meaning exercise."[12]

The loss of the material base of Christian identity also obscures its essential political, and thus potentially subversive, dimension. Bediako remarked on this dimension in relation to Christianity in the second century. Christianity, he noted, "was a newcomer, with no land to call its own. . . . Therefore, Greco-Roman Empire Christians had no settled identity and in order to fashion [one] they needed to come to terms with the various facets of that culture from which they emerged. . . . In a culture where identity was shaped simultaneously by nationality and religion the emergence of Christian faith was very disruptive."[13]

However, in his quest for "continuity" with Africa's religious past, and for a "unified" vision of African Christian identity, Bediako does not explore the implication of this observation for African Christianity. He does not do so, I suspect, because he already assumes the modern distinction between the political and religious spheres, according to which Christian conversion is an inner spiritual experience distinct from the social, cultural, and political processes around it. But by neatly assigning Christian identity to the spiritual realm, Bediako's theology not only obscures the essential material nature of Christian identity (and indeed of all identities) but overlooks the subversive and disruptive nature of Christian identity in relation to other (national, cultural, ethnic, racial) identities. It is this disruptive and subversive potential that makes Christian identity essentially political. A similar disappearance of the political nature of Christian identity is obvious in more recent theological contributions that assume Christian identity as an identity that builds upon one's "natural" identity, whether that "natural" identity is one's African or ethnic identity.

Building upon a "Natural" Identity

In *Jesus of Africa*, Diane Stinton concludes that as Bediako claimed in 1996, African theology has passed a crucial stage in its development, a transition from crisis to confidence. If in its initial stage African theology was a reaction to the Western onslaught on African culture, an attempt to affirm our identity as both Christian and African (countering the disdain in which local cultures had generally been held during colonial times), that era is past.[14] What we now witness is widespread African confidence in the Christian faith, giving rise to a "creative outburst of Christological reflection across the continent from the 1980s onward."[15] In trying to synthesize these Christologies arising out of Africa's social, political, religious, cultural, and economic contexts, Stinton identified four predominant faces of Jesus in Africa: Jesus as "life-giver," as "mediator," as "loved one," and as "leader." Her work complements an earlier publication, *The Faces of Jesus in Africa*, in which Robert Schreiter brings together ten essays by African theologians discussing different images— Jesus as Healer, Master of Initiation, Chief, Ancestor, Elder Brother— that African Christians use to describe the person of Jesus.

The more one examines these different images, however, the more it becomes clear that with the "confidence" that Stinton notes, African theology has indeed entered a new phase. It is no longer the identity of the African Christian that is in question but Jesus's identity. Accordingly the "outburst of Christological reflection" is focused on exploring if and how well Jesus can fit within the African cultural experience (and thus the theologies of inculturation), or how well he can advance the quest for liberation in the context of Africa's socioeconomic and political marginalization, as well as other forms of oppression such as poverty, sickness, hunger, ignorance, and gender subjugation (thus Jesus as liberator, healer, savior). It is not difficult to understand the confidence that accompanies the Christological quest for an "African Jesus" at this stage in the development of African theology. For as an academic discipline African theology was born amid crosswinds of sociopolitical, cultural, and theological change. With the Independence and the birth of African statehood, the reality of "Africa" and of "African identity" seemed to be assured, despite deterioration in social, political, and economic conditions in Africa, especially through the 1970s and 1980s. The confidence that Stinton speaks of therefore reflects, if not the reality, the hopes and ideological aspirations of post-Independence Africa. Concretely, what the confidence means culturally and politically is that now "African identity" comes to be assumed as the foundation upon which to build the African nation-state, whether this identity is defined in terms of a racial or a cultural oneness. In the previous chapter we highlighted Appiah's critical observations on these debates by the fathers of the African independence movement: Nkurumah, Senghor, Kaunda, Obote, and others. But the debates themselves would confirm the confidence as well as the optimism within this Independence and post-Independence moment regarding the fact of our being "Africans."

African theology has in many ways come to mirror these cultural and political developments. There is a feeling that the era of Africa's theology as a reaction to Western misrepresentation is now over. African Christian identity has been vindicated, so it is now "time to drink from our own wells." "African identity" thus is assumed to be an unquestionable and stable foundation not only for the nation-state but for the African theological project. The Ghanaian John Samuel Pobee best captured this sentiment in a book chapter revealingly entitled "I Am an African Christian." For one thing, Pobee writes, "In sober fact, before I became a Christian by baptism and confirmation, I was ensouled with Africanness, which was taken in with my mother's milk. Africanness is more than color of the skin. It is culture and worldview taken for granted, which cannot be erased."[16]

Here Pobee voices a sentiment that many Christians in Africa would come to assume and even take for granted from the 1970s on: being African is one's "natural" identity, and this identity is a stable and enduring reality that cannot be erased. Needless to say, this assumption involves all the problems and contradictions associated with the misleading essentialist conception of identity that we discussed in the previous chapter. Here we are interested in showing how such a view of African identity would by and large come to be taken for granted within the nascent field of African theology. Moreover, since the notion of "Africa" was, at least in the colonial imagination, connected with the idea of "tribe," the same view of African identity as our "natural" identity would soon be accorded to tribal identity, and to ethnic identity when the language of "tribe" became increasingly questionable and would from the 1970s on come to be replaced by the more politically correct notion of "ethnicity." Not only would ethnic identity be assumed to be one's "natural" identity, but theologians would begin to read back ethnic identity as part of God's plan for Africans since creation. David Kirwa Tarus and Stephanie Lowery capture this well when they note that in God's eschatological kingdom all ethnic communities are reconciled in Christ. Ethnicity, they argue, which is part of God's original creation, is not a negative reality: it only becomes negative when used as a marker of exclusion of people or to inspire physical or nonphysical conflict between ethnic groups.[17] *Restoring the Beauty and Blessing of Ethnic Diversity*, a training manual for Christian leaders in a reconciliation process, used by the African Leadership and Reconciliation Ministries (ALARM), goes even further by suggesting that ethnicity is not only good and God given but a reality that marks our lives here on earth and in heaven as well. "We will all die and resurrect as members of our various ethnic groups. . . . God values different ethnic groups and their languages."[18]

Does Christianity make any difference to this enduring "natural" identity? The sense one gets from both reflections cited above is that Christianity brings "reconciliation." But just as with Bediako, the reconciliation takes place on an altogether different (spiritual) plane, which does not obliterate or essentially change one's cultural or ethnic identity but incorporates it into a multiethnic community—the African nation. It is perhaps not difficult to see why the nation (not the church) now becomes the focal point and goal of the "reconciliation" of ethnic differences, given that as a scholarly discipline African theology was born out of the same struggle from which the African nation-state emerged as the political expression of an "Independent" Africa. Theologically, this would mean that for all their differences, African theological approaches such as "enculturation," "liberation," and "reconstruction" would be united at least in this one regard: they would all assume the "nation" as the ultimate political reality within which the theological enterprise was located.[19] This political reality of the nation-state is itself rarely questioned.

The attempt is to see if and how Christianity in general, and Christian identity in particular, can help advance the struggle for democracy, human rights, and the liberation of "our" nations (Kenya, Uganda, South Africa, and others).[20]

What the foregrounding of "African," "ethnic," or "national" identities takes for granted is that Christianity does not have a "politics" of its own. It makes a political contribution, and thus becomes socially relevant, when it advances the goals of these "natural" realities. Thus we find in this second trajectory of African theological exploration the same implicit assumption that Christianity operates on an altogether different plane than the level of "ethnicity," which is now assumed as a natural identity, and the level of the nation, which is assumed as the only political community there is. In this connection, the dangers of what Célestin Musekura and others describe as "negative ethnicity" are seen as a threat not so much to the church as to the nation. "Ethnic groups are a very strong foundation upon which a strong nation can be built. . . . Ethnicity (negative) . . . creates a loss of national culture—a culture which would be enriched immensely by the absorption of the existing different cultural backgrounds. If ethnic identity is positively appropriated, it can become a national value, together with the weaknesses and strengths of that ethnic group."[21]

What is missing from this view, as it is missing from Bediako's, is the reality of the church as a community, a recognizable community, a social body whose unique mission and membership cut across, not just mystically but concretely and visibly, the boundaries of race, ethnicity, tribe, and nation. What is missing is a vision of Christian identity as a journey of incorporation into a people—God's new people—whose identity does not simply build on the so-called natural identities of ethnicity, tribe, race, or nation but reconfigures them in a distinct way, even as it heals and reconciles them. What is missing is the vision of Christian life as a pilgrimage and the Christian as a pilgrim who has no real home in any assumed identity, be it of race, nation, tribe, or ethnicity. Christian life is a calling forth—a journey with an identifiable starting point (where the person happens to be as a member of a village, ethnicity, nation, etc.) but the goal of the journey is not simply to affirm that starting point. Rather, it is to offer the Christian a sense of direction and a way of living and navigating the ambiguities and contradictions of one's life—a life, to be sure, that is shaped by multiple identities, including race, nation, ethnicity, religion. To paraphrase Anthony Appiah, Christianity is more of a verb than a noun. Accordingly, Christian identity "is revealed as an activity, not a thing. And it is the nature of activities to bring change."[22]

An overlooked resource (and somewhat of an exception to the general trend of the sacralization of ethnic identity) that points to Christian life as a journey is the work of Congolese priest and theologian Vincent Mulago. Attending to his ideas, albeit briefly, will highlight this missing ecclesiological dimension that confirms not only the "forward-looking" nature of Christian identity but its political nature as well.

An Overlooked Resource, Vincent Mulago

A pioneer of African theology, Mulago played a key role in its early development. Described by Bénézet Bujo as "one of the precursors [of African theology] comparable to the Apostolic Fathers," Mulago contributed two chapters to *Des prêtres noirs s'interrogent*, considered by many to be the first concerted theological response by African theologians to the denigration of African culture within colonial Christianity.[23] A prolific author, Mulago covers a wide range of topics concerning the need to rethink Christian life within an African context. I find his views on Christian identity particularly relevant to our discussion here. For Mulago, Christian identity is universal, yet particular. The Incarnation makes this possible. As Lowery describes Mulago's thought, "In the Incarnation, the Son of God enters into a context to purify it, using elements within that context to reveal himself. He does not utterly demolish the context, but works with the elements there and fills them with a new reality."[24] In this paradigm, for the African Christian, African clan structures serve as "stepping stones" pointing to the church as a clan—a new clan—established through the blood of Christ. This new clan, Mulago contends, shares with the African clan the notion of vital participation, but unlike African clans it is not limited to the blood ties of its members; rather, it is made possible by the blood of Christ, its head. Thus its membership is open to all. Accordingly, for Mulago, the elements of "vital participation" and "incorporation" into Christ's Body make Christians "partners in God's life," ensuring that the church is not simply the sum total of its different cultural elements. While these cultural elements are not obliterated, they are "transformed," and through this transformation, "African identities are redeemed, to be made part of the overarching Christian identity."[25]

Mulago's "stepping stone" theology has been criticized by V. Y. Mudimbe, his former student, for its reliance on a Western outlook and methodology to advance "local" theology.[26] Others have also criticized his conception of the church as "a new clan," arguing that it is too hierarchical and does not reflect the Trinitarian vision of unity in diversity.[27] Even recognizing these criticisms, I find Mulago's theology particularly helpful in trying to understand the nature of Christian identity and its relation to other identities. Mulago's stepping-stones concept underscores Christian identity as a journey, whose direction or goal is becoming (Mulago uses "incorporation into" a "new people") in the world. This orientation in and of itself helps move the discussion of Christian identity from a focus that is backward-looking to one that is forward-looking. As Keith Ferdinando asserts in his critique of Bediako, New Testament theology is essentially forward-looking: "Identity in Christ in fact moves the orientation of [believers'] identity away from the past and toward the future, the center of gravity has shifted in a decisive way. . . . The identity of believers derives from the destination to which they are headed rather than from their present situation in this world, or the past from which they come. They are 'pilgrims looking for the city that is to come' (Heb 13:14)."[28]

Thus the sense of "journey" and "pilgrimage" is at the heart of what it means to be a Christian. But it is this aspect of Christian life as a journey with a particular direction and telos that has been greatly lacking in the discussion of African Christian identity. As a result, African Christian identity is conceived as a static spiritual reality that either stands above or simply builds on (but never questions) one's "natural" (African and ethnic) identity. At any rate, given its transcendental nature, Christian identity becomes powerless in the face of "natural identities" and therefore ceases to be a politically potent reality that could disrupt, transform, and redeem the inherent tribalism and ethnicization of Africa's politics.

On Becoming More Christian: A Personal Journey

Christian life is a journey, and Christian identity is a constant invitation into new forms of communities, "new we's" that cut across divides. The church is God's "new we" that reconciles and heals different forms of brokenness and identities that often divide us. So much of this conviction grows out of my own personal journey, which has been and remains a journey of crossing boundaries. I have always found myself in between communities, the bearer of multiple identities, and constantly negotiating the at times competing claims of those identities. I believe this is true of every Christian, indeed of every person. We never have (or are) one identity. The challenge for the Christian is how to negotiate these various identities so as to live into what we think God is calling us to be, into what we see as God's plans for the world. If we believe, as I do, indeed as every Christian should, that God "has reconciled the world . . . and has given us the ministry of reconciliation" and has thus invited us to be "ambassadors" of God's reconciling love in the world (2 Cor. 5:17–20), then Christian life and identity cannot but be a life of constant negotiation and boundary crossing. Here I can only testify to what this has meant for me, given the particular circumstances of my biography.

As already noted, my parents were born and raised in Rwanda, but I was born and raised in Uganda. For some this makes me really Rwandan, even though I have been to Rwanda only a few times and do not speak Kinyarwanda (instead Luganda is my mother tongue). I call Uganda home and I hold a Ugandan passport. My parents were not simply from Rwanda, one was Hutu and the other Tutsi. I guess that should make me a strange creature, a kind of Hutsirwandaseugandan. I grew up in a Catholic family, but after my father's death a Muslim teacher, Elias, became one of my "guardians." At my ordination he stood next to my mother as the two of them presented me to the bishop who ordained me. I think my ordination was valid. From 1991 to 1997, I studied and lived in Leuven—six years of eating Belgian frites and drinking Belgian beer (Hoegaarden was my favorite) and trying (unsuccessfully) to learn Flemish. I therefore like to claim that if you cut open my veins in the right place, you might see some European blood! At Leuven, I studied philosophy, even though I now find myself a professor of theology. My graduate students do refer to me now and again as a "recovering philosopher." Since 2001, I have been living in the United States, first as a nonresident alien (visitor), then as a resident alien (permanent resident), and since 2015 as a naturalized American citizen. Throughout this time, however, I have returned to Uganda, at least once every year, to visit my family and my diocese of Kampala, to do research and to work on various projects with grassroots communities, including the Bethany Land Institute (more on this later). I am therefore a dual citizen, who not only holds both an American and a Ugandan passport but actually owns a home in each of these countries.

In the United States, for twelve years, I lived and worked at Duke Divinity School, a Methodist seminary, where I taught not only Methodist seminarians but seminarians from a host of denominations, mainline, Evangelical, and a lot in between. I had never encountered so many denominations. The sheer range and variety of denominational affiliations often left me, a Catholic, totally confused and overwhelmed. But if I was confused, my students too were often confused by my Catholicism. To be sure, a number simply assumed that I was either Methodist or a Baptist. I remember how once, when lecturing in a class on the Eucharist and politics, I kept stressing the significance of the Eucharist and how it makes and reveals the church, much to the confusion of one student, who all along had thought I was a Baptist pastor and now couldn't see where all this interest in the Eucharist was coming from. "Are you some kind of Catholic?" he asked.

On the other hand, I must confess that by living among Protestants at Duke I came to a better appreciation of what it means to be Catholic and my identity as a Catholic priest. At first encounter, students would address me as "Professor Katongole." As they got more comfortable with me they would address me as "Dr. K" (much as they addressed the legendary Duke basketball coach Michael Krzyzewski as "Coach K"). However, I noticed those who got to know me pretty well would call me "Father Emmanuel." These seminarians would often stop me on the quad or come by my office for a chat, share more openly about their lives, and quite often ask me to pray for them, or with them.

At Duke, I was also privileged to work with Chris Rice to establish a Center for Reconciliation.[29] Working with Chris, a white Evangelical Presbyterian who had spent seventeen years in Mississippi in a ministry on racial reconciliation, introduced me to the treacherous challenges of race and racism in America. But my deepening friendship with Chris as we worked together to establish and lead the Center for Reconciliation also confirmed the possibility of friendships across divides and the possibilities of communities that are committed to forging a "new we" across boundaries of race, nation, tribe, religion, and denomination. In this connection, one of the unique gifts of my work with Chris at the Center for Reconciliation was discovering and bringing together (in CFR-sponsored "gatherings") various individuals and Christian groups, Catholics, mainline Protestants, and Evangelicals of different stripes, working across different divides and communities of brokenness. These gatherings, whether in East Africa, the US, or Southeast Asia, became a great opportunity not only for deepening a vision of reconciliation but for learning about these various denominations and for developing unlikely friendships between blacks and whites, between Catholics, Protestants, and Evangelicals, between Christians and Muslims, and between Africans, Americans, and Asians. But working with "practitioners" meant that I had to find a way to bridge the gap between the world of the academy and the broader world of the practitioners. I could not remain a standard academic but had to find a way to "translate" the dense theological jargon of the academy into graspable concepts, at the same time connecting the rich stories of the practitioners to theoretical frameworks and speculative notions of the academy. This was how the notions of narrative, story, and portraiture became central to my scholarship.[30]

I left Duke in 2012 to join Notre Dame, where I have been for seven years working both at the Kroc Institute for International Peace Studies and in the Theology Department. For a Catholic coming to and working at a Catholic university should feel like coming home. But I feel restless. Not only do I miss my Methodist, Baptist, and Evangelical friends at Duke, but I find myself alienated from both the "liberals" and the "conservatives" at Notre Dame. And many times I find the inward-looking complacency of the Catholic Church, especially of the Catholic Church in America, deeply troubling. I guess I am discovering how over the years I have become less Catholic—have become a "sort of Catholic." In 2005, I had led a Duke Divinity School–sponsored Pilgrimage of Pain and Hope to Uganda and Rwanda. One evening we visited with my mentor Cardinal Emmanuel Wamala, then archbishop of Kampala. Over dinner he joked with Dean Greg Jones that Duke should be canonized for putting up with me all these years. Greg responded by saying how it was a gift to have me at the Divinity School, and he (Greg) hoped that my working with Methodists, Protestants, and Evangelicals had helped make me more Catholic. The cardinal offered a striking response. "No," he said, "you have not made Emmanuel more Catholic, you have made him more Christian."

Becoming more Christian, if indeed that is what has happened to me over the years, and in the context of my journey, has led me simply to see more clearly how confused I am in terms of identity, and how at any rate I do not have anything like a "natural" identity—a stable enduring identity or essence (in terms of culture, race, tribe, ethnicity) upon which everything else builds. Instead, what I have—better, what I am—are several identities and a sense of the journey that has taken me from Malube, to Katigondo, to Leuven, to Duke, to Notre Dame, to Nandere (where I am working with rural youth through Bethany Land Institute), and a sense of the general direction in which my life is headed. Through this journey, the most determinative lens through which I interpret what is going on and assess the opportunities and challenges before me, and which shapes my day-to-day decisions as well as the overall direction of my commitments, is the Christian story. This story, which was introduced to me by my parents and teachers at an early age, and whose many facets and implications I continue to discover, has obviously had an overwhelming impact on my life, not least among which is to connect my life to (draw my life into) the drama of what God is doing in the world. With time I have learned that what God is doing is reconciling the world, which as Christians believe, has been realized in Christ. We are recipients of this gift of God's reconciliation, even as God invites us to participate in the divine drama as "ambassadors" of God's reconciling love, as we move toward its total realization in the eschaton.

I share my story of what it has meant for me to find myself as part of this divine drama, not because it is exemplary, and not because it is unique (although it certainly is, as all stories are), but because every Christian (or, as Paul says, "anyone in Christ"; 2 Cor. 5:17) is invited into the drama of God's new creation. How the Christian concretely lives out this drama depends on the "who," the "where," the "when," the "how," and other details of one's biography. But this in itself is another reason why identity in general, Christian identity in particular, does not render itself to definition but to narration. For, as an invitation into the drama of God's new creation, Christian life and identity is a journey. And journeys are unique and particular. Accordingly, I share my story with the hope that others may recognize a similar pattern in their own lives, a pattern of crossing boundaries, negotiating different identities and commitments, and developing an ever-expanding sense of "my people," as well as a tendency to become part of communities that reflect a "new we," defying and cutting across boundaries of race, nation, class, tribe, and ethnicity. And when they do (to the extent they do), they realize that they are part of a story, a movement, a "revolution"—a God drama! No doubt the invitation to be part of the drama always finds one somewhere: as a member of tribe, ethnicity, race, and nation. But its goal is not simply to affirm, not simply to build onto that (as though it were a foundation), but to turn that into a stepping-stone for the journey. The sense of one's culture as a stepping-stone explains why I find Miroslav Volf's *Exclusion and Embrace* helpful in understanding Christian life as a journey, even though there are aspects of Volf's view of culture that I find problematic. To get a deeper sense of what is involved in claiming Christian identity as a journey, it might be helpful to briefly attend to Volf's work.

Departing without Leaving—an Abrahamic Revolution

In Miroslav Volf's work, we find a similar vision of Christian life as a stepping out of one's culture. In *Exclusion and Embrace: A Theological Exploration of Identity, Otherness and Reconciliation*, Volf reflects on the tension between the message of the cross and a world of violence. How does a Christian remain faithful to the Gospel in a world of injustice, oppression, and violence, while continuing to struggle for justice, truth, and peace? The issue of identity is at the heart of this reflection. The

increasing violence and cultural conflict around the world are often related to the general tendency of people (including Christians) to give
ultimate allegiance to their cultures. The captivity to culture, Volf notes,
leads inevitably to a kind of "sacralization of cultural identity," and ultimately to an inappropriate dynamic between culture and self. What is
needed is cultivation of a "proper relation between *distance* from the
culture and *belonging* to it."[31]

Establishing this relation involves, in the first place, the recognition
that "departure" is part and parcel of Christian identity. Volf notes that
"at the very core of Christian identity lies an all-encompassing change
of loyalty, from a given culture with its gods to the God of all cultures."[32]
The story of Abraham provides support for this imperative. On the foundation of Christian faith stands the towering figure of Abraham, who,
Genesis informs us, "went forth" (12:1–4) even before the text tells us that
he "believed" (15:6). If Abraham is to be a blessing, he "cannot stay; he
must depart, cutting the ties that so profoundly define him."[33] He leaves
without even knowing where he is going. Volf elaborates: "The courage
to break his cultural and familial ties and abandon the gods of his ancestors (Joshua 24:2) out of allegiance to a God of all families and all
cultures was the original Abrahamic revolution. Departure from his native soil, no less than the trust that God will give him an heir, made Abraham the ancestor of us all (see Hebrews 11:8)." Christian faith is an
invitation to a similar Abrahamic revolution. "To be a child of Abraham
and Sarah and to respond to the call of their God means to make an
exodus, to start a voyage, become a stranger."[34]

However, even as Christians are called upon to "depart" from their
culture, Volf notes, they remain members of their particular culture or
nation or race. And so, in order to explore what "belonging" to a culture
might mean in the face of the imperative to "depart from it," Volf turns
to Paul, who faced this challenge, not as an abstract, but as a real tension
precipitated by Paul's mission to the Gentiles (non-Jews). How could
Paul's Gentile believers believe in and enjoy the blessings promised to
Abraham (a Jew) and his descendants (members of a particular tribe)?

Volf notes that Paul struggles with this question but eventually
comes to resolve it by turning to the person of Christ. "Christ, the seed
of Abraham, is both the fulfilment of the genealogical promise to Abra-

ham and the end of genealogy as a privileged locus of access to God."[35] At the center of Paul's logic are two central images: the cross and the body of Christ. In relation to the cross, Paul argues that the unity of the families of the earth is created through the self-giving sacrifice of Christ's cross: "The crucified Messiah creates unity by giving his own self. . . . Unity here is not the result of 'sacred violence,' which obliterates the particularity of 'bodies,' but a fruit of Christ's self-sacrifice, which breaks down the enmity between them."[36] A second central designation for the community created by the self-giving of Christ is "the *body* of Christ," for just "as the body is one but has many members . . . in the one spirit we are all baptized into one body" (1 Cor. 12:13). Baptism into Christ creates a people as the differentiated body of Christ. In this one body, "Bodily inscribed differences are brought together, not removed. . . . The Pauline move is not from the particularity of the body to the universality of the sprit, but from 'separated bodies to the community of interrelated bodies—the one *body in the Sprit* with many *discrete members.*'"[37]

The implication that Volf draws from this dialectic of departure and belonging is that

> each culture can retain its own cultural specificity; Christians need not "lose their cultural identity as Jew or Gentile and become one humanity which is neither." . . . At the same time, no culture can retain its own tribal deities; religion must be de-ethnicized so that ethnicity can be de-sacralized. . . . Through faith one must "depart" from one's culture because the ultimate allegiance is given to God and to God's Messiah who transcends every culture. And yet precisely because of the ultimate allegiance to God of *all* cultures and to Christ who offers his "body" as a home for all people, Christian children of Abraham can "depart" from their culture without having to leave it. . . . Departure is no longer a spatial category. It can take place *within the cultural space one inhabits.*

Thus, Volf concludes, "Distance from culture must never degenerate into flight from that culture, but must be a way of living in a culture."[38]

Volf's work is brilliant and quite illuminating on the dynamics of Christian identity, especially the relationship between distance from and belonging to a culture. My only problem with Volf is his conceptual imprisonment within the notion of culture. Not only does Volf assume culture to be univocal, or monolithic, thereby giving an impression that one deals always in the same way with every aspect of one's culture, but for Volf, as for Richard Niebuhr, culture seems to be inescapable.[39] Part of what brings him to this conclusion may be a thin ecclesiology; because Volf does not work with a substantive notion of the church as a people, a distinct community with a unique ethos shaped by a distinct memory, he does not have any other category to describe the reality of being a Christian than a relation to culture. Everything for Volf seems to be viewed through a cultural prism. Note for instance this conclusion: "The proper distance from a culture does not take Christians out of that culture. Christians are not the insiders who have taken flight to a new 'Christian culture' and become outsiders to their own culture; rather when they have responded to the call of the Gospel they have stepped, as it were, with one foot outside their own culture while with the other remaining firmly planted in it. They are distant and yet they belong. *Their difference is internal to the culture.*"[40] True, Christians are not insiders who have taken flight to a new "Christian culture." They are people who have become incorporated into a new people, for whom culture may not be the most determinative description. What Christians become in terms of culture is not something that can be determined a priori. What Volf fails to note is that the invitation to depart creates something new, something that did not exist before—a new community (just as it did for Abraham). This new people or community must be described on its own terms, not necessarily in terms of their "culture" or "tribe" or "nation." This also means that their relationship to their "culture" (out of which they are called to "depart") cannot be reduced to a single theory but rather is a practice that depends on what is happening as well as where and how. Christians are called to discern, and therefore negotiate in an ongoing way, which cultural elements are consistent with what it means to be God's new people and which elements represent resistance to God's reconciling love and thus need to be rejected. Thus the need for stories—another thing that is missing in Volf's otherwise brilliant analysis.

Another way to register the concern I am raising here is that Volf's notion of a journey does not go far enough. In other words, the Abrahamic "revolution" turns out not to be a real revolution: "Distance from culture is not flight from culture, but simply a way of living in one's culture." But this conclusion leaves things too neat, and the Christian journey, in the end, turns into merely a matter of the right attitude toward culture without capturing a sense of "displacement." Neither does it capture the possibility of being "unhinged" from one's cultural moorings or give a sense of "pilgrimage"—which may result in a sense of "confusion" in terms of one's cultural identity—especially as Christians realize that they are bearers of many cultural identities or find themselves at odds with particular cultural expectations. The Christian journey presses toward a Mestizo or "mixed" sense of identity, as my former colleague at Notre Dame the late Fr. Virgilio Elizondo reminded us.[41] To highlight this dimension of the journey of Christian identity, it might be worthwhile to attend, even if briefly, to Elizondo's work.

Christian Identity as "Mestizo"

The core of our existence, Elizondo writes, "is to be other," to embrace a "new identity," to live "in between" cultures—neither this nor that but fully both, always straining ("journeying") toward the fuller reality of a new humanity that Jesus himself represents.[42] For Elizondo, this understanding of Christian identity is grounded in the mystery of the Incarnation and in the Galilean Principle. In the Incarnation, Jesus is both divine and human. He is also a Galilean, or from a place known as "Galilee of the Gentiles" (Isa. 9:1–2). Occupied by many nations, its land and its people marked by centuries of continuous rebuilding, Galilee was a frontier region of Israel surrounded by foreign nations, a land of multiple borders! Being surrounded and even partially populated by various ethnicities, Galilee would inevitably have been a city of cultural encounters, tensions, and exchanges. This Galilean Principle, Elizondo notes, is central to understanding God's work in history: out of the rejects and ridiculed of society a new society of universal welcome and love emerges. From the margins Jesus initiates not a new center but rather a new movement of the Spirit that enables people to cross segregating boundaries and form a new human family based on love of God and love of neighbor.[43]

Speaking of his own Mestizo identity as a Mexican American and what it taught him about Christian identity, Elizondo writes, "Mestizo are part of both while not being exclusively either. . . . I am always both kin (at home) and foreigner at the same time." This "in-between" state is the pain and potential, the suffering and the joy, the confusion and the mystery, the darkness and the light of Mestizo life. And so notes Elizondo, "As I claim this ambiguity and recognize it for what it truly is, I become the bearer of a new civilization that is inclusive of all the previous ones. No longer do I carry the burden of the shameful news, but rather become the bearer of the good news of the future that has already begun in us."[44]

Elizondo uses various expressions to describe the goal of the Mestizo identity. Its telos is to create something new: a "new movement," a "new human family," and a "new civilization." Behind all of these is Elizondo's overriding conviction that Christian life does not leave us where we are but creates a "new future" out of our old identities. This future, Elizondo notes, is not a self-enclosed community but an ever-expanding journey of radical biological, cultural, and spiritual openness to others: "The mestizo 'in between' keeps expanding, as the 'frontera' keeps expanding both north and south at the same time it keeps including more and more peoples, more ethnicities, and races."[45]

I noted earlier how my biography and my journey had confirmed my own sense of "mestizo," leading the student to remark about my "confused" identity. But Bediako had noted a similar dynamic for the early Christians living in the Greco-Roman Empire. In a culture where identity was determined simultaneously by both nationality and religion (Roman pagan religion), Christians found themselves in an awkward space, claiming to be citizens, and yet not willing to follow the Roman religion. They were not only a "confused" and "confusing" group, they were socially, religiously, and politically very disruptive. Similarly, the disruptive and subversive nature of the "in-between" Mestizo identity can be glimpsed in the story of the "confused" Hutu boy who during the Rwanda Genocide fled to the bushes with the Tutsis. After two or three weeks, the Tutsis pointed out to him that he was Hutu and so could be saved. He left the marshes and was not attacked. But the mixed-up boy had spent so much time with Tutsis that he was confused. He didn't know how to draw the "proper" line between ethnic groups. Afterward, when he returned to his village, he did not get involved in the killings. The Interahamwe militias tried to force him to participate in the killing but eventually gave up on him because his mind was, in their words, "clearly overwhelmed."[46] In the face of entrenched national, racial, or ethnic identities, the goal of the journey of Christian life is to shape such "confused," Mestizo identities—identities for whom the questions of "Who am I?" and "Who are my people?" are never settled. Keeping these questions open is what makes Christian life a life of ongoing negotiation of identities, which involves an invitation not only to embrace the other (who is different) but to cross boundaries into an ever-expanding sense of community. As Elizondo notes in the already-quoted phrase, the "frontera" of "my people" keeps expanding, which is to say, keeps including more and more peoples, more ethnicities, and races.

The Goal of the Journey: A New People, a "New We"

Long before I read Volf's *Exclusion and Embrace*, and before I encountered Elizondo's Mestizo theology, I had already grasped the notion of Christian identity as a journey, thanks to the work of Stanley Hauerwas. For Hauerwas, Christian life is an invitation and a journey to follow Jesus. It is no coincidence, Hauerwas (and Willimon) write, that the Gospel writers chose to frame the Gospel in terms of a journey, reflecting not only Jesus's traveling from one place to another but also the invitation he extended to his disciples, "Follow me."[47] This "adventurous journey," as Hauerwas calls it, does not leave the Christian unchanged. It involves a willingness to step out, just as Abraham and Sarah did.[48] Much as their journey transforms Abraham and Sarah into the progenitors of a new people, the Christian invitation to "follow me," if accepted, will make us members of God's people. This is what explains the strong and repeated emphasis in Hauerwas's work on the church as a "people"— God's new people, who, like Israel in the Old Testament, are called to live by the memory of God's work in history. From a Christian point of view, the story of God's saving work has come to a unique realization in the life, death, and resurrection of Christ. This is the distinct memory that shapes the church as a community of memory, whose memory is kept alive through (preeminently) scripture and the Eucharist. Given the distinct memory that shapes the Christian community (which others may not necessarily share) and the social and practical implications for how Christians live, the church, Hauerwas and Willimon write in *Resident Aliens*, "is a colony: an island of one culture in the middle of another. In baptism our citizenship is transferred from one dominion to another, and we become, in whatever culture we find ourselves, resident aliens."[49]

While the image of "resident aliens" captures the thrust of the argument I am making here, Hauerwas and Willimon's reference to the church as a "colony" is both problematic and misleading. The word *colony* seems to imply a self-enclosed social group—"a group of people of one nationality or ethnic group living in a foreign city or country, going about its own affairs," is how one dictionary defines it.[50] Moreover, I suspect that it is this reference to the church as *colony* that leads many critics to dismiss Hauerwas work as a form of "sectarianism," which encourages Christians to withdraw into a Christian ghetto. Nothing, of course, could be further from the truth. For Hauerwas the whole purpose, the whole mission, of the church is not to carry out its own affairs but to exist "for the life of the world." In living true to this mission, the church's role is not simply to affirm cultural, national, or ethnic realities but to "witness," within those realities, the church's identity as a "people" (her unique "citizenship") formed by a distinct memory. At any rate, for Hauerwas Christian faith is not simply an "add-on" to what already exists; it involves a "stepping out," or, in the words of the Spiritan professor Elochukwu Uzukwu, a "primordial uprooting" so as to be "incorporated" into God's new people (a new clan, according to Mulago), which is not simply the sum total of ethnic identities.[51]

That is why, to get a clearer understanding of the goal or telos of the journey of Christian identity as the formation of a new people in the world, as a new sense of belonging, it is important to clarify the identity of this "new people." Are they simply another tribe, another culture, or another ethnicity? Clarifying these questions is important if we are to come to a better appreciation of why there can be no talk of Christian identity that does not refer to the reality of the church. The journey of Christian identity is not a Lone Ranger enterprise. A discussion of Christian identity is always an ecclesiological discussion. But clarifying these questions is also important if we are to highlight the social and political implications of Christian identity, more specifically why and how, in the face of entrenched national, cultural, ethnic, tribal, or national identities, the church can be that much-needed mischievous and subversive tradition that points to and makes real an ever-expanding *frontera* of who constitutes "my people."

More than anybody else, it was the missiologist Andrew Walls who helped me come to a better sense of the church as an activity and a "moment" that is constituted in and through what Walls describes as the "Ephesian Moments" of "coming together," "standing together," and "eating together."

In a now dated but highly influential essay, "The Gospel as Prisoner and Liberator of Culture" (1982), Walls introduces two principles of the Gospel's impact upon culture: the indigenizing and the pilgrim. Concerning the indigenizing principle, Walls notes that all churches are cultural churches:

> It is of the essence of the Gospel that God accepts us as we are, on the ground of Christ's work alone, not on the ground of what we have become or are trying to become. But, if He accepts us "as we are" that implies He does not take us as isolated, self-governing units, because we are not. We are conditioned by a particular time and place, by our family and group and society, by "culture" in fact. In Christ God accepts us together with our group relations; with that cultural conditioning that makes us feel at home in one part of human society and less at home in another.[52]

But throughout church history there has been another force in tension with this indigenizing principle—the pilgrim principle: Not only does God in Christ take people as they are, he takes them in order to transform them into what he wants them to be. "Along with the indigenizing principle which makes his faith a place to feel at home, the Christian inherits the pilgrim principle, which whispers to him that he has no abiding city and warns him that to be faithful to Christ will put him out of step with his society."[53]

In his essay, Walls's primary interest in these two principles is missiological—their implication for theology in the era of world Christianity. Accordingly, he notes that there is not just one theology; there are many theologies, each arising out of different cultural contexts, each with its own limitations and "cultural blinkers . . . which will prevent, or at least render it difficult for them to see some things."[54] This observation in itself is not novel, even though I might add, in light of the earlier discussion in this chapter, that clearly the pilgrim principle has not been sufficiently attended to in recent theological exploration on mission and culture.[55] More intriguing is Walls's argument about how these cultural limitations are overcome: "the great advantage, the crowning excitement which our own era of Church history has over all others" is the possibility for us to "come together" and to "read [the scriptures] together." This is what creates the church as that great multitude drawn from every nation, tribe, people, and tongue, and a revolutionary movement as "God causes yet more light and truth to break forth from his word."[56]

Walls returns to the themes of "reading together" and of "coming together" in another essay, "The Ephesian Moment: At Crossroads in Christian Mission."[57] This essay has more explicit lessons for the journey of Christian identity and for the church as a "new" community. The essay begins by noting a "crisis" (which you will see is similar to that described by Volf), precipitated by the spread of Christianity beyond the Jewish world into pagan territories. Traditionally, observant Jewish society and Hellenist pagan society could be viewed as distinct entities, and the distinctiveness of each was marked by the meal table. Jews ate with Jews, and Gentiles with Gentiles. But how was this division to be reconciled with shared membership in one church? The compromise reached at the Council of Jerusalem (Acts 15) produced two distinct Christian lifestyles corresponding to these ethnic and cultural divisions: the one for Jewish society, the other for Hellenistic society.

Paul was not comfortable with this compromise. Emphatically, there was to be only *one* Christian community.[58] God's purpose in Christ, Paul writes, was to create, out of many, "one new man" (Eph. 2:15) so that Jewish and Gentile Christians would now share "one Spirit" (2:18), "one hope" (4:4), "one Lord, one faith, one baptism, [as they are all children of] one God and Father of all" (4:5–6).

The original Ephesian Moment was the coming together for the first time of Jewish and Gentile Christians. It is this coming together of two communities historically separated—the breaking down of the wall of separation brought about by Christ's death (Eph. 2:13–18)—that Paul celebrates in the letter to the Ephesians. Jewish and Gentile Christians are "no longer strangers and sojourners" but "fellow citizens" and "members of God's household" (2:19). Thus, if the letter to the Ephesians recognizes the cultural and political realities of being Jewish and Gentile, this fact in itself was not theologically interesting. This is not what Paul celebrates, but the fact of their "coming together," of their being "made alive together" (2:5), of their being raised up together, sitting together (2:6). Jewish and Gentile Christians "belong together" like "bricks—used in the construction of a single building—the temple where the One God would live" (2:19–22). They constitute, not two separate communities, but one community, of which they are both members, constituting as it were (and now Paul uses another image, of the body) different parts of a single body of which "Christ is the head, the mind, the brain, under whose control the whole body works and is held together" (4:15–16).

Three elements of Walls's description of the original Ephesian Moment speak directly to an appreciation of Christian identity and the reality of the church. First, inherent in the Ephesian Moment is the realization that, on their own, Jewish and Gentile Christians remain but "fragments" of God's purpose. Together, and only together, can the fragments come to what Paul describes as "the height of Christ's full stature" (4:13). The implication seems obvious. On our own—as American, Asian, African, white, black, Hutu, Tutsi Christians—we remain but "fragments." Only by coming together are these different fragments "incorporated" into Christ's body and thus able to reveal the height of Christ's full stature. Second is the realization that the coming together of Jewish and Gentile Christians creates something new. "The full height of Christ's full stature" that Paul celebrates is about this new and odd communion of believers that is neither Jewish nor Gentile (Gal. 3:28). A similar phenomenon was under way at Antioch, where the term *Christian* was first used. In a unique Ephesian Moment, Jews and Gentiles came together and created a "new we" that required a new name. No one had needed such a term when they existed independently as only Jew and Gentile.

A third and very significant element of Walls's Ephesian Moment was the act of eating together, which was both the test and the expression of their coming together: "Two cultures historically separated by the meal table were now able to come together at table to share the knowledge of Christ."[59] Thus the meal table—the institution that had once symbolized the ethnic and cultural division—now became the hallmark of Christian living. This experience was reproduced at Antioch, Jerusalem, and other places as one of the most noticeable features of life in the Jesus community, as the followers of Jesus took every opportunity to eat together. It is particularly important for confirming how the coming together is not simply a "spiritual" fellowship. It is a true and genuine fellowship that is realized in and through working together and sharing the material—and thus economic—realities of everyday life. In fact, it is only through such collaborative efforts of "eating" that we become one. For indeed, as the Rwandan proverb goes, "Akamwa karya ntimumve, kavuza induru ntimumve," roughly translated as "Unless you hear the mouth eating, you cannot hear the mouth crying." The reality of new friendships arising out of and through working together is shown by the story of Father Andre Sibomana, a Rwandan priest, who narrowly survived the genocide in Rwanda. In the aftermath of the genocide, he mobilized his Christians for the reconstruction of schools, public places, and houses for genocide survivors. The Christians were both Hutu and Tutsi. At the beginning of the building project, the Hutus and Tutsis each kept to themselves and did not speak to one another. But the communal work helped to build bridges. At the inauguration of the first two hundred houses, on August 21, 2005, Hutu and Tutsi drank banana beer from the same jug.[60]

The overall implication from Walls's description of the original Ephesian Moment is that Christian identity is an invitation and journey of learning to eat together across national, racial, tribal, and ethnic boundaries. These opportunities of coming together across divides not only "break down the dividing walls of hostility" but create forms of catholicity that both reflect and reveal something of the church as Christ's body. The "height of Christ's full stature" that Paul celebrates means that the church cannot be a kind of "colony" or Christian "tribe" where Christians from different ethnic, cultural, national, or racial backgrounds learn to cooperate among themselves as Christians but have nothing to do with those outside the tribe. The "height of Christ's full stature" cannot mean that the church views itself as a self-sufficient community of "us" versus "them" (Muslims, Hindus, Jews, atheists, secularists, etc.). The church's identity and mission is to be a journey, and that means constantly being reconstituted as a new community, a new Ephesian Moment, as the *frontera* keeps expanding and new opportunities of collaboration and coming together even with those who "were once strangers" are grasped. In the end, the journey of Christian identity is to lead to the affirmation of our common humanity, or, as Paul says, to the realization that "all are children of one God, who is Father of all" (Eph. 4:5–6). The church is an Ephesian Moment in time and space of the reality of the "new we" beyond nation, race, tribe, and even religion.

The Journey as "Invention"

What our exploration in this chapter has demonstrated is that Christian identity is not a "static" essence, spiritual or otherwise, but an invitation to a journey, with a definite direction and telos. The goal of this journey is the creation of something new: variously described in the last section as a Mestizo or in-between existence, as an Abrahamic revolution, as a community of resident aliens, and as an Ephesian "new we." In describing Christian life as the life of "resident aliens" Stanley Hauerwas and William Willimon talked about a distinct memory. In discussing the relation between Christian and cultural identities, Volf invoked Paul's image of the "cross" and "Christ's body"—the same images that Paul uses in describing the Ephesian Moment. These theologians are pointing to what makes the Christian journey of identity possible and what propels it forward: the self-sacrificing love of God, revealed most preeminently in the life, death, and resurrection of Christ. It is this self-sacrificing love that the Christian journey of baptism recreates in the world by inviting Christians to "depart" from wherever they find themselves, to belong to new community that is "invented," which is to say, made possible by God's self-sacrificing love in the world.

But what does this "invention" of God's self-sacrificing love look like in the context of ethnic, religious, and ecological forms of violence in Africa? What kind of community and possibilities does it create? How are these communities able to interrupt the politics of violence? Can and, if so, how do its waters run deeper than the blood of tribalism? To respond to these and similar questions requires not only theoretical argument but stories that testify to the possibility and the reality of a different modernity in Africa. To this testimony of the invention of love in Africa we now turn, in the second part of the book.

PART II

Love's Invention in the Midst of Africa's Violent Modernity

Ethnic Violence and the Reinvention of Identity

Suffering is the true basis of human identity, the unifying factor that identifies us as humans.
—Fr. Jean Baptiste Mvukiyehe

My wounds can be a healing for others.
—Fr. Anthony

Love makes us inventors.
—Maggy Barankitse

Nyamata, August 1998

I am standing inside the church of Nyamata. Even though it has been four years since the genocide, the empty church carries fresh memories of what happened here. The corrugated tin roof has bullet holes and bears visible bloodstains; the main area of the church contains nothing except the bloodstained clothes of the victims. The cloth covering the altar, once white, is now dark with blood; a blood-stained machete, a spiked club, and a twisted metal cross lie on top of the altar. The marble baptismal font is chipped in a number of places, by either shrapnel from hand grenades or machete blows intended for some of the victims. The church basement, accessible down steep steps in the back, has been converted into a permanent catacomb. On either side of its narrow

67

hallways are racks of skulls, bones, coffins, and the personal belongings of the more than eight thousand people who were killed inside the church.

As I stand inside the empty church in horrified silence, I keep wondering about the contradictions that Nyamata represents. How to fathom that over eight thousand people were killed inside what was supposed to be a sanctuary? How to reconcile that genocide happened in this beautiful and deeply Christian country?[1] Why was the church unable to provide a bulwark against the slaughter, and why was it even, as some cases indicated, a contributing factor in the killing?[2] That the genocide started during Easter week only adds further irony to the contradictions. For obviously, many of the victims had celebrated Christ's resurrection from the dead, thus becoming the first fruit of God's new creation, here in this very church together with their killers who were also a part of the congregation. Was all the talk of a new identity, a new life with God—words that describe the life of the Christian—nothing but mere *spiritual* platitudes, words that actually mean very little in the "real" world? Could it be true that in the "real" world, the blood of tribalism runs deeper than the waters of baptism?

These and similar questions confront me every time I return to Nyamata. And not only Nyamata but elsewhere—Ntarama, Nyarubuye, Nyange—churches that became killing fields during the 1994 Genocide. I have visited the church of Nyange, in the Kibuye district of Western Rwanda, and heard Aloys Rwamasirabo, a former parishioner who lost his wife and five children in the church killing, tell the story of what happened. A few days after the genocide started, the priest there, Athanase Seromba, encouraged Tutsi Christians to take refuge in the church. A ten-day siege by the militia ensued. They threw grenades into the sanctuary and set a fire around the perimeter of the church, but the attacks proved unsuccessful. It was then that Fr. Seromba conspired with the mayor and the local police inspector to destroy the building. They brought in two bulldozers to knock down the church. The drivers of the bulldozers were reluctant to follow the orders. One of them even asked the priest three separate times if this was absolutely necessary. Seromba, who was later convicted by the International Criminal Court for crimes against humanity and is serving a life sentence at the Hague, gave them a go-ahead, saying: "We Hutus are many, we will build another church."

The drivers proceeded to batter the building until the walls and the roof collapsed, killing the over two thousand men, women, and children who had taken refuge inside the church.[3]

Every time I stand on the grounds of that erased church, under which over two thousand victims are buried, I feel an overwhelming sense of shame, bitterness, and anger. But I also wonder at the depth of hatred that would bring someone like Seromba (a Catholic priest) to *imagine* that the killing of over two thousand Tutsis was such a good thing that it justified even the destruction of his church? What brings one to such hatred? What is the role of memory (of injustice suffered or imagined) in fueling this hatred and the search for revenge by the destruction of the perceived perpetrator? How does one break or move out of the endless cycle of revenge and counter-revenge that the victims seem to be calling for?[4] What is the relationship between memory and identity? What kind of process is involved in forming an identity as Hutu, Tutsi, Igbo, or any other tribe that makes it so deeply rooted that being a Christian, a priest, or a religious does not seem able to alter it? Must identity always be an "us" against "them" zero-sum game? The more I ponder these questions on the ground of Nyamata and Nyange, the more I feel the need to think through the interrelated connections between identity, memory, and violence. The more I also wonder about the possibility of "reimagining" these issues in a way that would heed Paul's exhortation to "not be conformed to the patterns of the world" but instead to be "transformed" by the "renewing" of the mind so as to "grasp what is good, pleasing and perfect" (Rom. 12:2). In this chapter, I attempt that reimagining.

The Invention of "Tribe" and "Ethnicity": Making Nyamata and Seromba Thinkable

The journey through the interconnected realities of identity, memory, and violence lands one in the rough terrain of political imagination. Thus a crucial starting point in rethinking these realities lies in understanding the role of colonial and neocolonial politics in "inventing" Hutu and Tutsi as polar identities within Rwanda's politics. We are, of course, not used to thinking about "Hutu" and "Tutsi"—or for that matter "tribe" and "ethnicity"—in terms of their being invented. We tend to think about ethnicities as "natural" identities, the way that God created us, and about which we can do nothing. But that is misleading. For there is nothing "natural" about being white, being Hutu or Tutsi, Igbo or Ganda. These are identities, and like all identities, they are ideas, reflections of the way we have come to view ourselves, which are, in turn, connected to the way others view or imagine us. The story of Rwanda not only helps to confirm this, it makes nonsense of all so-called natural identities and their immutability.

For as mentioned before, the Rwanda Genocide tends to be depicted in terms of age-old animosities between Hutu and Tutsi tribes, which came to play out in 1994. Such a narrative assumes a cultural or biological difference between these two identities—differences that have existed for centuries and only came to be exploited within Rwanda's colonial and postcolonial politics, solidifying historical injustices and an exclusionary politics of "Tutsi" privilege versus "Hutu" marginalization, a politics of "us" against "them." The historical animosities finally exploded into "ethnic" violence during the 1994 Genocide. This account, however, is at best only half true, and is misleading in assuming Hutu and Tutsi as "natural" or "cultural" identities.[5] For Tutsi and Hutu speak the same language, share customs, share religious beliefs, and have a high degree of intermarriage. In fact, as mentioned in the first chapter of this book, Monsignor Louis de Lacger, writing in the 1950s, was able to note that there were fewer people in Europe "among whom one finds these three factors of national cohesion: one language, one faith, one law."[6] How then did such a homogenous, closely knit society succeed in becoming the Rwanda of 1994, in which Hutu and Tutsi were such polar identities, united in their hatred and desire for violent elimination of the other?

The key lies in understanding the dynamics of political imagination and the role that story plays in it. For whatever else can be said about Hutu and Tutsi in precolonial Rwanda, these identities do not reflect either a cultural or a biological difference. Rather, they are "political" identities produced and reproduced through the political history of modern Rwanda. To appreciate this conclusion, one needs to pay attention to the crucial distinction that the Ugandan political scientist Mahmood

Mamdani makes between "cultural" and "political" identities. According to Mamdani, cultural identities reflect something of the past—a shared history, a language, a set of customs or beliefs. Political identities, on the other hand, reflect a future political project, such as realizing specific political goals or allocating access to benefits and privileges.[7] In the case of Rwanda, colonial mythology played a key role in the process of state formation. Using the biblical story of the cursing of Ham, nineteenth-century Europeans obsessed with justifying domination came to cast ("imagine") Tutsi-Hutu differences operating in precolonial Rwanda as essentially racial, a reflection of ontological superiority and inferiority, and one that came to play out historically as the conflict between invaders and natives.

This is what is meant by the invention of Hutu and Tutsi identities. It is not that the Belgians entirely cooked up these notions. Hutu and Tutsi were part of the repertoire of cultural and political notions operative within precolonial Rwanda, as were the clans: the Basingo, Basigwa, Banyiginya, Baziga, and so on. Clans contained both Hutu and Tutsi and were in fact far more determinative when it came to political access in precolonial Rwanda than Hutu or Tutsi identities. That clans were not viewed as (and thus did not become) the decisive factor in the understanding and reorganization of Rwandan society by the Belgians is the work of political imagination. Instead, when it came to thinking about reorganizing Rwanda and its major economic, social, and political institutions in a modern way, the distinction between Hutu and Tutsi became the decisive factor in allocating and accessing privileges.

In the transformation of Hutu and Tutsi from cultural identities to modern political identities, the most effective and enduring tool was their deliberate codification. These identities came to be inscribed in the legal framework of modern Rwanda and enforced through the mandatory issuance of an identity card that bore one's *Ubwoko*. What is remarkable is that in spite of the so-called science of races with which Europeans mapped the differences in morphology between Tutsis and Hutus, when it came to the final determination of who was Tutsi and who was Hutu, the Belgians could not clearly tell those who were assumed to be tall with lean noses from their fellow Rwandans. They had to depend instead on a consideration as arbitrary as the number of cows that a

Rwandan owned! Anyone with more than five cows was legally declared to be Tutsi. And when the law recognized one as Tutsi, one became Tutsi.

No doubt, a legal framework did exist in precolonial Rwanda within which Hutu and Tutsi (as well as the clans) operated, but that legal framework operated differently from its modern counterpart. The former recognized and ensured some form of fluidity in identities and relations between Hutu and Tutsi and in fact encouraged it: the whole system was set up to accommodate a large degree of in-between possibility. But the modern legal framework, grounded in neoclassical essentialism and Cartesian dualism, would not tolerate any such flexibility in identity. One had to be either Hutu or Tutsi.

We can make a number of conclusions from this simple overview regarding the formation of Hutu and Tutsi as political identities within Rwanda's political history. First, just because we are referring to Hutu and Tutsi as "imagined" and as "invented" is not to say that these identities are any less real. To this point, Mamdani rightly notes:

> Whatever Hutu and Tutsi identity may have stood for in the pre-colonial state no longer mattered: The Belgians had made "ethnicity" the defining feature of Rwandan existence. Most Hutus and Tutsis still maintained fairly cordial relations, intermarriages went ahead, and the fortunes of "les petits Tutsis" in the hills remained quite indistinguishable from those of their Hutu neighbors. But with every schoolchild reared in the doctrine of racial superiority and inferiority, the idea of a collective national identity was steadily laid to waste, and on either side of the Hutu-Tutsi divide there developed mutually exclusionary discourses based on the competing claims of entitlement and injury.[8]

The second conclusion that we can draw is that political imagination has power. As Mamdani confirms, the Hamitic mythology of the separate origins of Hutu and Tutsi not only was used to explain distinctions among a people who originally spoke the same language, lived on the same hills, and shared the same culture but was the basis for successfully forming a society (modern Rwanda) where Hutu and Tutsi actually became separate political communities.

A third observation is that Rwanda helps illumine the kind of political imagination at work across much of modern Africa. "Tribe" was imagined by Europeans as the way Africans naturally lived and was therefore "invented" as an unquestionable building block of the politics of the modern African nation-state. The power of the invention is that, in being absorbed through the legal, economic, and political institutions of modern Africa, it succeeds in transforming a myth into a reality. Given the colonial and neocolonial politics of divide and rule, it is not difficult to see how "ethnic entitlement" (it is our turn to eat), "ethnic hatred," and "ethnic violence" became perpetual features of modern political life in Africa. Mamdani is therefore right to characterize Rwanda as a "metaphor for post-colonial political violence."[9] So we see that Rwanda in 1994 is not an exception but the most extreme manifestation of the same phenomenon of "ethnic violence" that we have witnessed in Burundi, South Sudan, Ivory Coast, and Kenya (following the 2007 elections).

A fourth conclusion has to do with how the politics of ethnicity both needs and creates registers of historical injustices and violence (violence suffered or perpetuated) that not only reinforce "our identity" but become a storeroom for volatile memories that easily unleash vengeance as a way either to "honor our dead" or to achieve a "final solution," ensuring that we will never become victims again. And so in Africa, the politics of ethnicity has only succeeded in creating endless cycles of violent reprisals (revenge and counter-revenge) where "victims become killers" (the memorable title of Mamdani's book) and the line between victims and perpetrators gets increasingly blurred.

Fifth, within this chemistry of political imagination, the appeal to ethnicity as a "natural" identity not only is misleading but becomes a dangerous myth. The appeal to "tribal unity" easily plays an ideological role that continues to blind us to the economic and political interests that often cut across "tribal" lines. Thus, as Appiah notes, "'Race' in Europe and 'tribe' in Africa are central to the way in which the objective interests of the worst-off are distorted."[10] What Rwanda also demonstrates is that the appeal to "racial" or "tribal" unity can be, and often is, in Africa, a dangerous call that leads to the unfortunate consequence of people actually killing totally innocent strangers or people they know and love—neighbors, family members—all in the name of ethnicity. Within this chemistry of state formation and an exclusionary politics of ethnic identity, Nyamata and Seromba become, if not justifiable, at least thinkable.

Finally, what is required, indeed what is an absolute necessity in our time, is, in the remarkable words of Thomas Sankara, the invention of a new future ("We must dare to invent the future").[11] This task, as Sankara notes, requires a "certain measure of madness," the madness to turn our backs on old formulas.[12] Tribe and ethnicity are part of the repertoire of the "old formulas" that need "reinvention." To see the possibility as well as the shape and form of this reinvention, we need stories of mad men and women, those who have "dared" to resist "tribe" and "ethnicity" as the ultimate definition of their identity.

Resisting Genocide and the Healing of Memory:
Jean Baptiste Mvukiyehe

Across the road from the Catholic parish of Nyange—where, during the genocide, more than two thousand refugees died when the church was bulldozed to the ground—is a high school, St. Joseph's School, run by the diocese. On the evening of March 18, 1997, three years after the genocide, students were in their classrooms doing prep work when an Interahamwe militia attacked the school. The rebels burst into the Senior 4 and Senior 5 classes and asked the students to separate into Tutsi and Hutu. The students refused. The rebels shot at them indiscriminately and threw grenades into the classroom. In all, eight students were killed and several were wounded.[13] Fr. Jean Baptiste Mvukiyehe was one of the students who survived. He is currently serving as rector and director of the shrine of Divine Mercy at Kabuga, east of Kigali. At the shrine, Jean Baptiste invites Christians, both victims and perpetrators of the genocide, to receive the gift of God's mercy and forgiveness so that healing and reconciliation can take place. Jean Baptiste's story helps illumine four things about resisting violence and healing its painful memories: (a) a sense of new family, (b) a personal journey from being healed to healing others, (c) a belief in divine providence, and (d) healing from "the burden of ethnicity." Attending to each of these elements through the story of Fr. Jean Baptiste and the places and people he introduced me to helps highlight the significance of the story of God's healing and reconciling love, which is behind the devotion to Divine Mercy, in the healing and reimagination of ethnic identity.

St. Joseph's School, Nyange: A New Family

I first met Fr. Jean Baptiste in August 2016, at the shrine of Divine Mercy at Kabuga. Deeply impressed by Jean Baptiste's work at Kabuga (more about that later), I invited him to a focus group discussion I planned to hold on the theme of "Christianity, Identity, and Belonging" in Entebbe, Uganda, in January 2017. At this workshop, as Jean Baptiste shared his story, I learned that he was one of the students at Nyange when the attack happened in 1997. He was born in Kibungo, in eastern Rwanda. In 1994, at the time of genocide, he was in Senior 2 on Easter break staying at home with his mother. They hid during the genocide, and when the Rwanda Patriotic Front (RPF) took over Kibungo they were sheltered in a neighboring school. After the war, he wished to return to his studies and enrolled in the only school that had a vacancy. That was St. Joseph School at Nyange. He was in Senior 5 when the 1997 attack happened, and his class was one of those on which the militia opened fire. Jean Baptiste was himself wounded. This is his account of those events:

> I remember that afternoon we had a normal day. Since it was toward April, it was the rainy season. That evening we went for our evening meal. . . . After dinner we come out chatting as usual. We saw people in military fatigues. I thought, they have deployed a new group of soldiers. . . . They said, you go and start your evening revising session. We thought they were normal soldiers. We started revising. After about twenty minutes we started hearing gunshots and heavy weapons. We noticed it was happening in our school. Two people broke into our class; they were shooting and shouting. They blocked the entrance, and we all hid under the desks. One man stood in the middle of the class and said, "Now, you should not waste our time. We need Hutu here and Tutsi the other side." We kept silent. Nobody said anything. The second and third time. No word. . . . Then he said, "Okay, you move out of your desks, I shall separate you

myself." Nobody moved. They grabbed two girls and cut their arms. But even with blood, they didn't separate. . . . Then they just put the gun under the desk and started shooting.[14]

I asked Fr. Jean Baptiste why he thinks the students remained united, even in the face of danger.

"Many people," he responded, "have tried to offer different views on this issue. However, what I believe is the simple fact that since our being together in the beginning of the school, we were like a family. . . . I do not remember the school authorities ever teaching us that you are one. We were just like a family."[15]

A year later, I was with Jean Baptiste driving from Kigali to Ruhango. I wanted to follow up on his remarks at the workshop, particularly his assessment of the resistance by Nyange students, which, according to him, was made possible by the "family" environment at the school. I asked him what it meant to be like a "family."[16]

"Ours was a small school, not more than three hundred or four hundred," he told me, "meaning you knew everybody. Seniors were in charge of junior students. It was like a small family." He added, "The leaders knew how to consider each student in his or her own needs. So we did not have a particular program of unity, but the setting and environment around there really made it easy for people to know one another and connect directly."

I was curious about the "setting and environment" that Jean Baptiste was talking about. So I asked him to explain further.

"Now and again the school would organize reconciliation workshops and days of recollection that brought students together. It was more the way the school was run and the way we were all committed and involved . . . the relationship we had with the school authorities and among us as students."

Jean Baptiste then talked about a sense of belonging and involvement in school activities.

"We had different clubs, and people would meet in movements like Catholic Action, and many other initiatives. And most importantly, we were involved in the school project and decision making. So we had so many student representatives and we had so many meetings with them."

But even with these factors—interpersonal interaction, good leadership, student involvement, and a sense of belonging, factors that created a family-like atmosphere at the school—Jean Baptiste admits, "We ourselves were surprised by the courage." He quotes the president of Komezubutwari Nyange—the Nyange student organization that was formed following the attack to encourage the culture of heroism, peace, and patriotism in other young people—who once remarked, "The heroism surprised us, but we now have to work to strengthen these values and principles."[17]

This sense of family and of gift ("We ourselves were surprised by the courage"—pointing to a sense of divine providence) are even more evident in the case of Ruhango. Jean Baptiste had told me about Ruhango following the Entebbe workshop in 2017 and described it as one of the few Catholic parishes that did not experience genocidal massacres during the 1994 Rwanda Genocide. He had encouraged me to visit the parish next time I was in Rwanda. The parish of Ruhango, originally founded by the White Fathers, was staffed by diocesan priests for a number of years until 1985, when the Pallottines took it over.[18]

The Miracle of Ruhango

When I was in Rwanda in January 2018, Jean Baptiste drove me from Kigali to Ruhango, south of Gitarama, to show me the parish where he had spent the first year of his ordination after he joined the Pallottines. He had returned for a few years to Ruhango after his study in Rome, helping to set up a retreat and pilgrimage center there and serving as its director for four years before he was transferred to Kabuga in 2014. I was eager to find out more about the parish and the reasons behind Ruhango's exceptional witness during the genocide.

As we drove from Kigali to Ruhango, I asked Jean Baptiste why he thought no massacres had taken place at Ruhango during the genocide. First of all, Jean Baptiste said, "You have to understand that it was divine protection. This is why people talk about the 'miracle' of Ruhango."[19]

As I learned from Jean Baptiste, the "miracle" of Ruhango was, in fact, a series of "miracles." First, there was the miraculous healing of the pastor, Fr. Stanislas Urbaniak, in 1991. Suffering from severe back pain, he had flown to Europe for treatment but returned without being cured. During a healing mass led by a Canadian Charismatic priest in Nyami-rambo Stadium, Urbaniak's back was healed. He saw his "miraculous" recovery as a call to help Jesus in healing others. Thus, on his return to the parish, he established a charismatic group focusing on prayer and on ministry to the sick. Most of the original members of the group were Christians from the parish who had been to Kibeho, where the Blessed Virgin Mary was said to have appeared to three young students with a message for conversion, prayer, and good works. With time, the group attracted more Christians, who joined the outreach to the sick in the community, praying over them and laying hands on them. There were many reports of sick people who were healed.

Then there was the miracle of divine providence during the geno-cide. As refugees flocked to the parish, the members of the charismatic group would go out to look for food in the villages. As tensions acceler-ated and it became impossible to send the Tutsi, Hutus would be the ones to go out to look for food. But when even that became impossible, they locked themselves up inside the church and continued in prayer and per-petual adoration of the Eucharist. They soon ran out of food but kept on praying and keeping hope alive (by boiling pots of water). When a trader from a nearby town delivered sacks of beans, maize meal, and rice to the starving refugees (arriving around 3 p.m., shortly before the start of the devotion to Divine Mercy), the community saw this as miracle—a clear sign of divine mercy.

What was perhaps by far the most talked-about miracle of the series was when the Interahamwe militia cut a hole through the door of the sacristy and entered the church. There they found the charismatic group together with the refugees in prayer and Eucharistic adoration. The leader of the charismatic group proceeded to thank God for the new brothers and sisters who had joined the group to "pray with us." The militia waited for the group to finish praying to begin killing, but of course this never happened, since the adoration was "perpetual." They left, promising to come back. Seven times the militia came back, each time finding the group in prayer and "perpetual" adoration.

These stories help to confirm in the minds of survivors and observ-ers that the fact that there were no massacres at Ruhango was indeed the result of divine providence. As one of the survivors recounted, "This is how the Lord saved us; it was the holy sacrament that saved our lives and *he* gave us what to eat."[20]

If the exceptional witness of Ruhango during the genocide was attributed to a divine miracle, it was also connected to the kind of community—an odd community—that Ruhango had become. At the head of this community was the parish priest, Fr. Urbaniak, a Polish Pallottine missionary. Both Jean Baptiste and Jean Paul (the current director of the Ruhango center) spoke of him as "a good man" who loved to "work in his flower gardens." They also described him as a very "stubborn priest" who could at times be "difficult to get along with." He was one of the few European priests who stayed in Rwanda during the genocide. When the UN sent a car to evacuate him, he sent the car back to Kigali, saying, "These are my parishioners, these are my people." Whenever the armed militia came to the church compound, he was there to courageously face them. At one time, they were about to kill a Tutsi priest and a seminarian who were hiding in the parish. Urbaniak confronted them and planted himself between the killers and the priest and seminarian. They would have to kill him first, he told the militia men, before they killed "his" brothers.[21]

A significant leader of the charismatic community and assistant to Fr. Stanislaus was a lay preacher named Gerard Ruvunabagabo. Both Jean Baptiste and Jean Paul described him as "an extraordinary preacher" whose words "always made a deep impact."[22] It is significant that Gerard was a "Mutwa" (a member of the minority and despised group of Rwandan pygmies). Perhaps because neither Fr. Urbaniak (a Muzungu) nor Gerard (a Mutwa) fit in the neat divisions of Hutu and Tutsi of Rwandan society, they were able to gather around them a community made up of both Hutu and Tutsi and to encourage the community to "take the faith seriously and stay united."[23]

From Being Healed to a Ministry of Healing

The stories of Nyange and of Ruhango highlight the courage needed to resist the violence of tribalism, a courage made possible by the sense and experience of a "new family" as well as the gift of divine providence. But the stories also point to another crucial dimension, that of healing, which was at work on a number of different levels: the healing of physical, spiritual, and emotional wounds, as well as healing from the "burden of history" and the "burden of ethnicity." Fr. Jean Baptiste's own story, which led him from Nyange to becoming a priest to his ministry of healing memories at Ruhango and now at Kabuga, is an example of this multilayered gift of healing. [24]

At Nyange Jean Baptiste had sustained a bullet wound in the leg. Recovering at the hospital and taking care of those critically wounded, he had met a Marist brother, a missionary at the Ecole des sciences, Byimana. He would soon join the Ecole and pass with grades high enough to take him to the university. But he had started to feel a call to become a priest. The Marist brother introduced him to the Pallottines, whose formation he would soon join.

As we drove back to Kigali from Ruhango, I asked Jean Baptiste about his journey to the priesthood and why he had chosen to become a priest. "I do not know," he said, paused, and then explained. "I was feeling this calling, which was getting stronger and stronger. At one time I could not resist it. That is why I decided to share with Brother Ray." Looking back, he explains, "There was also something 'mysterious' about becoming a priest. I had considered going to the university. And my mother really wanted me to (that way I could take care of her). I knew where the journey to the university would end. I would perhaps become an engineer. . . . That would be good, but being a priest was a larger perspective."

"So, you wanted something more," I pressed.

"Yes, being a priest was endless; it was a larger perspective."

"In what way?" I asked.

"There was something about becoming a priest that would engage the whole existence of a person for sure," he answered. "There was something extraordinary. Maybe that is what attracted me."

"But your mother wanted you to go to the university?"

"Yes, but I wanted to listen to my real thirst and make sure it was quenched."

"Why the Pallottines?" I asked.

"I did not know them. It was the community that Ray introduced me to. But when I encountered them I found their spirituality of the Divine Mercy quite meaningful."

The first Pallottine priests had arrived in Rwanda in 1973 from Poland. The Polish connection is important to understanding the special devotion to the Divine Mercy of the Pallottines in Rwanda. The devotion originated in Poland, with the reputed apparitions of Jesus to Faustina Kowalska. Pope John Paul II, himself a native of Poland who had great affinity toward the devotion, officially recognized the apparitions and declared the second Sunday after Easter Divine Mercy Sunday.

I asked Jean Baptiste about his formation and experiences at seminary with the Pallottines and what he remembered about that time.

"First and foremost," he noted, "formation was for me a time of purification" and a "time of healing." For until that time, Jean Baptiste explained, "I felt a heavy burden in me."

The "heavy burden" had to do with confusion about identity and the memory of violence. His extended family encompassed both Hutu and Tutsi. He had grown up with his mother only, his father having been killed in 1990 and his uncles living in exile in Tanzania. "This brought a lot of confusion in me." The formation, Jean Baptiste said, was an opportunity "to face my worries about who I am, and that was part of my own healing."

But Jean Baptiste, only sixteen at the time of the genocide, had witnessed the killing of a number of people before he himself was evacuated to a school by the Rwandan Patriotic Front (RPF). Consequently, he carried a deep sense of helplessness. He narrated the story of his fleeing and coming across, as his group ran, other refugees too weak to run anymore. One exhausted man asked him for a drink. Jean Baptiste found a dirty pot, fetched some water, and took it to the man. The man thanked him. "I looked into his eyes. He was suffering. Since I was pouring water for him, others were also looking for a drop. That was the last time I saw him. But we connected in that short time, and I always remember his eyes, his face, his misery." This and similar stories of suffering he had witnessed drew him to the spirituality of the Pallottines. "I loved the ministry of the Divine Mercy." He said, "It starts with human suffering." This might also be the reason, he concluded, "why after ordination I was sent to this ministry of reconciliation. My work in this ministry grew out of this personal journey."[25]

The ministry of Ruhango had grown out of another personal journey of healing—the story of Fr. Urbaniak. As already noted, the focus on
healing at Ruhango began with Fr. Urbaniak's own healing and the call
he felt upon being healed to "help Jesus to heal others." That's how
Urbaniak came to form the charismatic group, whose original focus was
on outreach to those who were physically sick, offering them prayer,
material support, and counseling. When genocide broke out in 1994 and
refugees flocked to Ruhango, Fr. Urbaniak's charismatic group welcomed them and looked after them as an extension of their pastoral outreach to the sick. The moving testimony of a survivor confirms the
reputation of Ruhango as a place of refuge where everyone, whether
Hutu or Tutsi, was welcomed. This survivor was a Tutsi woman who,
after losing all ten of her siblings and her parents during the early days
of the genocide, lived in the bush for weeks but held out hope that she
could find safety at Ruhango.

> I would tell myself [during the genocide] that if I could maybe get
> to Ruhango, I would live. There was someone I was living with
> during those hard times, and eventually she was able to get to Ru-
> hango before I did. She told of my story, and by the grace of God,
> three people came for me, risking their own lives in order to get
> me there. They would carry me most of the time and sometimes I
> would try to walk myself. . . . It was a miracle that we got to Ruhango
> Parish. We stayed there until the war was over.[26]

When the RPF finally arrived at Ruhango at the height of the genocide, they moved the refugees to the Bugesera district. After the genocide, when the people returned from Bugesera, the charismatic group
continued to play an active role in the parish. That is how Ruhango
became a pilgrimage and reconciliation center, which in the wake of the
genocide focused on offering both victims and perpetrators the opportunity to confront their "woundedness," to "unload their burdens," and
to find inner healing. Now, every first Sunday of the month, over fifteen
thousand pilgrims flock to the center to take part in the outdoor healing
mass. The testimony of Fr. Filipek offers a vivid illustration of the significance of this healing ministry:

In 1996 we started to build a Center for Reconciliation of the Merciful Jesus, with a chapel of perpetual adoration of the Blessed Sacrament, in Ruhango. Once, travelling from there to Kigali, I brought in my car someone who used to provide technical assistance to this project, a young man of 28 years. Along the way we talked and listened to a radio program that commented on the genocide with a lot of hatred against Hutu, even inciting revenge! I discovered that the man who was with me was a Hutu and that his family had been exterminated.

I asked him: "When you hear that sort of thing on the radio what are your feelings, how do you react?" And he replied: "At the beginning I was like a madman, I did not know what to do; I felt anger and a desire for revenge rising against those who killed my family. Fortunately, I later met a friend who invited me to a daily hour of adoration of the Blessed Sacrament. The first time I felt very upset, I wanted to flee the chapel, but out of respect for my friend I tried to spend that time. I accompanied him during the following days and, after some time, an inner peace returned to my heart and up until now I have remained faithful to adoration. Incentives for revenge have no more impact on me because I am reconciled with God and with myself—and I have forgiven others."[27]

This is the mystery of the healing that Jean Baptiste has been part of since his ordination, first at Ruhango and now at Kabuga, where he is the rector of another shrine of the Divine Mercy. At the shrine, he invites pilgrims to find healing by placing the wounds of their lives alongside the wounds of Jesus's own body. At Kabuga, he guides pilgrims through stations depicting Jesus's life: the Nativity, Crucifixion, and Resurrection. The Crucifixion scene is particularly striking. A life-size cross stands atop an elevated structure, suggesting the height of the hill of Golgotha. Directly below the station is the chapel of the tomb. In the rock formation built into the wall of this dimly lit chapel lies an image of Jesus's body, surrounded by a host of instruments used during the genocide—a machete, a club, a spear, and a grenade. Beside the weapons are a basket and slips of paper. Pilgrims, both survivors and perpetrators of the genocide, are invited to write the wounds for which they seek healing on the slips of paper and place them in the basket. On the last Friday of every month the papers are burned in front of the Divine Mercy Chapel of the Resurrection.[28]

What Jean Baptiste's (as well as Urbaniak's) story illumines is how the journey of personal healing is experienced as at the same time a "call" and an invitation to heal the wounds of others. But what these stories also demonstrate is how a personal journey of physical healing leads to a ministry of healing not only physical and spiritual wounds but also memories in the wake of the genocide. However, the more I explored the central role that the devotion to the Divine Mercy plays at Ruhango and at Kabuga, the clearer it became that a further dimension of healing, namely healing "the burden of ethnicity," was at stake in Fr. Jean Baptiste's ministry.

Divine Mercy: Healing from the "Burden of Ethnicity"

I was curious to see how and why the Pallottines at Ruhango saw the healing of inner woundedness and of memory as a natural development of their ministry, even though they had primarily focused on physical healing prior to the genocide. The key, Jean Baptiste told me, lies in the "spirituality" that animates the community and reflects a coming to-gether of the devotion to the Divine Mercy and the spirituality of the Emmanuel Community. Founded in 1976 in France, the Emmanuel Community grew out of the Charismatic Renewal Movement. Its aim was to encourage members to actively live their faith in their daily lives through adoration, compassion, and evangelization. Before the genocide, the Emmanuel Community was already working in Ruhango alongside the original charismatic group founded by Fr. Urbaniak. When the refu-gees returned from Bugesera after the war, the two groups joined hands and merged because "they realized they had the same spirituality. . . . They recognized that Jesus was healing not only from physical ailments but also from spiritual and moral wounds. They focused on reconcili-ation and healing through the Divine Mercy."[29]

Fr. Anthony heads the Emmanuel Community Center in Kigali, where Jean Baptiste and I found him.[30] His story reveals the same pattern of healing as "gift" and "mission" as Jean Baptiste's and Urbaniak's stories. But the conversation with him uncovered a further dimension of healing—namely from the "burden of ethnicity." This is a healing that the spirituality of the Emmanuel Community invites people to experience. The Emmanuel Community, Anthony explained, is not a congregation or a society or an institution but a spirituality whose heart is God's healing mercy. The spirituality is based on two biblical texts. First, the text of Isaiah 53:11: "By his suffering my servant will justify many." Jesus, Anthony explained, is God's suffering servant, who through his outstretched hands on the cross draws together God's scattered and wounded children. "In his wounds a suffering world is healed." The second text is Matthew 11:28, in which Jesus invites all who "labor and are over-burdened" to come to him and find rest. Anthony described his own journey and how he had found "rest" through the Emmanuel Community. He had lost his family in the genocide, leaving him bitter and filled with desire for revenge. When he joined the Emmanuel Community, he not only found healing but also discovered that his "wounds can be a healing for others." From Anthony's story, it becomes obvious that the "rest" that the text of Matthew refers to is not stasis, or coming to a stop, but rather a movement toward being subsumed within a more determinative story. The "rest" that Anthony received though the practices of perpetual adoration and the devotion to the Divine Mercy within the Emmanuel Community was the "rest" of placing his suffering under the story of God's own suffering servant. The "rest" he received was both a gift and a mission: the healing of his bitterness and pain, and a call for his "wounds to be a healing for others."

As Anthony and I talked about the healing of memories, he confessed that after the genocide he had "carried a heavy burden" of memory, for which he had found personal healing. He then talked about the "burden of our history," which also needs healing. I asked him what the healing from the "burden of our history" might mean in relation to the issue of ethnicity in Rwanda.

"Our identities are limited," he told me. "Being Hutu, Tutsi, or Rwandan is not enough. First and foremost I am a child of God. We are all God's children!"

Without this truth, Anthony tells us, our identities can be a heavy load. He then described the history of ethnic hatred in Rwanda and the historical injustices/violence suffered and perpetuated in the name of identity. Such violent history needs to be healed, he said. However, we cannot heal by simply trying to forget (or denying it ever happened) or by violently suppressing all ethnicities—a veiled reference to the official government policy that has banned the use of ethnic labels and vigorously promotes a national ("We are all Rwandans) identity. Instead, we must allow ourselves to be drawn into a new communion of self-sacrificing love. "There is no point in hiding who one is," Anthony told me. "We need to be open and talk about these identities of Hutu and Tutsi. That helps us to understand not only our pain but also the pain of the other."

The perpetual adoration of Jesus in the Eucharist, as well as the devotion to the Divine Mercy that the Emmanuel Community promotes, is one way to encourage individuals to face their pain and the pain of others by contemplating God's own suffering and embracing God's mercy, which heals and reconciles.

"Is the goal then," I asked Anthony, "to invite everyone to become a member of the Emmanuel Community?"

"Emmanuel Community is not so much a community," he answered, "as a spirituality. The goal is to accept one another, in all our differences, and learn to journey together."

"Journey together toward what?" I asked.

"To journey toward Jesus on the cross—to the suffering Jesus, whose wounds heal us." And here Anthony again mentioned the text of Isaiah 53:11: "By his suffering my servant shall justify many."

The stories of Jean Baptiste, Urbaniak, and Anthony converge on a number of significant points. First, they are all stories of personal healing, whether physical healing or healing from the "heavy burden" they felt in the wake of the genocide. It is also significant that all three men understand their being healed in terms of both a "gift" and at the same time a call to "heal others."

Their stories and words highlight the need for healing on various levels: physical, spiritual, and emotional, also the healing of memories, of the "burden of our history," and, finally, of identity, which Anthony described as healing from the "burden of ethnicity."

These various levels of healing indicate different kinds of wounds, wounds that have caused suffering, which has manifested in brokenness.

Present in both Jean Baptiste's and Anthony's stories and ministries is the conviction that healing these wounds and their associated "burdens" can begin only when the suffering is placed under the story of God's own suffering. Thus both Anthony (within the Emmanuel Community) and Jean Baptiste (within Divine Mercy) not only have received their own healing through the story of God's own suffering but also invite others to the same experience of God's suffering love through perpetual adoration and the devotion to the Divine Mercy. Accordingly, Jean Baptiste would say, "I love the ministry of the Divine Mercy [because] it starts with the acknowledgment of human suffering."

One hears echoes of Vincent Mulago's "stepping stones" in both Jean Baptiste's and Anthony's stories and words. Both acknowledge that while being Hutu or Tutsi or Rwandan may be real, it is not destiny. Indeed, those identities can and have become a "burden"—what Anthony described as the "burden of our history" and the "burden of ethnicity." Anthony's observation that "our identities are limited. Being Hutu, Tutsi or Rwandan is not enough" seems, even without saying so explicitly, to be making a claim like Mulago's for these identities to become (in the words of Mulago) a "stepping stone" toward a new communion of divine love and mercy, or, as Anthony puts it, "to the cross whose suffering heals." It is this communion with God's own suffering love that reconciles, heals, and renews one's true identity.

But what I am also hearing behind both Anthony's and Jean Baptiste's stories and words is that if the goal—the telos of the journey of identity—is the new communion of divine love and mercy, that community is a communion of "compassion," in terms of both "suffering with" and outreach to the wounded and most vulnerable. Thus reconciliation, the healing of memory, identity, and compassion all belong together in the economy of God's merciful love manifested on the cross. This is the spirituality that was promoted at Ruhango through the devotion to the Divine Mercy, perpetual adoration, and the outreach to the sick and vulnerable members of the community. By living out this spirituality, the community at Ruhango came to discover not only healing for their physical and spiritual wounds but also healing from the "burden of history" and the "burden of ethnicity." The visible social manifestation of the healing was an "odd," "mixed-up" community of Hutu, Tutsi, Twa, and Musungu that remained united and was therefore able to resist the genocide and at least provide an alternative to the violent politics of ethnicity. Compassion in this sense, as shown in the stories of Jean Baptiste, Urbaniak, and Anthony, is the antidote to tribalism, reinventing ethnicity into a "new we." The next story of Maggy Barankitse and Maison Shalom will bring this process into even clearer focus and further illumine both the possibility and the rich dimensions of love's invention in the midst of "ethnic violence."

Oasis of Peace: Maggy Barankitse and the Invention of a "New We"

Kigali, January 19, 2018

It is a bright and beautiful Saturday afternoon on a hilltop overlooking the city of Kigali. Here on the site of a former hotel stands Oasis of Peace, a community center for Burundian refugees. Maggy Barankitse established the center after she was forced into exile from her country of Burundi, where she had criticized President Nkurunziza for seeking to change the constitution so as to extend his stay in power. Today is the graduation ceremony for the first class of students, who have been attending training in various vocational skills (culinary services, embroidery, painting, tailoring, and car mechanics).[31] As the graduates and invited guests gather for the procession into the hall, loudspeakers hanging from the trees fill the air with lively discotheque music, proclaiming "*maison shalom . . . nyumba ya mahoro . . . orakarange*" (long live Maison Shalom, house of peace). Inside the hall, the seventy-four young men and women come up one by one to the stage as their names are called to receive their diplomas. You would not be able to tell, given the graduation gowns, the sense of dignity and confidence in their gait, and the radiance on their faces, that all seventy-four are refugees. Less than a year ago, they were living in refugee camps, full of fear and bitterness from the painful memories of the flight from their homes and loss of everything they had, in order to escape Nkurunziza's violence. It was in the camps that Maggy, herself driven from her home in Ruyigi, found them and enrolled them in the various courses.

In her speech to the graduates, Maggy speaks of her journey from the tears and darkness of exile to her determination not to allow hatred

to make her "lose her tenderness" but to live with the dignity of knowing that she is a child of God. "Love is our true identity," she tells the
graduates. Reminding them that "hatred will never have the last word,"
she urges them to always "work hard to change violence into peace,"
while inviting them to "celebrate today the victory of love over hatred."

A beautiful celebration it indeed is. The diploma service is followed
by a sumptuous candlelit dinner in the gardens of the Oasis of Peace—a
dinner for all the graduates and their invited guests, with plenty of good
food, a live band, and at a certain point in the evening, Maggy dancing
with her graduates. Throughout the evening my mind keeps returning
to a line of Psalm 23, "A banquet he prepares for me in the presence of
my enemies," and to the image of rich food and the choicest wine that
God has prepared for all people, according to Isaiah (25:6). I remember
that Isaiah was offering this vision as a prophecy to people who were
facing difficult times and the threat of exile. Just a few verses earlier, the
prophet predicted the impending destruction in vivid images: the foundations of the earth shaking (24:18), the earth mourning and fading, both
heaven and the earth languishing (24:4), the inhabitants of the earth
turning pale (24:6). In the midst of this terrible devastation where "all
joy has disappeared, and all cheer has left the land" (24:11), the prophet
now promises that "on this mountain the LORD Almighty will prepare
a feast of rich food for all peoples, a banquet of aged wine—the best of
meats and the finest of wines." But something is not right. Shouldn't the
banquet wait until after restoration, after the return from exile, after reconstruction, and after total reconciliation? But there it is in the midst.
Not just a meal, but a feast! What I am now witnessing on a beautiful
Saturday in January has a similar odd logic. For right here in the midst
of exile and displacement, springing out of Burundi's violence, there is
an "oasis of peace"; at a time of desolation, there is joy; in the midst of
loss and hatred, there is a banquet of good food, wine, music, and dance.
A celebration of the victory of love over hatred.

What kind of victory is this? How does one account for its logic?
What drives someone like Maggy Barankitse, who is not satisfied with
giving refugees just some rationed food to keep them going and tents to
sleep in within the refugee camps (that itself would be admirable) but
invites them out of the camps up on "this mountain" to give them

diplomas, graduation gowns, rich food, music, dancing, joy, dignity, and employment possibilities right here in the land of exile!

Maggy's story is a story of compassion, which is to say, a story of God's reconciling love. Two apparently contradictory elements characterize this love, its "simplicity" and its "excess." As Øystein Rakkenes, a Norwegian journalist who has followed Maggy and is now working on a documentary about her, explained to me: "What drives Maggy is a simple message (God's love) that however keeps being played out in endless and rich practical manifestations of courage, beauty, compassion, and service to the least of these."[32] The Oasis of Peace is but another chapter in Maggy's life of endless innovation on behalf of vulnerable children, about which she herself proclaims, "Love has made me an inventor."[33]

I have previously discussed Maggy Barankitse's story.[34] I have, however, found it necessary to revisit it here mainly for two connected reasons. First, Maggy now finds herself in exile in Rwanda, having fled from the violence in her native Burundi that threatened her life. However, even in exile in Rwanda where she now lives, she is unwavering in her advocacy on behalf of the victims of violence and unfaltering in her conviction that love always wins. Whence the confidence? And, what does this new chapter of Maggy's life reveal about how the reinvention of love must continue even in the midst of challenges and setbacks? Second, Maggy's current work with the refugees shares much with the ongoing work of resisting violence and healing from the wounds of violence that we have traced in the stories of Jean Baptiste and Anthony in the previous section. Thus, reading her story alongside their stories confirms some crucial conclusions about the need for these kinds of "redemptive spaces" if we are to grasp the possibility of healing from what Anthony describes as the "burden of identity." Even though there may be no need to retell Maggy's story in great detail here, providing an outline of her story might be helpful, especially for those who may not be familiar with it.

Love Has Made Me an Inventor

The winner of the 2008 Opus Prize, the 2016 Aurora Prize for Awakening Humanity, and numerous other awards, Maggy Barankitse has been

described variously as the Mother Teresa of Africa, the mother of Burundi, and a crazy woman. All of these epitaphs are fitting. Here I will
attempt to capture in broad strokes her "madness," her ongoing reinvention of ethnic politics, the possibilities and challenges of her work, and
the "simplicity" and "excess" of the message that drives it. To appreciate
her story, one must locate it within the broader one of political violence
in Burundi, where "ethnicity" was reinforced and reproduced as an un-
questioned building block of Burundian society. A German colony until
1919, Burundi then came under Belgian rule. The Belgians, using the
same Hamitic mythology that they used in Rwanda, divided the country
neatly into Hutu, Tutsi, and Twa identities. Tutsi privilege was affirmed
by establishing a system of political and economic administration that
marginalized the majority Hutu. Unlike Rwanda to the north, Burundi's
independence in 1962 left the Tutsi in power, but the "ethnic" hatred
between the groups set the framework for Burundi's post-Independence
history, which has been marked by political instability, a series of military
takeovers, and massacres that have pitted Hutus and Tutsis in an endless
cycle of revenge and counter-revenge. The fact that Burundi's ten million people speak the same language and that more than 80 percent are
Christian, with Catholicism as the dominant religion, seems not to have
made much difference.

In 1993, following the assassination of President Ndadaye, the
country erupted in Hutu-Tutsi ethnic massacres and countermassacres.
Maggy, a Tutsi, had adopted seven children, three Tutsi and four Hutu.
Together with her children and other Hutu families she sought refuge
in the bishop's residence, where Tutsi militias, including members of
her own family, found her, set the place on fire, and killed seventy-two
people. She was spared but was forced to watch the massacre of the
seventy-two people. After the massacre, Maggy, crying and trembling,
crawled into the chapel. There, looking at the cross, she cried out: "Why,
oh God? How could you allow such hatred? What kind of God are you?
Mother told us that you are a God of love. Did she lie to us? And why
was I spared?"

Two surprising gifts ("miracles" she calls them) were to emerge in
the midst of Maggy's anguish as she beheld the crucified God. First, one
of Maggy's adopted children cried out from the sacristy, "Mama, we are

all here, all of us are here." The children had escaped the massacre and were hiding in the sacristy. Second, with the gift of her children also came "the gift of love"—of realizing that her life was intimately connected to God's love. But this was true not only for her, for Maggy was now able to see that "love is our true identity" and the unique purpose of each individual—that "love is the most beautiful calling of human beings. We are created out of love and to love." The surprising discovery of love in the midst of her lament not only filled her with inexplicable strength but liberated her from fear and confirmed a new calling for her: to raise the children in the spirit of love, "beyond the hatred and bitterness" that she had seen in the killers' eyes.

This is how Maison Shalom (house of peace) was born at Ruyigi in Burundi, not as an orphanage, but as an attempt to raise children in the story of God's love and to confirm their identity as "members of a family, princes and princesses in God's household." This purpose also explains Maggy's often-quoted statement "Love has made me a rebel." Among other things, for Maggy the rebellion requires saying "no" to what she describes as "the lies of ethnicity"—lies that have become so naturalized that they are now unquestioningly accepted as "our way of life." We are crazy, she says, because "we are not afraid to kill one another. We have accepted hatred because of ethnicity and have forgotten the most noble gift of belonging to the family of God." And because Christianity in Burundi has not been able to challenge the lies of ethnicity, but rather has accommodated itself to them, it has given rise to what Maggy describes as "practical hypocrisy."

If love has made Maggy a rebel, it has also made her an inventor. It was "the needs of the children that drove and inspired me," she explains. "They needed love, they needed safety, and they needed food and clothing. I simply had to invent ways to help them." The invention of love took many forms, first the gathering of orphaned children, beginning with her seven, then other orphaned children around her hometown of Ruyigi. Soon she had over a hundred children in her care. To date more than thirty thousand children have been raised under Maison Shalom. Maggy had to create homes for the children and services to support their needs, including schools, businesses, farms, a cinema, and even a swimming pool. Then, as the work of Maison Shalom expanded in the community, she established a microfinance credit union, a hospital, and a radio station. Impressive as these programs are, Maggy insists, "Maison Shalom is not about these projects; Maison Shalom is the message."[35] That message is the message of what it means to be God's children whose true identity is love.

The invention of love also involved the creation of a new family, a new community, and a "new tribe," which brings together children from different ethnicities and countries. Once asked by a journalist whether they were Tutsi or Hutu, the children of Maison Shalom responded, "We are Husitwacongozungu."[36]

A New Tribe—a New We

We can draw many lessons from Maggy's efforts to "invent" a "new tribe." Foremost, perhaps, is that these efforts are a form of "madness." For Maggy this is at the heart of the Christian vocation and connected to the identity of being God's children. To be a Christian is to be invited into a drama of madness. In a testimony to commemorate the five-hundredth anniversary of Lutheran Reformation in Sweden, on November 2, 2016, Maggy reminded the audience, which included Pope Francis, that the first crazy man was Jesus. She invited the audience to "accept the unique vocation of love" and to be "crazy for love." Maggy sees herself as caught up in the same drama as Jesus, who in the midst of the identity politics of his day—a politics of who was in and who was out among Greeks, Jews, Samaritans, heathens—reminded his audience that in God's love everyone belongs, that there are "many rooms in my Father's House."

It is important to note that Maggy's new tribe" is not a self-enclosed community but an ever-expanding community that does not consist merely of those baptized (that would simply be a religious version of the ethnicity that she is trying to overcome) or simply of "we" Burundians (that would be a bigger form of tribalism). Rather, that baptism, whose gift of love she rediscovered during the 1993 event, set her on a journey along which she discovered that her village, her ethnicity, the nation of Burundi, even her Catholic Church could no longer contain her. Her sense of "my people" was constantly being reconstituted as it expanded. In this connection, Maggy describes Maison Shalom as a "train" that cannot be stopped, in which "God will continue to gather" his scattered children. That is also the reason that with all the pain of the closing of Maison Shalom headquarters in Burundi and Maggy's own exile, she sees these events as another chapter in the unfolding of the story of invention of God's reconciling love. "Who knows," she says, "perhaps God sent me into exile in order to expand the work of Maison Shalom outside Burundi, in Rwanda and beyond."[37]

What is unique about Maggy's invention of love—the "gathering" of God's family—is the kind of family that Maison Shalom is. In Burundi, the majority of children Maggy welcomed to Maison Shalom were orphans, former child soldiers, and street children. Many had been discarded as "bastards" and "illegitimate." Most were abandoned. And now, in exile in Rwanda, she works with refugees exiled from their homes and living in camps. This policy of ministering does, of course, reflect a profound theological conviction about God's love, which is extended to all, but especially to the poor, the weak, and the vulnerable. It is in these "crucified peoples" of history that God's abundant love is made evident. Accordingly, if God's love invents a new social reality in history, that reality begins, not in the centers of power, but at the margins of society, with overlooked and wounded individuals and communities.

While Maggy's Maison Shalom has not solved Burundi's ethnic politics and Ruhango and Kabuga have not solved Rwanda's ethnic problem, they are what one might describe as "redemptive spaces" for healing both the victims and, equally important, the imaginative grip of the burden of ethnicity. This means that within these redemptive spaces, one is now able to view oneself and be viewed by others differently—that is, not through a tribal or an ethnic prism. The spaces provide an opportunity, in Maggy's words, for "discovering our true identity." That identity, it turns out, is a gift—God's love poured out for all, but especially the weak and vulnerable, with whom we stand as "members of God's household." In this way Maison Shalom provides a much-needed interruption of the dominant imagination by reinventing identity. It creates a "new we"—a "we" that cannot be plotted in the familiar sociological landscape. Herein lies the significance of Maison Shalom's center at the outskirts of Kigali. The "oasis of peace" is an "oasis" where a different logic is at work.

If Maison Shalom, Ruhango, and Kabuga are spaces of redemptive love, they are also spaces of suffering love. But then all love is a form of suffering. Both Anthony and Jean Baptiste spoke of finding healing in God's suffering; and Jean Baptiste described suffering as "the true basis of human identity, the unifying factor that identifies us as humans."[38] Maggy expressed a similar sentiment when, at the graduation event, using her story as an example, she exhorted the graduates not to allow hatred to make them "lose the tenderness." She was encouraging the refugees to keep, in spite of what they have suffered, their lives open to God's love and to the suffering within that love. Tenderness is what allows them to "risk" community and friendship, including community with the potential enemy, thus exposing their lives to the ever-present possibility of betrayal. This is what makes the tenderness itself a form of violence, what the late El Salvadorian archbishop and martyr Archbishop Oscar Romero described as the "violence of love."[39]

Finally, at the graduation event, Maggy asked the graduates, using one of her favorite expressions, to always remember that "evil will never have the last word," and that "love always wins." One time pressed for "evidence" for this claim, she pointed at herself and her recent experience, now in exile, with Maison Shalom's bank accounts confiscated and with all its operations in Burundi shut down by the Nkurunziza government. "Look at me," she told the audience at the five-hundredth anniversary of the Lutheran Reformation. "Some people think that I have lost everything. . . . No, I did not lose everything, I fled with my treasure— love, and love makes us inventors."[40] What we learn from Maggy's evidence is that the "new we" remains an eschatological reality that is never fully realized, that is always scattered. This, however, does not mean it is not real. It simply means that the journey of identity and the invitation into "a new we" remains a journey of hope. What makes communities like Maison Shalom and Ruhango so essential for the Christian journey of identity is that they provide both evidence and historical reference points for the "already" and the "not yet fully" of the story of God's love, whose final realization is yet to be revealed.

The Invention of Stories

The discussion in this chapter supports at least three crucial conclusions. First, stories matter. They have the power to destroy and build, to kill but also to heal and save. Nyamata, Ntarama, Seromba, and the entire 1994 Rwanda Genocide cannot make sense outside the political imagining of modern Rwanda. At the basis of this imagining is a story or set of stories organized around the Hamitic mythology of civilized light-skinned invaders versus black, lazy, backward natives that was first told by colonialists. Assumed in the social, political, and cultural institutions of modern Rwanda, the story succeeded in creating ("inventing") not only Hutu and Tutsi as political communities but a post-Independence exclusionary form of politics that pitted one group against the other in a constant struggle for power. Not surprisingly, the zero-sum politics of ethnic identity was to shape a register of historical memories as well as a sense of victimhood and entitlement, which would in turn fuel an endless cycle of revenge and counter-revenge on either side of the ethnic divide. The violence of 1994 grows out of this story, which Fr. Anthony appropriately described as "the burden of our history."

Second, the way out of this madness, out of this story and its endless cycles of "ethnic violence," is through another story or set of stories that can engender courage to resist violence but also shape a politics committed to healing. The stories of the young students at Nyange, the parish of Ruhango, Fr. Jean Baptiste, Urbaniak, and Anthony all lead to the story of God's suffering love and mercy. What these testimonies offer is a glimpse into the dynamics of the story of God's love and its potential to create a new sense of belonging ("family") and to heal not just physical wounds but spiritual and moral wounds as well as the burdens of history and ethnicity.

Finally, what we witness in these stories, most explicitly in the story of Maggy, is the invention of love. Speaking of Maggy, the Norwegian journalist Øystein Rakkenes noted that what drives her is a simple message (God's love).[41] In other words, outside that story Maggy, her relentless innovation, her invention not only of Maison Shalom with its impressive programs for the children but also of the Oasis of Peace and her sense of community—a new we—does not make sense. A similar "invention" is at work at Ruhango, again arising out of a "simple" story and message: God's love. And just as Maggy insists that Maison Shalom is not a project but a "message," so Anthony notes that Emmanuel Community is not a congregation or an institution but a "spirituality." What

Ruhango and Maggy's Maison Shalom confirm is that "spirituality" is indeed a rich politics—not in the banal way of the "spirituality of politics" but in the radical sense of the "politics of spirituality." In the end, the claim that both Ruhango and Maison Shalom make is that this politics—shaped by the "simple" story of God's love—has the power to resist, interrupt, and heal the politics of ethnic violence.

The healing begins by discovering our true identity, which is both a gift and an invitation into the drama of God's self-sacrificing love. For Jean Baptiste, Anthony, and Maggy the identity was reaffirmed at the most painful time of their "woundedness," and they received it as the gift of healing, "liberation" "rest," "inexpressible strength," and the confirmation of their own identity as "loved." They also received it as an invitation to become agents within the story of God's reconciling love, thus to use their healing to heal others. This is the essence and telos of Christian identity, which both redirects ethnic identity to its true end and invents a "new we" that transcends the boundaries of race, nation, and ethnicity.

In the end, what the stories of Ruhango and Maison Shalom demonstrate is that the antidote to the madness of the story that shaped and continues to shape the violent politics of (ethnic) identity in Africa is another form of politics, another type of madness, another invention, and another form of violence—the "violence of love" (Oscar Romero), which Jean Baptiste describes as the "suffering" of love and Maggy embraces as the "tenderness" of love. In this chapter we have been tracing the tenderness of love in the context of ethnic violence. But a similar "invention" is needed in the context of religious violence in Africa, as the case of the Central African Republic confirms. To that story we now turn.

The first graduation at Oasis of Peace, Maison Shalom, Kigali, January 9, 2018.

Maggy Barankitse celebrating with the graduates.

Ruhango Parish Church, Rwanda. Photo credit: Mvukiyehe.

Inner courtyard of Ruhango Church compound.

Inside Ruhango
Church.

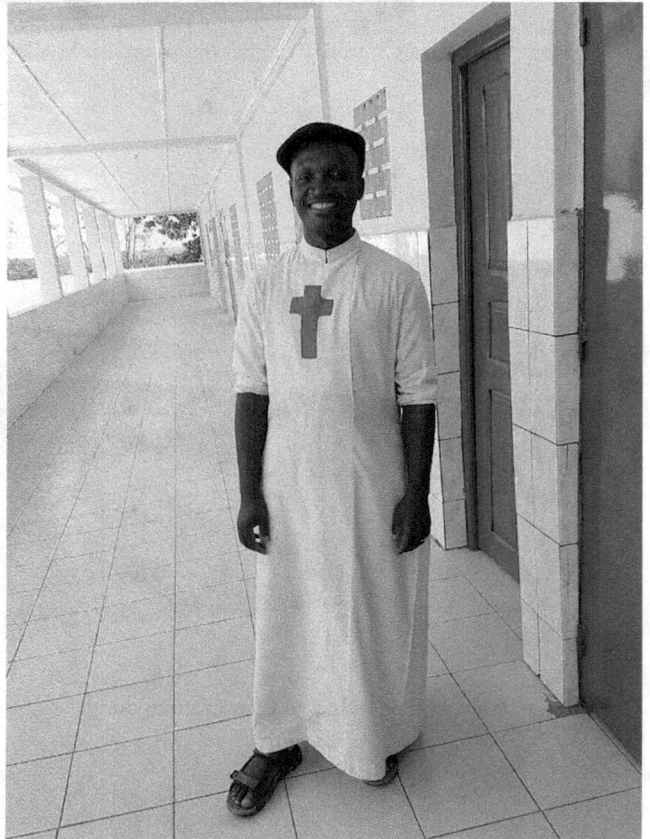

Father Bernard Kinvi
in front of the
new hospital he built
at Bossemptele,
March 2018.

AFRICA

☆ National capital
○ Major City
——— International boundary

Map of Africa. © Copyright: One World—Nations Online, OWNO, nationsonline.org.

Fr. Godfrey Nzamujo at Songhai Center, Porto Novo, Benin. Photo credit AFP.

Katwe slum near Kampala (in Uganda). Photo credit: Love Uganda Foundation.

Map of Rwanda.

Father Jean Baptiste Mvukiyehe at Kabuga, near Kigali.

CHAPTER FOUR

Religious Violence and the Reinvention of Politics

We don't have the kinds of mouths that can speak to the government.
—A militia leader

I took a vow to remain with the sick and to serve them even at the
danger of my life.
—Bernard Kinvi

Bordering Congo, the Democratic Republic of Congo (DRC), Sudan, Chad, and Cameroon, the Central African Republic (CAR) is rich in timber, diamonds, gold, uranium, and oil. And yet, for all its natural wealth, CAR remains one of the poorest countries in the world, ranking last but one on the 2017 UN Human Development Index.[1] In March 2013, Séléka rebels, made up of loosely organized militia groups that drew primarily from the Northeast, ousted President François and installed their own leader, Michel Djotodia. Even though the Séléka would soon be officially disbanded, its members continued to commit crimes such as pillaging, looting, rape, and murder. During the nine months of ad hoc Séléka rule and widespread criminality, a violent response began to build, drawing initially on local self-defense groups. The fighters became known as "anti-balaka." Soon the conflict in the nation took on the mantle of a religious war, as anti-balaka militias, many of them Christians, began attacking Muslims out of revenge for the Séléka's acts. By the time of the Bangui Forum, organized by the interim president, Catherine Samba-Panza, to bring together Central Africans from all regions and backgrounds to find a solution to the crisis, more than ten thousand people had been killed, some 390,000 Muslims had fled CAR, and nearly 1 million of the country's 4.5 million residents had been displaced.[2]

How does one explain the civil war in CAR, where Muslims constitute 15 percent, Christians 80 percent, and traditionalists 5 percent of the population? How does one account for the "religious" violence given that there had been no history of religious animosity in CAR, and that Christians, Muslims, and traditionalists had until now lived peacefully with and among one another?

Much of the answer lies within the unique history of CAR, specifically in the way the nation-state, power, and the country itself have been imagined. Attending to the history of Central Africa reveals a consistent pattern: Central Africa has been successively "owned" and controlled by powerful outside and local interests, who have abused, used, or simply neglected the majority of the population. The area that would eventually become CAR had been "settled" from at least the seventh century on by overlapping empires, including the Kanem-Bornu, Ouddai, Baguirmi, and Darfur groups based in the Lake Chad region and along the Upper Nile. Slave-trading sultans who controlled the area in the early part of the nineteenth century depleted the area demographically, leaving it "an archipelago of scattered ethnic groups . . . isolated from one another by unclaimed buffer zones."[3] The French annexed the area (Oubangui-Chari) in the 1890s, making it part of the French Equatorial Africa territory (which includes present-day Chad, Cameroon, the Republic of Congo, and Gabon). French colonization was alternately brutal and neglectful.[4] France had very little interest in the territory. Its conquest was intended to preempt further Belgian, German, and British colonial ambitions. Finding the area inaccessible, and therefore difficult to administer, France leased the territory to forty private companies, giving them virtually unlimited power to exploit the "vacant and unowned land." Employing a method of exploitation copied from King Leopold's Congo Free State, the concessionary companies levied a head tax on the local population and conscripted them as forced labor in the gathering of wild rubber or on newly established cotton plantations. Jean-Bédel

Bokassa, the army commander who seized power in 1965 shortly after the country's independence, perpetuated the politics of control and extraction and the "ownership" of the state as personal property. A captain of the French army, Bokassa's model was France's self-made emperor Napoleon. In 1977, in a direct imitation of Napoleon's self-coronation in 1804, Bokassa spent $200 million on a lavish coronation ceremony for himself as the Emperor Bokassa I of the newly renamed Central African Empire.

The imagining of the state as a "cake" to be shared out greatly explains the constant logic of "fighting" and the many (a total of six) military coups d'état (see table 4.1) as various political and military elites have struggled to control the state, demanding, in the memorable words of Michele Wrong, that "it is our turn to eat."[5]

Table 4.1. Central African Republic (CAR) Post-Independence History

1960	CAR attains independence under David Dacko.
1965	A coup is led by Col. Jean-Bédel Bokassa.
1979	French paratroops stage a coup that sends Bokassa into exile and reinstates David Dacko, the Independence leader, as president.
1981	Dacko is toppled in a military coup headed by André Kolingba. Like Bokassa, Kolingba has a dozen years in power, but he exercises a more conventional military dictatorship.
1993	Civil unrest follows a wave of pressure for multiparty elections across much of sub-Saharan Africa. Kolingba is defeated in the presidential election by Ange-Félix Patassé.
1996–2001	A series of mutinies occur and in 2001 an attempted coup. Patassé, propped up by French, African, and UN peacekeepers, survives a military coup, and Bozizé, the army chief of staff, flees with his supporters to Chad.
March 2003	While Patassé is abroad, rebels move into Bangui and install their commander, General François Bozizé, as president.
2005	Bozizé organizes and contests the March 13, 2005, presidential elections, which he wins. While Bozizé's government appears stable, a number of rebel groups form and are active, especially in the North and Northeast.
March 2013	The Séléka, backed by heavily armed mercenary fighters from Chad and Sudan, overthrow Bozizé. The group's leader, Michel Djotodia, becomes the first Muslim president.

Figure 4.1. Central African Republic (CAR) and neighboring countries.

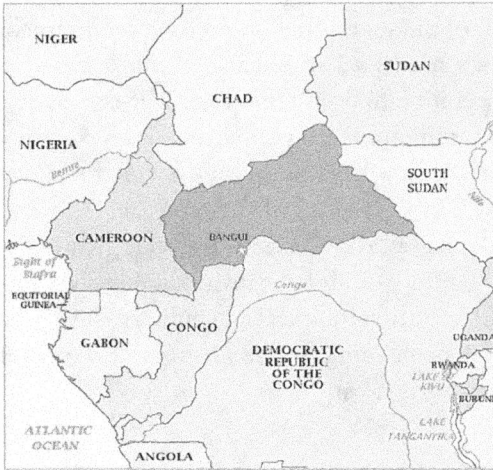

Figure 4.2. Map of CAR.

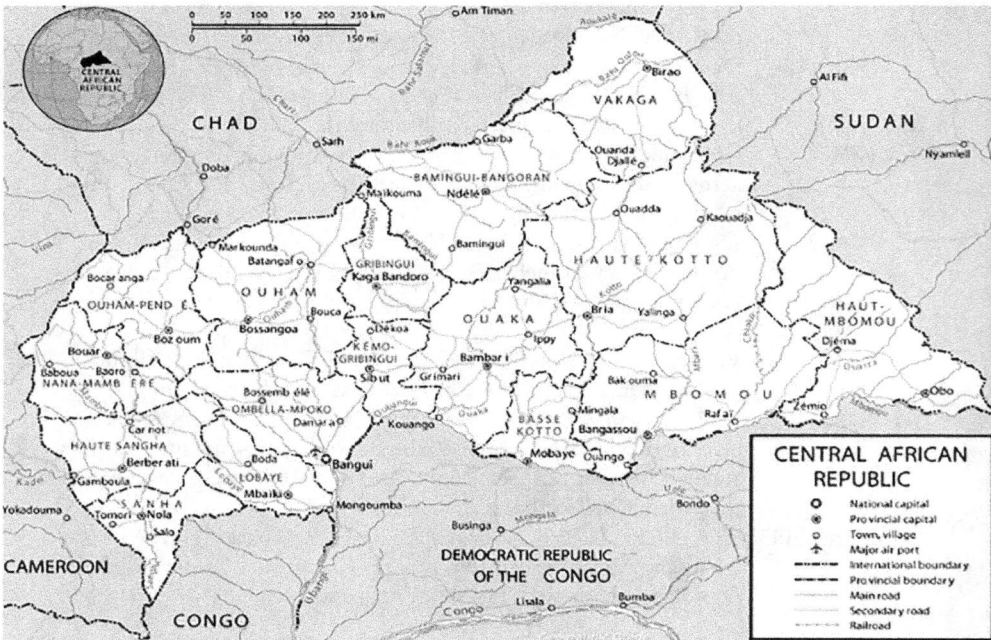

The foreign element stands out as a critical factor in the struggle for state control by the local political and military elite. It is represented first and foremost by France's continued power and influence but also by the role that CAR's neighbors, especially Chad, DRC, and Sudan, play in determining political developments in CAR, directly or indirectly. This became particularly evident in 2002–3 when several of the region's leaders—chief among them Chad's Idriss Derby—decided to replace CAR's truculent Patassé with François Bozizé. Bozizé captured Bangui in March 2003 with a force that was seven-eighths Chadians. "These fighters," Lomard and Carayannis note, "as well as the DR-Congolese rebels Patassé had called on for support, looted, raped, and murdered along the way."[6] The disproportionate involvement of foreign players in determining CAR's history is in stark contrast to the lack, or near lack, of local involvement in shaping politics in CAR. Politics has been, and continues to be, about the state and who controls state power.

The 2012–13 crisis that gave rise to the Séléka—their government takeover as well as the subsequent rise of the anti-balaka and the ensuing "religious" violence—must be located within this history. The more one locates it within this larger context, the more it becomes obvious that the term *crisis* is a misleading characterization. Referring to the events as a crisis is to assume that the war that began in 2012 was an aberration, or a break with a normal past. We see, though, even from the condensed time line above, that the war was a continuation, only the latest instantiation, of the disorder that is an endemic part of CAR's history, evident at both the local and regional levels, "where the boundary between peace and wartime has been increasingly blurred."[7] As Carayannis and Lombard note, for CAR, "There has never been such a thing as 'normalcy.' Life before the onset of violence in 2013 was one of permanent insecurity, internal displacement, and absent state services. In this forgotten country . . . civilians live in a chronic crisis marked by periods of low intensity violence that are punctuated by spikes in fighting."[8]

In the same way that the events of 2012–13 were not a crisis, they also did not constitute a "religious" war between Christians and Muslims. The events were instead another development in CAR's "politics of the belly" (to use the term popularized by François Bayart), a struggle for state power in which the questions of who owns/controls state power, who is included and who is excluded from that ownership, are endlessly redefined. In this case, CAR is not unique but represents a recognizable pattern within Africa's modern politics. The elite, in their struggle to control state resources, "discover" and "recruit" sections of the population who in Africa's political modernity have been systematically excluded and dismissed as "mere peasants," representing interests that are "backward," "primitive," "animist," "rural," "pagan"—in a word, as those who do not matter. These excluded "local," "primitive," "ethnic," and religious interests now are mobilized in the struggle for power.

Making the Religious War in CAR Thinkable

To understand how religion became a flash point in the fighting in CAR in 2012–13, one needs to view those events not only within the social history of the Central African Republic but also within the microdynamics of Central African society—which is to say, within the way that Central African society works given its particular history of state formation and its politics.

To get a sense of some of these microdynamics of CAR society, I made my first trip to CAR at the end of February 2018. I wanted to experience the effects of the 2013 violence and to find out how the Central Africans themselves experienced and thought about the war. I was also interested to hear the people's views on the future of their country and to research grassroots initiatives that represented hope for the future. I talked to various sections of the population: youth, women, chiefs, politicians, and religious leaders. I spoke to people in and around Bangui, the capital, and also in Bossemptele, three hundred miles northwest of Bangui. My research illumined four paradoxes of Central African society that together make the "religious" violence of 2013 thinkable.

A Phantom State

Upon my arrival at Bangui M'Poko International Airport I was met by Soh Keugne Nouthak Jules, a young Jesuit priest and my guide and translator for the two weeks I was to be in CAR. Originally from Cameroon, Soh had been stationed in CAR, living with the Jesuit community and working mostly with the youth in campus ministry at the University of Bangui. I was grateful that he was there to meet me, for I would not have known how to begin to navigate the linguistic, cultural, and bureaucratic systems that faced me. There seemed to be chaos everywhere inside the small terminal as everyone crowded around the tiny immigration window trying to get their documents stamped. Jules took my passport and disappeared behind one of the cubicles. When he returned after ten minutes, he told me that he had to talk to somebody because my visa had not yet come through. We had been cleared to go but would have to return on Monday for the visa to be fixed in my passport.

The road to the airport was lined with makeshift markets where lots of young people were selling fruits, French baguettes, handbags, and an assortment of used clothes. Soh drove to the center of town to show me the monument to Bathlomey Boganda, the ex-priest who had negotiated CAR's independence from France; he also showed me the presidential office, the prime minister's residence, the university, and the cathedral (of the Immaculate Conception), where in 2015 Pope Francis had opened the Jubilee Year of Mercy. We drove by Bangui River as Soh pointed out the DRC on the other side. We stopped at the very first Catholic parish (established in 1894 by Spiritan missionaries). Even the church is run down and in disrepair. The country, Soh explained, has nine Catholic dioceses, all of them, except one, run by missionary congregations.[9]

"Why is that?" I asked.

"The local clergy have an image problem. No one trusts local clergy, but," he added, "no one trusts anything Central African anyway."

Notre Dame Guest House, where I would be staying for the next two weeks, is a moderate and clean guesthouse connected to the pastoral center. It is run by religious sisters from Benin. Before we checked in, Soh wanted to show me the Ledger, the biggest hotel in town. The compound and expansive lobby was full of UN and other foreign personnel.

"This is where everything happens," Soh told me. "This is where the real power lies."

"But," I said to Soh, "I thought one of the problems of CAR is the endless struggle for power by local politicians and military elites."

"Yes, that is true, but these leaders, Dacko, Kolingmba, Patassé, Bozizé, they are all puppets of France and other foreign interests. Everything in this country is controlled by foreigners: the politics by France, the economics by the Lebanese, and the church by foreign missionary congregations."

"What is then left for the Central Africans, the local people?" I asked.

"There are really three options for people to survive: join politics, go abroad, or join the militia."

On the plane, I had read *Making Sense of the Central African Republic*, a collection of essays edited by Tatiana Carayannis and Louisa Lombard. In one of the essays, the author, Steven Smith, notes that CAR cannot be described as either a "successful" or a "failed" state so much as a "phantom state" that for most Central Africans is experienced as a "painful absence *and* a hurtful presence."[10] Smith also notes that all Central Africans are united in always trying to find a way around state control. I found the irony in both Smith's and now Soh's observation striking: one obvious way to survive CAR phantom politics is to join politics. As Dalby notes, "To launch a rebellion in CAR is to claim a place at the negotiating table."[11]

"How many militias," I asked Soh, "are still active in CAR?"

"The UN is leading a heavy disarmament and demobilization program," he told me, "but it is very difficult to know how many militias. You see, the government has very little control outside Bangui."

Later in the week, I had a chance to talk to Jean Pierre Meme (not real name), an officer working in the president's office in charge of disarmament. He expressed total frustration: "The program is poorly funded, and time bound, but every time we turn around there are new militias to register. At times it is difficult to know who is a militia and who is not."[12]

The ultimate irony seems to be that many of the militias trying to get a place at the negotiating table of CAR's phantom politics are themselves phantom militias!

An Abandoned Population

By Central African standards, Alex Gumba is a successful businessman. He owns and runs the only Western Union franchise in CAR. His father, the late Abel Gumba, served with Boganda in the interim government leading to Independence and became Dacko's prime minister. "The professor," as Alex referred to his father, formed his own party, Front Patriotique le Progres (FPP), contested the 1981 elections, which he lost, and ended up as government ombudsman. The younger Gumba took over the FPP presidency, but under Bozizé a series of bogus legal challenges (instigated by Bozizé's government) created internal factions and weakened the party, which Alex was now trying to rebuild. I met him at his Western Union office in downtown Bangui. I asked him to assess CAR's post-Independence governments and their legacies.[13]

"The problem of CAR has been the problem of power—the abuse of power," he surmised. "All the governments since Independence have continued to abuse power."

Gumba did not, however, blame this on the political system inherited from the French.

"It is the responsibility of the Central African state," he told me. "It has the power and political responsibility. We are Central Africans, and the country is for Central Africans, and we are responsible for its management. France, America, Britain have their interests. But if you are not prudent, not serious, and if the country is under mismanagement, with high levels of corruption, nepotism, you can be sure you will be manipulated."

I wanted to follow up on Soh's observation that the government has very little control outside Bangui and asked Gumba for his opinion. He responded with an image: "The country is like a kid who has a very big head and a very small body. Bangui, the capital, is the big head, and the rest of the country from north to south to west and east is just malnourished and not fed at all."

"The government," Gumba explained, "stays in Bangui. Outside Bangui, there are no roads, no electricity, no water, no hospitals, no good schools. The government has completely abandoned the population."

As a result, Gumba noted, "There is a total loss of confidence in the government, and the population distrusts the government."

I asked him if he was surprised by the rise of the Séléka.

"No, not totally," he said, "for as I said, the country [outside Bangui], especially the North and Northeast [where the baraka formed], is totally abandoned. When the little groups of militias form, they tell the population, 'We are here to protect you because the government has failed.'

But what happens is that there are many militias and they begin to attack one another. Each group is competing for power in the local areas."

Gumba's observation that the experience of state absence outside Bangui gave rise to multiple and contested pluralized authorities (militias) in many parts of the country seemed insightful. I followed up and asked, "So, was the genius of the Séléka that it succeeded in forging an 'alliance' [*séléka* means alliance] of various military groups?"

"Exactly," Gumba responded. "But that did not happen until the Séléka were halfway to Bangui; that was when a large number of Central Africans joined the movement. At first, everyone thought they were just a local militia group in the Northeast."

"What is the way forward?" I asked Gumba.

"The government needs to be close to the population. The government must provide security and the social services the population needs. That is how you can begin to build trust. The solution is to decentralize. If this had been the case, we should not have had a revolution and the Séléka would not have come."

I asked whether decentralization was going to be FPP's platform going forward. "Definitely," he confirmed.

Later that evening I reflected on my conversation with Gumba as I read Louisa Lombard's essay "The Autonomous Zone Conundrum." In it she makes the point that if CAR is a forgotten and marginalized country, the Northeast is the "periphery of the peripheries."[14] She describes the Northeast as an example of an "autonomous zone," an area marked by a minimal government presence, where government has treated the residents as foreigners and ignored them.[15] Stuck "between their *lived reality* of abandonment by any government and their *formal reality* of being bound to CAR," the residents often feel that "their only way of getting 'the state' to pay attention to them is by threatening rebellion and armed disorder."[16] As one rebel explained, "We don't have the kinds of mouths that can speak to the government."[17]

While this is true particularly of the Northeast, the sense of rural abandonment is palpable in other parts of the country. A week later, as Soh and I drove to Bossemptele, three hundred miles northwest of Bangui, on the only paved road (now filled with huge potholes) outside Bangui (only a total of 267 miles in CAR are paved), the sense of rural abandonment was obvious: no infrastructure, no schools, no apparent economic activity save for a few stalls by the roadside where villagers sold charcoal, fruits, and trapped rats! The irony that became apparent was that the relation between France and its French Equatorial Africa (AEF) colony, which it viewed as an "autonomous district" and largely ignored but exploited, had come to be reflected in the state's relation to its hinterland, particularly the Northeast. It was from within these marginalized, abandoned villages that both the Séléka and anti-balaka drew their strongest support.

Autochthony and the Dubious Citizenship of Muslims

If the majority of CAR feel marginalized, Muslims in CAR feel a double, often triple, sense of marginalization. They form only 5 to 15 percent of the population, the majority live in the autonomous zone of the Northeast, and in the eyes of many they are "not from the land." Part of this feeling reflects the colonial legacy. As Louisa Lombard observes, "The French colonial view of the north-easterners as exploitative, slave-raiding foreigners remained in place after independence. Though educated elites from the North East have ascended to ministerial positions, Central African nationalism (to the extent it exists) is strongly coded Christian, and non-north-eastern. The North East is associated with Islam and foreignness—regardless of how many generations a Muslim family has lived in the country."[18] The feeling that Muslims are foreigners is reinforced by the fact that many Muslims do not speak Sango, the national language. They speak pidgin Arabic (also spoken in Chad and Sudan).

But for all their "marginalization" Muslims dominate the economy, and they are on the whole better off than non-Muslim Central Africans. This irony partly helps to explain the rise of the Séléka and the anti-Muslim crusade of the anti-balaka.

Bridget is a Catholic lay leader and the head of Christian Life Community, which promotes Ignatian spirituality in parish communities in the Archdiocese of Bangui. She formerly worked with the ministry of social affairs and as adviser on gender and women's development but now runs a private transportation company. I met her on Saturday morning after mass and was interested to find out from her who she thought was to blame for the current mess that is Central Africa.[19]

"France," she responded without hesitation, "has the primary responsibility."

"How is that so?" I asked.

"France left a mindset that has been copied in Central Africa. It taught us to see that the only respectable work is indoors; there is no dignity for manual work."

I was at once surprised and curious as to how this was behind the problem of CAR.

"You see," she explained, "all educated Central Africans desire to work as civil servants and to get the benefits of office, car, and government house. No creativity at all. . . . Even those who have no high education, they aspire for high positions. This is why many youths joined the Séléka rebellion; they expected to be rewarded with high offices."

The second major problem, Bridget told me, stems from "Muslims who tried to take over 'our' country. Muslim intellectuals manipulated the masses promising jobs in administration to other Muslims."

"Wasn't the Séléka rebellion justified given that the government had completely neglected the Northeast?" I inquired.

"No, not at all. The majority of the population in the Northeast are Muslims, and their leaders used to get a lot of money from the gold and diamonds in the area. But the money was not used to develop the area; instead it was sent to foreign countries. If they had invested the money here, there would have been a lot of schools and hospitals."

"Why was the money not invested here, is it because the country was unsafe?" I asked.

"No," she said emphatically, "it is because the majority of the Muslims are foreigners, they came from elsewhere."

"But," I asked, "are there no native Muslims?"

"There are some who are 'native,' but even these have external links."

This sense of Muslims as dubious Central Africans, aliens disguised as nationals to claim a seat at the table, explains Bridget's lack of sympathy for the Séléka and her more sympathetic assessment of the anti-balaka. I asked her if she was surprised by the rise of the anti-balaka.

"No, when the Séléka came to Bangui, within one week of taking over the government, they killed a lot of people. The anti-balaka wanted to defend the population, even though in the end they also killed people. But Séléka killed more than the anti-balaka."

Imam Yacoub (not his real name) is the vice president of the National Council for Nonviolence, an initiative founded by Fr. Barwendé Médard Sané at the Catholic Center in Bangui. Originally a Christian, Yacoub had converted in 1974. In introducing himself to me he was keen to highlight the fact that he was a Central African "native" and a Muslim.[20]

"Why did you stress the fact that you are native?" I asked him.

"Because I belong to those who have been there right from the beginning. The ethnic group I belong to did not come from elsewhere. They have been here, and they are sons of the soil."

This seemed to contradict Bridget's claim that Muslims, even native Muslims, were not true sons of the soil.

I asked, "What does it mean to be Muslim in CAR?"

"People look at Muslims as nothing, and when you are Muslim here, you are just marginalized. People who convert from Christian to Muslim, like me, are looked at as if they just lost their citizenship; they start calling us Arabs."

He explained that Muslims are considered foreigners and that this makes life difficult. He offered his own story as an example.

"It took me six months to get a passport simply because of my name, yet it takes only one month for any Central African to get a passport. And when you are traveling, if you are dressed the way I am, the police stop you and ask you how you got the documents because they think you are a foreigner."

But for all this perception of Muslims as "foreigners," Imam Yacoub reiterated the same view that most people I had talked to had shared, namely that before the Séléka uprising Christians and Muslims had lived together peacefully.

"Why did that change during the crisis? Why did Muslims kill Christians and the other way round?" I asked.

"The problem started with Bozizé's failed coup [in 2001], when he fled to Chad," Yacoub explained. "He returned [in 2003] with many Chadian mercenaries, whom he promised 25 million CFA each when he took over power. However, when Bozizé ousted Patassé and became president, he forgot his promise to his Chadian [Muslim] freedom fighters. Some of them returned to Chad, but others withdrew to the Northeast and eventually became part of the Séléka alliance. . . . The same people who helped Bozizé become president were the same people who were now trying to overthrow him. When Bozizé realized this he started claiming that 'Muslims are coming to invade our country.'"

Yacoub continued, "Not all Séléka were Muslims. There were Christians among the Séléka." Elsewhere I had read that 20 percent of the Séléka were Christians. "Bozizé wanted to unite the country against the rebellion," Yacoub told me. "He was on the radio saying, 'Be aware of our enemies. They are coming. Muslims are coming from Chad to take over *our* country.'"

According to Yacoub, it was Bozizé more than anybody else who had helped to frame the conflict as a "religious war." Just as Patassé in the 1990s had used "ethnicity" to reinforce his flagging hold on power, so now Bozizé was using religion as an effective tool for political mobilization. To accomplish this he played off not only the long-standing view of Muslims as "foreigners" but also his own membership in his Pentecostal Christian Congregation, for whom the language of "religious war" seemed to be particularly resonant. For as Yacoub was saying, "While the Séléka were still moving toward Bangui, Bozizé was claiming over the radio that Séléka had killed many people and destroyed many churches."

"But it is true the Séléka were killing people?"

"President Bozizé had promised these people 25 million francs," he explained, "and he did not give to them. So they were killing people because they were just angry and they wanted to pay themselves and revenge at the same time."

"Was this before or after they took power in Bangui?"

"This started about three months before the Séléka took power, and after they just continued killing people, looting, and doing bad things."

Yacoub paused briefly, as if trying to recall something, and took another approach that threw light on what Bridget had said about the colonial mentality of Central Africans wanting to work indoors.

"For me I think the conflict was not simply a religious conflict because Muslims in this country own over 75 percent of the economy."

"So," I inquired, "why then do Muslims feel they are discriminated against if they own 75 percent of the economy?"

"We are marginalized because of jealousy," he said. "Most Central Africans do not want to work and they like only indoor jobs. Muslims, they do not want to go to schools, and they are taught outdoor jobs right from childhood. They are taught business and commerce. If you look at the statistics of those who work in the natural resources and diamond industry, for example, you will find only 2 percent non-Muslims. Even a Muslim who does not know how to speak French and has never gone to school, he owns a big house, but you find non-Muslims who went to schools and speak excellent French, and they don't even have a house."

"This is interesting," I noted. "Muslims control the diamonds, the trade, commerce, and are generally much better off than non-Muslims. Is this just in the Northeast?"

"No, everywhere in Central Africa."

A clear picture was emerging. Even though the violence was expressed using the idiom of religion, it had less to do with doctrinal differences or hatred than with a "concatenation of several [factors] all of which exacerbated the others: the fact that Muslims are never considered 'true' Central Africans; the dominance of commerce by 'foreign' Muslims; the rise of Pentecostal churches, the regionalization of Central African political instability, and particularly the increasing involvement of mercenaries in changes in power in Bangui."[21]

The Violence of the Anti-Balaka

Roland Marchal notes that state building in CAR over the last two centuries is a history of oppression, coercion, mass killings, and dispossession.[22] The effect is a profound sense of insecurity felt by the majority of Central Africans, experienced on many levels. There is, in the first place, physical insecurity based on the tumultuous history of migrations to escape slave raids, brutal colonialism, predatory regimes, and militia control. In addition, there is economic insecurity provoked by widespread poverty, lack of employment, and the control of the market (commerce/economy) by what are perceived as "non-native" and foreign operators. The cumulative effect of these two insecurities has been to reduce the majority of the Central African population to a life of "mere survival" and to underwrite another form of insecurity, what Adam Ashforth describes as "spiritual insecurity"—the unease arising from the conditions of knowing that invisible forces are acting upon one's life but not knowing what they are and how to relate to them.[23] According to Ashforth, the resurgence of witchcraft within postcolonial African societies (Ashforth is studying South Africa) is not simply an indication of the persistence of "traditional African culture" but a modern phenomenon, an attempt to make sense and protect oneself from the insecurity of modern daily life in Africa.[24]

I find Ashforth's notion of spiritual insecurity helpful to understand the heavy reliance on fetishes and magical concoctions by the anti-balaka. The excess of violence by the anti-balaka can also be seen as a reaction to the profound sense of insecurity and frustration that had been building up within a population so long neglected, exploited, and left to feel defenseless.

Francis Mtingo is the president of the National Council for Youth in CAR. I met him in his office at the National Stadium. The youth, he told me, were very angry: "There is so much anger that for a small thing they can just start fighting."[25]

I asked him why the youth were angry.

"There are no opportunities for them. There is nothing here to do. The model that is put before the youth today is two sides. You can earn your dreams by either joining the militia or joining government forces."

Either way, Francis was saying, fighting (violence) was the only option.

A conversation with Barwendé highlighted yet another dimension of the violence of the anti-balaka. A Jesuit priest originally from Burkina Faso, Barwendé directs the Catholic Center at the University of Bangui. He talked about the "tiredness" and lack of energy in the general population, even among the youth:[26] "With the crisis since 1980s there have been many challenges in this country: tribalism, coups d'état, and the majority of the people are tired and passive. Even the youth are tired, and you cannot feel any kind of energy like what you see in other parts of Africa."

Barwendé also noted that there is a flip side of the general sense of despondence and resignation. "There is something I call a magical faith," he explained, "having a kind of belief and expecting from God to respond to your situation magically. If you go to church you will see people praying and fasting and saying, 'Only God will bring peace in this country. If God wants it we shall have peace.'"

I mentioned to Barwendé how on the Friday I arrived in CAR, I passed by many churches where people were observing the Way of the Cross. Barwendé did not seem to be impressed.

"People think that the more we are praying, the better the situation will become. Like 'Let us fast,' 'Let us take holy water,' and even when they come to talk to you as a priest, they ask, 'Give us a blessing and please show us some verses we can read, then be able to respond to some situation.'"

This magical belief, Barwendé explained, was exploited by the anti-balaka. They told people that if they took some traditional charms and herbs, the bullets would not hit them. When four days later I got a chance to talk to Poko (not his real name), a former member of an anti-balaka militia, I could sense the anger, resignation, and belief in magical faith (practice) that both Barwendé and Francis talked about.[27] In his late thirties, Poko had had three kids, but only one was still living, two having died in their infancy. He lived in the village where he was born on a small field where he grew cassava and other food crops. He had heard about a place that was rumored to have gold and had gone to look for work there, but he did not find any. When he returned to the village he heard that Séléka were coming; he fled to the bush, where he started feeling anger against the Séléka.

"Why were you feeling angry?" I asked.

"I heard they were beating up everyone. They had attacked my mother and beaten her. But also the Peul [a group of Muslim cattle herders who for centuries had moved with their herds throughout the region] had lived here with us for many years. We welcomed them and we were living peacefully. We needed their meat, and they needed our cassava. But now we heard that they had sided with the Séléka."

"You felt betrayed?"

"Yes, they were siding with the foreigners because they were Muslims, and yet we were their neighbors. The Séléka were also taking away weapons, guns, pangas, and machetes from the people except the Peul. One of the seers said that he had received a message in the night from the protecting spirit, who had shown him which herbs and charms to use to protect ourselves but also to fight against the Séléka. Many young people came together and began to be trained."

I asked Poko if there was really a protecting spirit. He explained that many years ago the Zaragina (highway robbers) had terrorized the area. The same protecting spirit had revealed what kind of herbs and charms to use against the Zaragina. And the local population had repelled the Zaragina. The same spirit was now revealing the herbs and charms to protect the people.

"What kind of training did you receive? Was this military training?"

"Yes," he responded, "we had some people who had been soldiers and they knew how to fight. But we trained spiritually."

"How?" I asked.

"They gave us some charms and a concoction, which we always had with us to drink. For the medicine to work you had to abstain from sexual intercourse, and also not eat food prepared by a woman during her period. This is how we protected ourselves against bullets of the Séléka." (Thus the name "anti-balaka," meaning both anti-*matchete* and anti-*balles à ti laka*', or anti-AK-47 bullets.)

"Did you actually call yourselves the anti-balaka?" I asked.

"No, our local group was called 'Siriri' [which means peace]."

"Who organized your Siriri group, and how did it operate?"

"The spiritual leader organized us; other local groups were also organized, and one local group would support another."

"Did your Siriri group actually achieve peace?"

"Yes, we felt God was working for us; even though we had simple weapons, yet we were able to chase the Séléka and their guns!"

"So you continued to believe in God even when you were using charms, fetishes, and concoctions."

"Yes, I am a Christian. I believe in God, even though I use the herbs and roots to protect myself."

I thought of Ashforth's observation about how "spiritual insecurity" evokes the quest for spiritual power, taking it from wherever one can find it in order to protect oneself against the many invisible forces. Accordingly, the wearing of fetishes along with the Christian cross or rosary does not seem to pose a problem. I was also thinking about the extent of the violence of the anti-balaka, which by many accounts exceeded that of the Séléka. So I asked Poko about the killings.

"We killed," he said, "because the Séléka were also killing."

"Did you only target the Séléka?"

"Yes, but also the Peul who had betrayed us."

I asked him whether he had any regrets looking back.

While earlier Poko had talked about the "success" of their efforts in getting rid of the Séléka, now he was quiet for a long time. Something seemed to be bothering him. When he spoke, he said he regretted the violence and did not seem to see much hope from their efforts.

"There was a lot of killing and looting, too much," he said. He wished the Peul, who had all been driven out, would come back, even though he doubted they ever would. He lamented the fact that the spiritual leader was dead. Another spiritual leader (in the neighboring village) had been burned alive after he was suspected of killing someone. There were many cases of domestic violence. Now that the Siriri group had been disbanded, there was a lot of idleness in the community, where men "just sit and drink!"

The conversations with Francis, Barwendé, and Poko were helping expose the violence of the anti-balaka, not as "religious" violence, but as the violence of an angry, downtrodden, and defenseless people—a people without much hope. The problem with this kind of violence, as Fr. Joseph, the secretary-general of the Bishops' Conference, later told me, is that once it is unleashed, "there is no limit to the violence. . . . Today they will say the violence is against the oppressors, but tomorrow the violence will go to even their neighbors."[28] I thought of Frantz Fanon and his insight that the last war of the colonized will not be the oppressed against the oppressors but the oppressed against the oppressed. I also thought about Mamdani's book *When Victims Become Killers*, in which Mamdani seeks to account for the popular agency of otherwise peaceful Rwandans during the genocide. I was seeing a similar pattern of mass violence here in CAR. The irony of such violence is that local militia groups set up to defend themselves against "foreigners" ended up directing most of the violence against their neighbors. Supposedly "Christian" militias fighting "Muslims" ended up exercising more violence against fellow Christians, in the end exacerbating the very situation they had set out to confront: killing innocent people, looting, raping women, and destroying homes.

The Hope of CAR

Throughout my time in CAR, the question of hope was uppermost on my mind. What hope was there for a country and a people so long exploited and forgotten? What visible signs of hope might there be in the aftermath of the Séléka and anti-balaka violence? Given CAR's political history and the multiple contradictions within the microdynamics of CAR society whose overall effect was abysmal failure of which the violence of 2013 was but one manifestation, it is not difficult to see why one might easily give up hope on CAR. I encountered many sentiments (explicit and implicit) of hopelessness, none perhaps as outright as those of two foreign humanitarian workers. Today, there are over seventy-five international aid organizations delivering all types of humanitarian assistance, with a combined budget of 515 million francs for 2018, all now coordinated under one office, the United Nations Office for the Coordination of Humanitarian Affairs (OCHA). Over a meal, I asked Louise, the Dutch director of OCHA, what hope she saw for CAR.

"I do not see much hope here," she confessed. She ran off a number of reasons: "Five hundred fifteen million francs is too little for a crisis of this magnitude; all we are doing is 'crisis management,' that is our mandate; there is no long-term vision or programs for long-term development; local NGOs have little capacity; the international agencies contribute to the same marginalization of local efforts even as we seek to empower the local efforts."[29]

Louise went on to identify the underlying problem.

"Even as we care for the people here, the truth is that CAR does not matter much in the eyes of the international community. We will all leave as soon as another international crisis pops up, and funds become directed to a more pressing crisis."

Jonathan, a French national, a monitoring and evaluation expert for the UN-funded refugee resettlement program, sounded even more hopeless. "We try to make life a little better," he said, "but we should be realistic. CAR is the least developed country—the last on every development index. It will never become a Singapore! If life for the ordinary Central African can improve a little bit . . . but the situation is not easy. There is nothing here; the feeling that CAR is a 'rich' country is simply misplaced nostalgia!"[30]

But one does not have to take such a hopeless view. To claim that "there is nothing here" is to overlook local initiatives like the Interfaith Platform (IFP), which many people point to as a sign of hope. The IFP brings together religious communities at the national and local levels. It was established at the height of the Séléka crisis by the three most senior religious leaders in CAR—Archbishop (now Cardinal) Dieudonne Nzapalainga (Catholic), Imam Omar Kobine Layama (Muslim), and Reverend Nicolas Guerekoyame-Gbangou (Pentecostal). When I met the soft-spoken Imam Kobine, IFP cofounder and president of the Central African Islamic Community, at the IFP office in Bangui, he was quick to point out that the problem in CAR is not a problem of religion.[31]

"The crisis of 2012–13 was a crisis of leadership and the way of governing this country, which has many causes, including regionalism, tribalism, corruption, marginalization, and the rejection of others."

I asked him about the IFP, its work, and the hope it represents.

"We work to bring people of different faiths together to show that we can live in peace," Imam Kobine explained. "During the crisis, we went around the entire country, including villages occupied by Séléka. We brought together the different religious communities and religious leaders—imams, pastors, and priests—and encouraged them to continue working together so that we could not be instrumentalized by politics."

Similar efforts for social cohesion and sensitization are represented by the over two thousand youth volunteers for peace, a network founded by Fr. Barwendé at the Catholic Center (Chaplaincy) at Bangui University. The volunteers, many of them university students, organize meetings for youth around the country and instruct them on the basic principles of peacemaking and peacebuilding. Fr. Barwendé also founded the National Council for Active Nonviolence, which works with leaders in the community, promoting the culture and principles of active nonviolence. Imam Yacoub is an active member and vice president of the network.

Given that over 80 percent of CAR's population is Christian, the Catholic Church's presence and work in CAR is another sign of hope for many people. Both Gumba and Stanislaus Kembe (former CAR ambassador to the United States) talked about the church as the "conscience of the nation" and pointed out that some priests had lost their lives for speaking out. Bridget had observed how during the crisis the church was a place of refuge for many displaced people, a situation that continues today in some parishes. Moreover, given the "dysfunctional" nature of the CAR state and the absence of government services in most of the country, the Catholic Church with its extensive network of schools and health care centers in parishes throughout the country seems to be the only institution that can create social cohesion. Some even wanted Cardinal Nzapalainga to serve as president (citing the example of Barthélemy Boganda, the first CAR ordained Catholic priest, who served as the first prime minister of CAR), reflecting a widespread sentiment that the Catholic Church in particular has a unique role to play in bringing peace to CAR. As an example of the church's role, many remarked on the pope's visit in 2015. Almost everyone I spoke to said it was the pope's visit, more than any other single event, that brought an end to the Séléka–anti-balaka violence and improved Christian-Muslim relations. (Pope Francis not only said mass in the stadium but went to the predominantly Muslim neighborhood of PK5.) The pope's visit also gave the Central Africans a sense of unity and hope for their country, especially after France had opposed the visit. "We felt proud to be Central Africans," Fideli Modat, a former member of parliament during the transition, remarked about the papal visit.[32]

It is therefore not totally true that in CAR "there is nothing here." There are also the efforts of the government since 2014, when Michel Djotodia was forced to step down and was replaced by a transitional government headed by Catherine Samba-Panza. Even though the current president Faustin-Archange Touadéra and his government face enormous challenges, the fact that the 2015–16 elections (which brought Touadéra to power) were mostly peaceful is itself significant.

Although these efforts are contributing to a better CAR, they are still insufficient. They all lack a new vision for Central Africa and are driven not by imagination but by "realism." This is to say that they all take the reality of CAR's politics—its broken, dysfunctional, and violent nature—for granted. The goal is to manage and improve the brokenness ("if the life of the average Central African can be a little better!") and ameliorate its violent outbursts, of which the Séléka–anti-balaka was the most recent. But given the dominant imagining that has driven politics in CAR, and the history and society these imaginings have shaped—a society mired in various contradictions—it is clear that what is needed is not simply managing or relief or development, or even peaceful coexistence (though that would be a significant first step). What is needed is the "reinvention" of CAR. This requires much more than a cease-fire, much more than a new constitution, much more than a change of government, even much more than religious tolerance. It requires rewiring society with a fresh vision of politics. It requires rediscovering the soul of politics, which could generate a new identity and a new sense of belonging for Central Africans.

It is the need for that "much more" and the lack of progress toward it that seem to be at the heart of Barwendé's critique of the IFP. Asked about his assessment of the organization, Barwendé gave this response: "They received a lot of trust from the people at first, and it was nice to see a bishop, pastor, and imam together. But people are hungry for *something more*. They were expecting a lot from them and not just to be together." I take the "something more" that people are hungry for to be a new sense of personal and social identity and a new vision of society. As Barwendé remarked, "When you listen to the cardinal and the other leaders of the Platform, you cannot get . . . clear teaching [a distinct vision of society] out of the Platform—except 'Let's live together in peace.'"[33]

The Catholic Church, which seems to suffer not only from institutional weakness but also from a cultivated reticence in matters political and deference to the state born out of its Constantinian legacy of church-state relations, also seems unable to provide or inspire that "much more." When I talked with Fr. Joseph, the secretary-general to the Bishops' Conference, he highlighted the church's traditional role in education, health care, and peacebuilding efforts and spoke of the church's advocacy for peace and justice and the pastoral letters of various bishops speaking out against abuses. However, when I asked what the church could do differently, Joseph thought for a few minutes and said, "I do not know, perhaps more education of the population, and more catechesis." But he immediately added, "With the level of unemployment, poverty, and lack of education, the impunity and absence of justice . . . we are facing an uphill task!" He also noted, "There is a limit to what the church can do. We are the church; we are not the government. The policy of the church is to support what the state is doing, and where the government is lacking, the church tries to supplement, while at the same time providing a prophetic voice and distance."[34]

How does one think about, let alone realize, that "much more" than politics as usual in light of Central Africa's history and performance? This question came up in my conversation with Barwendé. Since he had described how Central African politics had generated a sense of "tiredness" even among the youth and had succeeded in eroding people's trust not only in the government but in one another and in themselves, I asked him how such a dispirited people could regain confidence.

"What we need here," Barwendé suggested, "is a revolution, similar to what Sankara did in my country of Burkina Faso, giving the Burkinabe people a new identity and sense of pride and confidence."[35] I offered Barwendé my favorite quote from Sankara: "You cannot carry out fundamental change without a certain amount of madness. In this case, it comes from nonconformity, the courage to turn your back on the old formulas, the courage to invent the future."[36]

Barwendé immediately lit up. "That is precisely the problem here. Even though people have no trust in politics, they cannot see any alternative. They continue to hope that the very institutions that have failed them in the past will somehow, as if magically, become the solution. When you talk to people about the future—students, religious leaders, civic leaders—they always come back with the same answers: it is the government, France, the UN, the international community."

I asked him what it would take for people to begin to see and imagine alternatives.

"It begins with helping people to regain a sense of trust in themselves, for when you have a person living in fatalism, you cannot bring about change. This is what I am trying to get at in my workshops with young people."

"How do you do that?" I asked.

"I tell the stories of people like Thomas Sankara, Patrice Lumumba, Nelson Mandela, and others to help students see these fellow Africans as role models and develop a sense of self-confidence: we are black Africans, but we have great values. We do not need to continue to be beggars."

Barwendé explained that what he wanted to see was "a new kind of imagination, a kind of understanding that we can do something from our own capabilities."

"We can build the space," he told me, "and can change society from the trust we can develop from ourselves."

Barwendé also explained that the new imagination came at a price.

"The price one is willing to pay and what one is willing to sacrifice, because peace does not come cheaply. What I have noticed is that people want peace, but they are not willing to suffer for it. Again, that is what I am trying to get at in the network of volunteers for peace. I stress the point of volunteerism, which is about what each student can do and is willing to sacrifice to achieve peace."

I asked Barwendé what the role of the church was in creating this revolutionary transformation of identity and imagination of a new society.

"The church can act as a midwife," Barwendé said, and expanded on the image. "You cannot force the revolution, it is like giving birth. Only the mother can push the child. I wish to see the church and all the international community and NGOs helping Central Africans to understand that positive peace is your baby to be pushed out by you from your own acceptance of and paying the price for peace."

Barwendé also described how the church can help this process,

"The [way the] church can contribute is to educate the people by giving examples."

"What kind of examples?" I asked him.

"The prophetic role of the church," he responded, "is to denounce injustice and announce the good news. The prophetic role is to renounce personal interest and show good examples of renouncing personal interest and a willingness to sacrifice."

I was extremely interested in the themes that Barwendé spoke of—revolution (Sankara-like), imagination, stories, sacrifice (self-sacrificing love), and the church as a midwife. They all seemed to be at the heart of any efforts at social reimagination. But our conversation, even with the example of his volunteers for peace, was still abstract. I needed a more concrete, practical, and compelling "demonstration" of the church as a midwife, of a revolutionary praxis of self-sacrificing love, which represents a fresh political imagining and thus is capable of giving birth to new social possibilities and a new sense of belonging in Central Africa. I found the demonstration in the story of Fr. Bernard Kinvi at Bossemptele.

Fr. Bernard Kinvi and the Mission Hospital in Bossemptele

Bossemptele lies three hundred miles northwest of Bangui. The Catholic parish runs a rudimentary hospital, the only one in a seventy-mile radius. In 2010, a young Camillian priest, a native of Togo, was sent to Bossemptele to be in charge of both the mission and the hospital. Fr. Bernard Kinvi was twenty-eight. When the violence from the Séléka takeover reached Bossemptele in 2013, the mission and hospital became a place of refuge. At first it was Christians fleeing from the Séléka who found sanctuary in the mission; then, when anti-balaka militias formed, it was the Muslims who sought shelter at the parish. At the height of the anti-balaka purge, over a thousand Muslim refugees, mostly women and children, lived at the mission hospital. During this time, Father Kinvi not only fed the refugees and treated the wounded (both Séléka and anti-balaka) but buried the dead (many decomposing bodies lay in the streets and threatened a cholera outbreak). The anti-balaka would sometimes call him after they killed someone, saying, "We have our work, you have yours. We kill, you bury."[37] Sometimes they would demand ransom from him in exchange for someone's life. On more than one occasion, he was threatened by both the Séléka and the anti-balaka for being on the side of the "enemy."

For his extraordinary courage during the crisis, Kinvi has received a number of awards. He was given the Alison Des Forges Human Rights Watch Award for Activism in 2014 and was named on *Time* magazine's 2014 list of 100 most influential people. He was a 2016 Aurora Award finalist and has been hailed as a great humanitarian hero. But "humanitarian" does not capture the full range of motivations behind Kinvi's work at Bossemptele and the imagination that drives it. His concern for the refugees and the sick during the crisis does not flow only from sympathy and a desire to minister to the needy. The more closely I explored and considered his work at Bossemptele, the more I appreciated its political nature. In addition to refuge and care, Kinvi supplies all—but especially the sick, the poor, and the suffering—with a revolutionary vision of identity and an expansive sense of "my" people, made possible by God's love. This self-sacrificing love of God, which Kinvi first encountered through the Camillian order, is what he has sought to recreate at Bossemptele, both during the war and after.

As a non–Central African national, Kinvi had an option to leave during the crisis. I asked him why he stayed in Bossemptele even when his life was threatened. He stayed, he said, because as a Camillian he had taken a vow "to remain with the sick and to serve them" even if his life was endangered. I had never heard of the Camillians and was curious to find out about them.

A Roman Catholic religious order dedicated to the care of the sick, the Camillians operate in thirty-five countries, where they run hospitals and provide trained physical as well as spiritual care for the sick. They were founded in 1582 by St. Camillus de Lellis (1550–1614). Camillus had dedicated most of his youth to soldiering, gambling, and drunkenness. While staying at a hospital in Rome when suffering from an incurable leg sore, Camillus noticed the poor quality of care given to the sick and dying. It was then that he realized that God was calling him to care for the sick. He invited some other young men to join him to care for the ailing as a concrete expression of their faith. Before and throughout the 1800s, frequent epidemics, including the Black Plague, decimated the "Servants of the Sick," but the order continued to grow throughout Europe and worldwide. Many joined because they were inspired by Camillus's own example and words. One of Camillus's favorite sayings was that the poor and sick are the way to God's heart. In serving them, we serve Jesus, the Christ.[38] In their profession, members of the order take not only the three traditional religious vows of poverty, chastity, and obedience but a fourth vow to care for the sick even when one's own life is endangered.

This is the order Kinvi joined when he was nineteen. I was curious how he'd found his way to the Camillians and how compassion for the sick and dying had found its way to his heart.

He'd grown up in a polygamous family. When he was six, he lost his young sister (electrocuted), and soon after, his stepsister (killed by her boyfriend). During the years of political unrest in Togo, he and his family spent six months as refugees. When he was ten his father had a stroke and was paralyzed, and the young Kinvi was often at his side taking care of him.

"I knew the pain of losing my sisters, of being a refugee, and of having a sick father." These experiences, he explained, "helped me, I think, to become more empathetic. . . . I could feel the pain of others." Kinvi had also read a small book about Luigi Scrosoppi, a priest who had dedicated his whole life to serving the sick and orphans and had founded a female congregation (Sœurs de la Providence de saint Gaétan de Thiène). He went to the sisters and asked if they had a male community that looked after the sick. They directed him to the Camillians, who had a formation house in Benin.

During his formation with the Camillians, Kinvi remembers four things that touched him the most. First was the life of Camillus himself and his dedication to the sick and dying. A story is told that during the plague in Europe, while everyone was running away from the afflicted, Camillus and his band were running into the plague-infested villages to take care of the sick and dying. This and other stories of self-sacrificing love would come to shape Kinvi's spirituality and courage. He remembers the particular influence of the stories of Maggy Barankitse (of Maison Shalom in Burundi) and of the Seminarians of Buta (Burundi) who stood together, Hutu and Tutsi, and were willing to face death. "Every time, I felt like giving up during the crisis, I remembered these stories, and they encouraged me."

Second, his internship at a hospice had great impact. "At first it was very difficult for me to stay with the sick and dying, to bathe, feed, and smell them, but gradually I got used to it and even became happy. For I knew that in touching the sick, I was touching Jesus."

Third, the course on Catholic social tradition, especially the principle of the preferential option for the poor, made a deep impression. "Every time I go near the poor, I remember the church's calling to minister to the poor."

Fourth, the course on eschatology, which stressed the vision of Christian hope in the world, also helped Kinvi to see that our hope is not limited to the here and now, that "there is life beyond this world."

These four elements in Kinvi's formation continue to shape his life as a Camillian priest. They also allow one to appreciate how his ministry

at Bossemptele is not merely "pastoral" but a revolutionary form of politics, which offers a counternarrative to CAR's politics of violence and
dispossession. In his pastoral ministry Kinvi is reinventing CAR's politics
from the ground up. A closer look at some key factors in Kinvi's ministry
helps to bring Kinvi's political imagination into sharper focus.

Kinvi's Counter-Politics of Compassion

Kinvi's incarnational ministry at the mission and hospital at Bossemptele
has endeared him to the local population, who all (Christians, Muslims,
traditionalists) refer to him as "our priest." Kinvi's commitment to this
local place and its people must be seen against CAR's politics of abandonment and the generalized sentiment that CAR does not matter.
Rooted in CAR's colonial history, this sentiment has translated into de-
spair, especially among the rural communities. If Gumba rightly noted
that one of the greatest challenges of politics in CAR was the state's
"abandonment" of the people and called on the government to be "close
to the people," Kinvi provides a compelling example of what being "close
to the people" means and concretely looks like. In New York, after Kinvi
was honored with the Alison Des Forges Human Rights Watch Award,
he was asked what he planned to do with the award and whether he was
going to use the "international" platform to try to bring change to CAR.
Kinvi's response seemed to indicate that he was already bringing change
to CAR and that Bossemptele was his international platform. "I told
them," he said, "that I very much want to return to 'my' community and
continue to serve the sick and poor in Bossemptele. . . . This is what I
am currently doing. I go in the neighborhood and visit the sick people,
the elderly, and the handicapped." The commitment not only to place
but to a rural village is a key factor in Kinvi's reimagination of CAR. Not
in Paris, not in Bangui, not in the city, but in the abandoned village—not
in Jerusalem but in Nazareth—a new vision of society is emerging.

As we have noted, autochthony (belonging to the soil) has been an
underlying feature in CAR's politics, with Muslims constantly suspected
as "foreigners" and not true sons of the soil. Even though (perhaps because) Kinvi himself is not a "son of the soil," he is helping to redefine
the sense of belonging. "I do not feel I am a foreigner here," he told me.
"Actually I am more comfortable here than when I am in Togo." Even

though he has been here only eight years, he says he speaks the local language Sango "better than I speak my mother tongue." Kinvi's feeling of belonging to this "local place" even more than his native Togo is based, not on blood or soil, but on his sense of identity as a child of God who "belongs" to God.[39] This, according to Kinvi, is our one true identity. All other forms of belonging are secondary. What his Camillian formation helped him see is that to serve the sick and poor is one way to get to God's heart. To get to God's heart is to discover the same lesson he learned from his father's generosity and hospitality, that "there is always room"—and that everyone has a place there.[40] Kinvi's hospitality and care for the vulnerable (which became particularly evident during the crisis) regardless of their religion, origin, or nationality are just a reflection of this expansive sense of belonging within God's love.

Kinvi's hospitality transformed the Catholic mission at Bossemptele into a community offering a rare Ephesian Moment that revealed the reality and possibility of a new Central African society. Even after Kinvi had helped evacuate many Muslims to Chad and Cameroon, a few remained at the parish: a traumatized teenage boy, two Peul girls with polio, and an elderly blind woman who had been left in a river after being attacked with machetes. The town's imam, married to a Christian woman, was also living at the parish (until last year when he passed), contributing what he could to Father Bernard's work. An experienced tailor, he earned his keep at the mission by sewing school uniforms.[41] These wounded, "left-behind" people under Kinvi's care were helping to transform the Catholic mission into an odd, "catholic" community—a "new we"!

Behind CAR's politics has been the struggle for power to control CAR's resources. This self-serving "politics of the belly" has succeeded in turning CAR into an ongoing battlefield and impoverished the majority of the population. Given this politics, which has become the "norm," Kinvi's commitment to serving the poor and sick offers a refreshing alternative. Moreover, compared to the Bangui-based politics shaped around abstract concepts like power, resources, state bureaucracy, and statistics, the concrete materiality of Kinvi's local engagement— feeding, treating, bathing—in a word, "touching"—the poor offers a reminder of the true goal of politics. For in the end, the measure of any true polity is how well it treats its weakest members: the poor, the stranger, the homeless, the sick. This is what makes Kinvi's work at once Eucharistic (in touching the poor, I touch Jesus) and prophetic in that it is both a renunciation (critique) of politics as a struggle for power and a proclamation of the good news. This is what true politics is about. In this sense one can refer to Kinvi's efforts at Bossemptele as a revolutionary reinvention of politics. I think Barwendé was hinting at this when he said, "People are looking for something more"—something more, that is, than politics as usual.

Even though the 2012–13 crisis was not a "religious" war, our investigation has confirmed that a deep spiritual wound, an ongoing spiritual insecurity, fueled much of the violence. Through his work at the mission hospital, lovingly tending to the physical needs of patients, Kinvi is helping to heal their spiritual wounds as well. His story illumines that healing the "spiritual" wound at the heart of CAR's politics takes concrete "material" commitment and action: touching, feeding, bathing, treating the bodies of the most vulnerable and helpless members of the body politic. But that in itself is almost unimaginable unless one is driven, just as Kinvi is, not by a quest for power, but by love—the self-sacrificing love one encounters in the heart of God. This excess of love is the only credible and hopeful antidote to the politics of violence. Those who bring hope to CAR are not the generals, or the international agencies and power brokers, or the self-seeking politicians, or even the institutional church, but the likes of Kinvi.

The Church as a Field Hospital

Kinvi's story reveals deep theological sensibilities that shape his life and work. What drives Kinvi, and what Kinvi is driving at, is a unique theological politics—more specifically, an ecclesiology that is a vision of the church as God's new people—an odd community that is "gathered" (as the Greek word *ecclesia* connotes) from every race, tribe, tongue, and nation. This is the great multitude of Revelation 7:9. What is different about this crowd, impossible to count, is that it is "gathered" around the lamb that was slain. It is also a crowd of people who through their own suffering "have washed their robes and made them white in the blood of the Lamb" (Rev. 7:14). They are marked by the same self-sacrificing love as the lamb. Their willingness to suffer as they extend God's love especially to the poor, the sick, the vulnerable is what characterizes God's new people in the world. Their sacrifice, more than anything else, constitutes their politics. That is why the church as God's new people is not so much a "space" or an entity (thing) as an event, an action. Pope Francis evokes this sense of church as action when he refers to the church as a field hospital.[42] The church's unique location and mission, Pope Francis states, is at the "frontiers," where it enacts the social process of healing—the healing of all sorts of wounds. In this action, the pope tells us, the church reveals what it means to be human—our shared identity as created in God's image—and initiates new historical processes and social possibilities that reflect God's compassion in the world. In this way, the church becomes at once the midwife, agent, and demonstration of the revolution—a revolution of tenderness, of God's tender love in the world. It is this vision of the church as a field hospital and its politics of love that Kinvi is seeking to recreate at the mission hospital at Bossemptele, thereby reinventing CAR's politics from the inside out.

CHAPTER FIVE

Ecological Violence and the Reinvention of Land

The ways of your ancestors are good . . . their roots reach deep into the soil.

—Okot p'Bitek, *Song of Lawino*

The more we become connected with the earth, the more we discover that death leads to life, and that just like the rest of creation, we are dying every day, and every day being resurrected.

—Godfrey Nzamujo

Africa's Ecological Crisis

When I think of the ecological crisis in modern Africa, three images come to mind: the village, the slum, and deforestation. Together, these portray the reality of a "slow violence" due to the environmental degradation under way across much of Africa. First, the image of a village reveals the growing impoverishment of life in rural Africa, characterized by increasing water poverty, food insecurity, and lack of viable economic possibilities. My own village, Malube, sixteen miles to the west of Kampala, off the Kampala–Fort Portal highway, paints the picture of the changes that are occurring. When I was growing up there in the 1960s, our lives and daily routines were shaped by and centered on the three-acre plot of land that my parents had bought when they migrated from

Rwanda in the late 1940s. My parents would wake us up at dawn and send us to the garden, where we grew coffee, beans, maize, bananas, and other food crops. A couple of hours later, our morning work in the garden done, we would trek down the forest path to draw water from a spring. We would then wash up quickly and run two miles to school in order to be there before the opening bell at eight. When school got out at four in the afternoon, we ran home and ate quickly before joining our parents in the garden. Ours was a small piece of land, but it produced enough food to feed our family and occasionally provide a surplus, which our parents would sell, together with the coffee, to earn money to pay for our school fees and buy other essential commodities in the home.

To be sure, there was nothing romantic about growing up in Malube. Life was tough. But if ours was a simple and "primitive" lifestyle, it was marked by a deep sense of belonging—to the family, to the community, to the land (that supplied our food), and to the forest (where we collected firewood and drew water, and on whose outskirts we played). That was then. Now when I visit Malube, there are more people living in it, the forest that surrounded it has all disappeared, the spring has dried up, and where it used to run young men are burning bricks. There is an acute "water poverty" in the village;[1] the land looks dry, and the banana trees and other crops on it all look miserable. It is not surprising that little food is produced on the land. Where in the past we carried produce from the village to our relatives living in the city, now whenever I visit home I have to buy food and groceries in the city to bring to the village.

The slum and the slum dweller are the new face of poverty in Africa. The road to Malube passes through Nateete, a sprawling slum on the southwestern edge of the city of Kampala. In the 1980s, Nateete, five miles from the city center, was a small town with a few shops lining the highway. In recent years, its population has surged. With over two hundred thousand residents, Nateete is now one of the most densely populated slums around Kampala. Grain milling, retail shops, and motorcycle passenger taxis (*boda boda*) are its main businesses. There is also a huge outdoor market where everything is sold, from farm produce, secondhand clothing, charcoal, and firewood to household goods and motorcycle and car parts. Two roads come to an intersection in Nateete, creating a semipermanent jam of traffic and people. When it rains, given the poor drainage, water blocks most of the roads. The two-mile commute through Nateete to the Busega traffic circle—where the highway to Fort Portal and on to the Democratic Republic of the Congo (to the west) splits off the highway to Masaka, Mbarara, and on to Kigali in Rwanda (to the south)—becomes an agonizing one, lasting two hours or more.

Nateete represents a growing phenomenon across much of Africa: slums are growing at twice the speed of the continent's exploding cities. In 2007, in *Planet of Slums*, Mike Davis noted how for the first time in history the urban population of the world was about to outnumber its rural population.[2] Even more remarkably, he pointed out, UN statistics showed that by 2015, Black Africa would have 332 million slum dwellers, a number set to double every fifteen years.[3] That prediction turned out to be an underestimate. The World Economic Forum on Africa predicts that Africa's population of 1.1 billion is expected to double by 2050, with more than 80 percent of that population, more than 1.5 billion Africans, living in cities, the majority in slums: Kibera (Nairobi), Kroo Bay (Sierra Leone), Mathare (Kenya), Westport (Monrovia), and Makoko (Lagos) lead the trend as the biggest and perhaps best known.[4] UN-Habitat estimates in 2010 put about 62 percent of sub-Saharan Africa's urban population as living in these "informal settlements," where poverty is widespread, violent crime is rampant, and basic public utilities, including clean water, reliable electricity, and law enforcement services, are absent.[5] As Davis noted, "Instead of cities of light soaring toward heaven, much of the twenty-first century urban world squats in squalor, surrounded by pollution, excrement, and decay."[6]

The third image that represents the growing ecological crisis in Africa is deforestation. As of 2008, according to the UN Food and Agriculture Organization (FAO), indigenous or "old growth" forests in Africa were being cut down at a rate of more than four million hectares per year, which was twice the world's deforestation average, and between 1980 and 1995 alone forest losses totaled more than 10 percent of the continent's overall forest cover.[7] This grim picture is vivid in Uganda, as Musasizi Josephat of Makerere University shows in his paper "Deforestation in Uganda: Population Increase, Forest Loss and Climate Change." He notes that forest cover, in Uganda, has diminished from 10.8 million hectares in 1980 to 4.9 million in 1995, a rate that continues unabated. In fact, at the current rate, it is feared that over 70 percent of Uganda's forest cover will be lost by 2050.[8]

The factors that drive this rapid rate of deforestation in Uganda (and in Africa generally) are many and interrelated. They include commercial logging (both legal and illegal); the conversion of forests to commercial farming (especially of "cash crops," like sugarcane and palm oil); the lack of alternative energy sources (the majority of Africa's population use fuelwood for cooking); and population growth (which drives encroachment on forest land for subsistence farming). The politics of deforestation in Africa has been widely discussed, so there's no need to discuss it here.[9] Whatever the contributing factors, the consequences of deforestation are already evident in irregular rainfall patterns, extended droughts, decreasing soil fertility, and increasing mudslides due to loss of soil cover. Buduuda District in eastern Uganda is a case in point. The villages on the slopes of Mt. Elgon in Buduuda have been experiencing devastating landslides. More than one hundred people were buried by mudslides in 2010, fifty in 2010, more than ninety in 2012, and over forty in 2018.[10]

I draw attention to these three faces of Africa's ecological crisis—village, slum, and forest—to illumine through a kind of kaleidoscope lens Africa's unique form of modernity, which, in the words of Christian Parenti, is a "catastrophic convergence of poverty, violence, and climate change."[11] The three images reflect what is often not recognized as the heart of Africa's modernity and thus the root of Africa's ecological crisis—a shifting relationship and attitude to nature in general and land in particular. Perhaps the most obvious evidence of this shift is the rapid rate of deforestation, but no less important are the rural-urban exodus (which contributes to the growth of slums) and the abandonment of the "village." The changing relationship to the land is the result of a modern worldview that sees nature primarily as a "resource." Modern development economics is based on this worldview and therefore not only centers on a "cash economy" but tends to encourage an exploitative and extractive relation to the land.

The images represent forms of the "slow violence" that is under way across much of sub-Saharan Africa.[12] As forms of slow violence, these calamities remain largely imperceptible, undetected, and untreated. "Incidents" like the Buduuda landslides make visible the ongoing erosion of the fragile relationship between the human community and the natural earth community. That is why to refer to climate change and ecological degradation as "slow violence" is not simply to say that they lead to violent outcomes (destruction of lives and property as in Buduuda) or that they trigger violence (conflicts over diminishing land and water resources), though they obviously do.[13] Rather, to refer to them as "slow violence," as O'Brien rightly points out, is to see climate change and ecological degradation "as the product of a destructive system that degrades human lives, other species, and the world upon which all living beings depend."[14]

The effects of the slow violence of ecological degradation, especially on poor communities, are many: food insecurity, diminishing livelihoods, loss of water, and overall ongoing vulnerability to unpredictable climatic and weather conditions. Whereas the physical, social, and economic effects might be easily graspable, the spiritual wounds are far less obvious and yet more elemental. For without attending to the spiritual wounds, all forms of technical, economic, and political adaptations fall short of addressing the ecological crisis that the world, and Africa in particular, faces.[15] The goal of this chapter is to highlight the spiritual wound at the heart of Africa's ecological crisis and display it as "a crisis of belonging" within Africa's unique modernity. Modern Africa is built on the wholesale rejection of the spirituality of native African peoples as "primitive," "backward," and "pagan," and on the promotion of a problematic vision of "civilization," "progress," and "development." Africa's ecological crisis grows out of and reflects this rejection of the traditional worldview and uncritical embrace of Western modernity. The chapter argues that addressing ecological violence in Africa requires a recovery of a spirituality that affirms human beings' connection and belonging to the earth. The chapter advances in four sections. In the first, I will highlight the spiritual wound at the heart of the ecological crisis by drawing attention to Pope Francis's 2015 encyclical, *Laudato Si': On Care for Our Common Home*. In the second section, I will locate Africa's ecological crisis within the modern aspirations for progress, civilization, and development, which are built on an ideological rejection of African native spiritualities that foregrounded a mystical and intimate sense of belonging to the earth. In the third section, I will display the effects of development economics in Africa as the catastrophic convergence of poverty, conflict, and ecological degradation. In the fourth and last section, using the story of Godfrey Nzamujo and the Songhai Center, I offer an example of what a return to a spirituality of belonging to the earth—and thus a healing of Africa's ecological violence—might look like.

Pope Francis, the Ecological Crisis, and the Spiritual Wound

In his 2015 encyclical letter *Laudato Si': On Care of Our Common Home*, Pope Francis draws attention to the immensity of the ecological crisis of our time.[16] The world, "our sister," as Francis calls her, is "crying" under the weight of various burdens: global pollution, water poverty, loss of biodiversity, global inequality, and an overall decline in quality of human life (*LS* 15).

Two insights make *Laudato Si'* a particularly useful resource in understanding and responding to the ecological crisis in Africa. First, Francis observes that there is a deep connection between the ecological and social crisis. He makes the case that we are faced, not with two separate crises, one environmental and the other social, but rather with one complex crisis. That the cry of the earth and the cry of the poor go hand in hand means that the "the deterioration of the environment and of society affects the most vulnerable people on the planet" (*LS* 48).

Second, while Francis highlights the complex economic, social, cultural, and political factors that contribute to the ecological crisis, he notes that at their root lies a spiritual "wound," which he also calls a "sin" (*LS* 2). The wound is the crisis of belonging, in this case, the failure to see and acknowledge our deep connection with the land: "We have forgotten that we ourselves are dust of the earth (Gen. 2:7), our very bodies are made of her elements, we breathe her air and we receive life and refreshment from her waters." Pope Francis traces the failure to understand ourselves as "belonging" to the earth to a "distorted" anthropocentrism that shapes modern forms of production and consumption. The latter places human beings at the center and thus "sees everything as irrelevant unless it serves one's own immediate interests" (*LS* 122).

Modern anthropocentricism also ends up prizing technical thought over reality, since the technological mind "sees nature as an insensate order, a cold body of facts, as a mere 'given,' as an object of utility, as raw material to be hammered into useful shape" (*LS* 115). This "anthropocentric" view of the universe, with its roots in the Copernican revolution, which gave rise to modern science and the Industrial Revolution, has no doubt led to remarkable advances in all spheres of human life, such as technology, medicine, travel, and economics. However, this paradigm sets up humans as the subjects who view and approach nature as an external object to be controlled and manipulated (*LS* 106)—a conception that has often been supported by a "misreading" and misleading application of the Genesis account of Creation whereby humans are given "dominion" over the earth (Gen. 1:28). According to this reading, nature is given to humans, who must exercise control and dominion over it and in so doing fulfill their God-given mandate. For as beings "made in God's image," humans extend God's work of creation and thus become "co-creators" with God. Popular as it might be, Francis notes, this is not a correct interpretation of the Bible: "We must forcefully reject the notion that our being created in God's image and given dominion over the earth justifies absolute domination of other creatures" (*LS* 67). Another reading of this biblical account of Creation must be recognized which invites man to "till and keep" the garden of the world (Gen. 2:15). "Tilling," Francis notes, refers to cultivating, ploughing, or working, while "keeping" means caring, protecting, overseeing, and preserving. A proper attention to the biblical tradition, Francis concludes, suggests "that human life is grounded in three fundamental and closely intertwined relationships: with God, with our neighbour and with the earth itself" (*LS* 66).

The rupture of these three vital relationships is what has transformed both our view of and our interaction with nature and has led to an economic system built on a mentality of "plunder." For a long time, Francis notes, our relationship with nature was based on acknowledging and "respecting the possibilities offered by the things themselves." "It was a matter of receiving what nature itself allowed, as if from its own hand. Now, by contrast, we are the ones to lay our hands on things, attempting to extract everything possible from them. . . . Human beings and material objects no longer extend a friendly hand to one another; the relationship has become confrontational" (*LS* 106).

Going hand in hand with the mentality of plunder is the idea of infinite or unlimited growth or progress, which "proves so attractive to economists, financiers and experts in technology." The idea, Francis notes, "is based on the lie that there is an infinite supply of the earth's goods," a lie that leads to "the planet being squeezed dry beyond every limit" (*LS* 106).

Although others before him—Bill McKibben, Norman Wirzba, Fred Bahnson, Wendell Berry, and Wes Jackson, for example—have drawn attention to the unsustainable patterns of production and consumerism and, like Francis, have described the adverse effects of the ecological crisis, not only on our sister Earth but also on the poor around the world, they have not sufficiently addressed the spiritual roots of ecological degradation. Particularly in his discussion of the spiritual wound, Pope Francis significantly advances the analysis of the ecological crisis facing the world. For this reason, along with policy or economic adjustments (necessary as these are), Francis insists that addressing the ecological crisis requires a spiritual conversion: "Ecological culture cannot be reduced to a series of urgent and partial responses to the immediate problems of pollution, environmental decay and the depletion of natural resources. There needs to be a distinctive way of looking at things, a way of thinking, policies, an educational programme, a lifestyle and a *spirituality* [author's emphasis] which together generate resistance to the assault of the technocratic paradigm" (*LS* 111).

This emphasis on a "spirituality" and a "distinctive way of looking at things" is behind Francis's call for a "conversion," the goal of which is to think differently about ourselves and reimagine our relationship with nature. Such a reinvention not only will allow the cultivation of various "ecological virtues"—nobility in the care of creation, self-esteem, a sense of beauty, a spirit of service, gratitude, tenderness—but, most importantly, will reestablish our "ecological citizenship" (*LS* 211). Through this renewed sense of belonging the rupture in the intertwined relationships with God, with our neighbor, and with the earth begins to be healed.

Pope Francis's diagnosis of the "wound" at the heart of the global ecological crisis is spot on, and his call for spiritual conversion as a necessary step in addressing the twin cries of the earth and of the poor is a vital contribution. But what does the "wound" that Francis talks about look like in the context of Africa? What shape does it take? How does it perpetuate itself, thus deepening Africa's ecological crisis? Part of the answer to these questions—a major part of the answer—requires understanding the unique outlook that is the basis for how modern Africa operates. It is an outlook that rejects as "primitive" and "backward" the spirituality of Africa's native peoples.

Becoming Modern in Africa, Rejecting a "Primitive" Worldview

An adequate assessment of the "wound" at the heart of Africa's ecological crisis must first locate it against the backdrop of African native spiritualities, within which human life and activity are marked by a deep connection to and sense of belonging to the earth.

Belonging to the Earth

In *Cry of the Earth, Cry of the Poor*, the famed theologian Leonardo Boff draws insights from liberation theology to address the urgent twin cries of poverty and ecological degradation. Even though his focus is not on Africa but on the threatened Amazon of his native Brazil, his description of the spirituality of the Amazon's "original peoples" rings true in many ways of African spiritualties. To reclaim the dignity of the earth, Boff argues, we need to "listen to the permanent message of the native people."[17] This message is captured in the profound words of the great champions of the indigenous peoples, the Villas Boas brothers: "If we want to be rich, accumulate power, and rule the earth, there is no point in asking the native peoples. But if we want to be happy, combine being human with being divine, integrate life and death, put the person in nature, connect work and leisure, harmonize relations between generations, then let us listen to the indigenous peoples. They have wise lessons to impart to us."[18]

Boff goes on to identify five distinctive but interrelated lessons that can be learned from indigenous peoples. First is ancestral wisdom, which is set down in great stories and myths focused on the mysteries of the universe and on the depth of the human psyche in relation to it. This wisdom, Boff notes, is "built particularly on observation of the universe and listening to the Earth. . . . The elders, those who have accumulated the most experience, are the sages. When consulted by the community, they look attentively around them, contemplate the mountains, breathe air deeply, stamp on the ground, and only then speak."[19] Behind Boff's observation is the significance of "listening" to the earth and to the wisdom accumulated over the years and passed down by the elders from one generation to the next through myths and stories.

The second lesson to be learned from indigenous people is the mystique of nature. For native peoples, earth is not merely a means of production but an extension of life and of the body. It is Pacha Mama, the Great Mother who gives birth, feels, and envelops all. A Kuna chief from Panama elaborates on this point: "The earth is our mother and is also culture. The elements of our culture are born there . . . all the foods eaten in our traditional celebrations; the materials that our artisans use and that we use to build houses, all come from the hills. If we were to lose these lands, there would be neither culture nor soul."[20]

The third lesson is that work is never merely a means of production but a collaboration between human beings and Mother Earth to provide for human needs. "She is bountiful and sustains and nourishes all. But human beings help her in her mission. Hence, indigenous people work enough to supply their human needs and enjoy life. Work is always a community activity and one of pleasure, the aim of which is not to produce profit but live well."[21]

Celebration and dance comprise the fourth lesson. Original peoples are deeply mystical. They experience the Mystery of the God of a thousand names. Through celebration and dance they create the conditions for experiencing the divinity. But also, "Celebration and dancing—practices of sheer gratuity and lightness—give bodily substance to humankind's original vocation. They exist in order to grasp the majesty of the universe, the beauty of Earth, and the vitality of all things. If everything exists in order to shine, human beings exist to celebrate and dance that shining."[22]

The final and most profound of the lessons is indigenous peoples' intense and constant experience of God. God fills and pervades all. Human beings feel immersed in the world of the gods and of the ancestors, who live with them in another dimension. "The tree is not just a tree, closed in on itself. It is a being with many arms (branches) and thousands of tongues (leaves); it sleeps in winter, smiles in spring, is a bountiful mother in summer, and a harsh old woman in autumn. God is made present in all these manifestations."[23]

The descriptions in Boff's *Cry of the Earth, Cry of the Poor* of the wisdom of native peoples of the Amazon in many ways also hold true for the spirituality of African peoples. Boff's five lessons from the Amazon especially help highlight two crucial dimensions or elements of indigenous African ecospirituality. First is the sacredness of nature, which for many African peoples is not simply one aspect of life but the very essence of it. Accordingly, there is always a "more" to nature. A tree, as Wangari Maathai notes, is not merely "a source of food, medicine, and building material, but a place of healing consolation, and connection—with other human beings and with the divine."[24] The "more" of nature evokes a sense of majesty and wonder and respect. For African peoples, this sense of mystique is preserved through stories (that humanize and give agency to nature) and taboos and proscriptions that are intended to spell out clearly what ought not be done so as to preserve the balance and harmony in nature. The mystique also means that nature is suffused with a spiritual meaning. The individual lives in an enchanted universe—so thoroughly enchanted that it is not possible to separate the "sacred" from the "mundane." This is perhaps why the African, as John Mbiti remarks, is notoriously religious.[25] For the individual lives in close kinship with nature—a kinship that is not merely physical but spiritual. For nature is not just a physical entity; it has an inbuilt spirit that reflects something of God, the creator of the universe. This is also why, just as for Amazon peoples, celebration and dance are integral to the African way of life. Again as Wangari Maathai notes, one reason why the community appeared to have so much time to celebrate and enjoy the natural world was that they weren't looking at it through acquisitive, materialistic eyes but through the lens of spiritual kinship.[26]

The other dimension of African spirituality that the lessons from the Amazon help illumine is a sense of participation and belonging. Individuals are at one with, and part of, this dynamic universe. They participate wholly in its life and through this belonging discover their connections not only to its divine manifestations but also to the community, including those living now, future generations, those recently deceased (the "living dead"), and ancestors long deceased. As Laurenti Magesa rightly points out, the African sense of belonging is inexorably connected to the soil (land), which in many ways serves as the "umbilical cord" that links the past, present, and future; the spiritual and mundane; the individual and the community; the earth and the world above and the underworld.[27] Thus, though legally informal, the individual's relationship to the land is deep, providing identity through a sense of belonging to family, clan, community, and to the earth. Equally significant in this context of belonging is the emphasis in African spirituality on ritual, dance, and story, elements that, Boff points out, reflect and reinforce a sense of sacredness and participation as well as a sense of providence and gratitude, the ideals of communal solidarity, and an attitude of contentment.

Walking into Progress and Civilization

The deep sense of connection and belonging to the earth and community outlined above has been the object of ongoing attack and erosion by the technocratic paradigm of modernity in Africa. Under the banner of modern ideas of "progress" and "civilization," as well as some forms of Christian mission, there has been a concerted effort to uproot Africans from this vision of nature as sacred and from their deep connection to the soil—in short, from their intimate sense of belonging to the earth. If these efforts have triggered an ongoing identity crisis in Africa, they have also underwritten an exploitative relationship to the earth, which has heightened the cry of the earth and the cry of the poor in Africa. In *Song of Lawino and Song of Ocol*, the late Ugandan poet Okot p'Bitek aptly captures the source of Africa's crisis of belonging. By attending to p'Bitek's "diagnostic poetics," to his characters of Lawino and Ocol, we can gain insight into Africa's spiritual and ecological crisis.[28]

Song of Lawino is a bitter complaint—a lamentation by Lawino about her educated husband Ocol, who has not only left her but abandoned the traditional ways of his people, which he now looks down upon as primitive and pagan. He abuses all things Acholi and considers all the ways of his people backward. Lawino places the blame for Ocol's attitude on "the shyness [he] ate in the church" and on the impact of Western education: Lawino complains that her husband "has lost his head in the forest of books":[29]

> And the reading
> Has killed my man,
> In the ways of his people
> He has become
> A stump.
>
> (113)

Lawino also describes how Ocol has become a "slave"—slavishly mimicking Western ways of thinking.

> he lives on borrowed foods,
> He borrows the clothes he wears
> And the ideas in his head
> And his actions and behaviours
> Are to please somebody else
>
> (116)

In the end, all that Lawino asks is for Ocol not to "uproot the pumpkin" but to "return home" and learn to respect the traditions of her people.

> The ways of your ancestors are good,
> Their customs are solid
> And not hollow
> They are not thin, not easily breakable
> They cannot be blown away
> By the winds
> Because their roots reach deep into the soil
>
> (41)

P'Bitek's *Song of Ocol* is shorter, and even more spare, stark, and direct in its presentation. It is Ocol's rebuttal to Lawino's "primitive" views. What becomes obvious from Ocol's response is that while Lawino expresses the great attachment of her people to place, their roots reaching deep into the African soil, Ocol sees Africa only as a "thing," a flawed "object" that needs fixing:

> What is Africa to me?
> Blackness,
> Deep, deep fathomless
> Darkness . . .
>
> Diseased with a chronic illness,
> Choking with black ignorance,
> Chained to the rock
> Of poverty.
> (125)

For Ocol the deep sense of belonging and attachment to the traditional values and customs that Lawino celebrates is not a form of wisdom but a sign of Africa's backwardness and timidity.

> Unweaned
> Clinging to mother's milkless breasts
> Clinging to brother,
> To clan,
> To tribe,
> To blackness
> To Africa,
> Africa, this rich granary
> Of taboos, customs and
> Traditions
> (126)

Rather than looking backward, rather than the "return home" that Lawino is calling for, Ocol seeks to move forward. He seeks Progress, and for this he is happy to leave behind "primitive" Africa and all she stands for:

To hell with your pumpkins
And your old homesteads
To hell with your old husks
Of old traditions and
Meaningless customs
We will smash
The taboos, one by one . . .
                    (126)

The customs are too little to bear the weight of civilization. And the taboos are nothing but chains of enslavement to the past—"chains around the neck."

Child,
Lover of toys
Look at his toy weapons
His utensils, his hut . . .
Toy garden, toy chickens
Toy cattle
Toy children
                    (125)

The desires and dreams that drive Ocol are not the little (what he calls "toy") concerns for village, soil, community but the big dreams of Independence, Progress, and Civilization represented by the City:

Weep long
For the village world
That you know and love so well,
Is gone,
Swept away
By the fierce fires
Of progress and civilization. . . .

Bid farewell
To your ancestral spirits

Fleeing from the demolished
Homestead

. . . I see the great gate
Of the City flung open,
I see men and women
Walking in . . .
Why don't you walk in with the others?

(147)

For Ocol, Progress and Modernity represent an inevitable path for
everyone, so in the final appeal to Lawino, Ocol encourages Lawino to
dare to walk in—even as he reminds her that she really has no choice:

Why don't you walk in with the others
Are you feeling homesick
For the deserted Homestead
Or are you frightened
Of the new City?
You have only two alternatives my sister
Either you come in through the City Gate
Or take the rope and hang yourself.

(149)

This powerful literary masterpiece, though dated, reveals much
about Africa's current spiritual and ecological crisis. It accurately captures the ideological mindset prevalent in how modern Africa operates.
Represented by Ocol, the mindset views traditional patterns of life as
"primitive," accepts "development" and "progress" as inevitable, and is
characterized by a slavish imitation of Western modes of production and
consumption. This ideological framework and its attendant models of
development help explain the poverty and growing desperation in African villages, the urban exodus and the growth of slums, and ecological
degradation. These faces of explicit and slow violence in Africa cannot
be explained outside the logic of modern development economics. For
as prominent economist Jeff Sachs notes, the "ladder of economic development" involves a "progression of development that moves from sub-

sistence agriculture toward light manufacturing and urbanization, and on to high tech services."[30] This progression begins with peasants who "typically know how to build their own houses, grow and cook their food, tend to animals, and make their own clothing. . . . They do all, and their abilities are deeply impressive." But they are also deeply "inefficient." A modern economy, notes Sachs, involves

> a shift of people from overwhelmingly agrarian activities to industrial activities, giving rise to urbanization, social mobility, new gender and family roles, a demographic transition, and specialization in labor. Modern economic growth is accompanied first and foremost by urbanization, that is, by a rising share of a nation's population living in urban areas. There are two basic reasons why economic growth and urbanization go hand in hand. The first is rising agricultural productivity. As food production per farmer rises, an economy needs fewer and fewer farmers to feed the overall population. As food production per farmer rises, food prices fall, inducing farmers and especially their children to seek employment in nonfarm activities. The second is the advantage of high-density urban life for most nonfarm economic activities, especially the face-to-face demands of commerce.[31]

What has become increasingly obvious is that the walk into Progress, or climb up the "ladder of economic development," is leaving a huge ecological footprint of increasing deforestation, mass poverty, pollution, and mass unemployment in much of sub-Saharan Africa.

Ultimately, the bombastic logic of "inevitable" development that both Ocol and Sachs represent, one that is advanced through the modern institutions of politics and economics in Africa, has succeeded in shaping a unique modernity in Africa. While Lawino's pumpkin ("the ways of my people") has been uprooted, the promised dreams of "development" and "progress" continue to be elusive. As a result, the majority of Africans now find themselves in a "zone of exile,"[32] an awkward intermediate stage of belonging and not belonging, of instinctively feeling a sense of connection with earth, spirituality, family, customs (the traditional outlook) and at the same time feeling the need to despise and reject all that "primitive" outlook and connections so as to become "modern" and "civilized" and to economically advance. The awkward in-between stage is the context within which the slow violence of Africa's ecological crisis festers and grows, contributing to poverty in African villages and triggering, now and again, various forms of open conflict. Land is in many ways a flash point of the awkwardness, which is most clearly evident in the love-hate relationship with the village, increasing land conflicts, and the economics of land exploitation. By exploring these three primary modalities of relating to land, we can shed light on the contradictions within the in-between stage of Africa's awkward modernity and better understand the forms that ecological violence takes within it.

Development Economics in Africa: A Catastrophic Convergence

Living in a Zone of Exile

In p'Bitek's poem, Lawino is a "village" girl. That is why Ocol, her educated husband, no longer finds her attractive. He has fallen in love with Clementina, a city girl. If the colonial project in Africa had as one of its chief objectives the transformation of "primitive" African societies into "developed" nation-states after the model of Europe, the "village" represented all that was primitive and backward (customs, animism, superstition, etc.) in Africa—all that had to be left behind if Africa was to be ushered into the sunny future of civilized modernity, which the "city" represents. What is noteworthy is that Ocol's disdain for Lawino the village girl and the ways of "your people" (Ocol no longer regards them as "my people," even though they once were) and his view of the "inevitability" of the "city" are things that Ocol has "learnt." It is a vision he has "acquired" through his education and his "forest of books." For as Basil Davidson notes, with a play on Dante's *Inferno*: "Above the entrance to every school there was an invisible but always insistent directive to those who passed within the magic gate to the 'white man's world': *Abandon Africa, all ye who enter here.*"[33]

By reinforcing the vision of the village as a place of "backwardness," a place of no hope, and the city as a place of forwardness, of all hope, the institutions of education, politics, and economics in Africa succeed in creating the very poverty and "hopelessness" they have presumed exist in the village. In this way, the poverty and backwardness of African villages become a self-fulfilling prophecy. The rural-urban exodus is both contributing factor to and reflection of the increasing impoverishment of villages in Africa. As mentioned at the beginning of this chapter, World Economic Forum projections indicate that by 2050 more than 1.5 billion people—80 percent of the African population—will live in cities. But the fact that the vast majority of these urban dwellers, over 65 percent, will live in so-called informal settlements or slums confirms that the road from the poverty and backwardness of the village does not necessarily lead to the towering dreams of city life and in fact is most likely to lead to the slum, a unique "zone of exile" characterized, as Davis notes, by a life of "marginality within marginality."[34]

In the summer of 2018, I carried out a random series of interviews in the slums of Nateete, Kalerwe, and Kamwokya on the outskirts of Kampala city to get a sense of how the young people living in these slums thought about their former life in the village. I interviewed a cross section of the slum dwellers, which included traders, *boda boda* riders, housemaids, market vendors, hawkers, and others doing all sorts of odd jobs ("whatever kind of job I can get," as one interviewee told me). They ranged in educational background from primary and secondary school dropouts, to high school graduates, to some university degree holders. The majority said the main reason they had come to the city was "to look for a job" or to "try to get money." Many described life in the village as "very hard" with no opportunities, "nothing there to do except to dig," and said the village was a place where money was hard to come by. Not a few described their moving from the village to the city as a kind of "escape" (*Nawona ekyalo!*).

Robert, a twenty-three-year-old Senior 4 (high school) graduate from Kisolo, has been in Nateete for over a year, where he rides a *boda boda*. He talked about the village as a "challenging place" where there are "high illiteracy rates and no room for one to properly utilize his or her talent." In the village, he notes, "There is no way you can put your talent to better use," while "In the city your thinking capacity goes high, unlike the village." He adds, "There is a lot of jealousy in the village, and at times when villagers see someone who may have bought a new car, they will plan to kill him, yet in the city everyone minds his own business and people here are not jealous." Asked if he would ever consider returning to live in the village, he responds with a definite "No." "I escaped the village [*Nawona ekyalo*]," he answers. ". . . I want to develop myself in the city and not to backslide again to village life."[35]

Others, like Apollo, a thirty-year-old university graduate, used the image of "running away" from village life (in Kamuli). Life in the village is very hard, he says. "There is no electricity and it is very hard to access other social services like hospitals, schools, shops, and others." True, he noted, "There is a lot to eat in the village. We had so many mangoes, jackfruits, oranges, and every kind of fruit. . . . In the village they are free." But, he complained, "There is very limited exposure to important things. Here in the town, you get to meet so many people and ideas that can bring positive change in your life." Apollo did not have a "steady job" (he was working as a part-time volunteer at the L'Arche community and as a gas pump attendant over the weekend) and was clearly aware (and articulate) about the problems of living in the city, saying, "There is congestion and pollution in the city; the food is not fresh and very expensive; at times I do not have money for rent, and other things." Even so, there was no way he would consider ever going back to live in the village. Not only is he now used to life in the city, he'd run away from the village because "there was nothing there for me to do."[36]

What is ironic is that even though a number of respondents openly spoke of urban life as a place of opportunities (jobs, money, ideas), many admitted that those opportunities were not easy to come by. Thus most spoke of their life in the city as one of "hustling and gambling" to "try to get something to eat." Still, returning to the village did not seem much of an option. This was especially true among the younger slum dwellers, with older ones (generally above thirty) expressing more ambivalence about village life and a sense of their just being "stuck" in the city.

Shifah, a thirty-year-old Senior 3 graduate, had come to the city when she was in Senior 2 (sophomore in high school) to attend a better secondary school. "My parents made the decision because education standards in the village were bad. Teachers in the village do not care as much as those in the towns. But you cannot blame them because they also have challenges, as they have got a life to live. You find a teacher wakes up and goes to the garden before coming to school, then by the time they reach school they are tired because most of them walk long distances to reach school." In Senior 3, Shifah got pregnant and dropped out of school. She is now a single mother with three children. She has sent her two elder children (nine and five) to the village, where her parents take care of them. The youngest child (three) lives with her, and Shifah brings her to her market stall. She misses the fresh food available in the village. "We could go and pick fresh jackfruit from a nearby tree and start eating while fresh. . . . Mangoes, pineapples, maize, all fruits in the village are fresh. But look at these things we sell here . . . most of them are not fresh and they are tasteless."[37]

She does not like living in the city because of its noise, pollution, and lack of sanitation: "When it rains people open up their latrines so that running water can clear the waste. This creates a lot of diseases that sometimes kill people." Her remarks remind me of the irony of the point Davis made, mentioned earlier, namely that while many rural poor move to the cities in order to "escape" poverty, the majority end up "squat[ting] in squalor, surrounded by pollution, excrement, and decay."[38] Even with these living conditions, Shifah feels she cannot go back to live in the village because she has to earn money to support her parents back home (in the village) as well as her children. She therefore feels a sense of being "trapped": "*Ekibuga kinsibidde wano*" (The city has "locked" me here), she admits.

Joseph, a forty-two-year-old trader who has been living in Nateete for over ten years, expressed a similar sentiment of being "stuck" in the city. He left his home village of Naggalama for the city in order to get money to support his wife and children, who still live in the village. Joseph visits them every month. Like Shifah, Joseph does not like living in Kampala—he does not like the thieves and thugs in Nateete. He likes the simplicity and honesty of village living. "But what can I do, I have to support my family. . . . I just stay in my own lifestyle. I am just looking for money in the city."[39]

Also telling is that even those city dwellers like Robert and Apollo who are glad that they "escaped" the hardship and poverty of the village and cannot imagine themselves ever returning to live there maintain a deep connection to village life. They talk (thanks to Warid and other cellphone networks) to their relatives in the village frequently, they send them money, they return to the village to celebrate feast days like Christmas and Idi el Fitri with their families, and they even dream of building a house or setting up business there. Robert's dream is "to work hard and make money . . . [so] I build a house on my *kibanja* [plot of land], and when I go to the village I can stay in it."[40] Sam, another *boda* rider, has a similar dream. "The only plan I have of going back to the village is to go and build my own country home so that when I go there, me and my family can sleep in it and after our trip we come back to the city. That is the life I want, including starting other projects like cattle raising. I hire someone who will always be there taking care of my belongings, but I don't want to go back to stay there."[41]

Still others see the village as a place to fall back on in case everything else (in the city) fails. When Zaina, thirty-two, first came to Kalerwe after her father died and her stepmother made "life hell" for her in the village, she started off as a housemaid. She soon moved in with a boyfriend and had two children with him before he left her and them. Together with three other women, Zaina now owns a stall that sells secondhand clothes. Through her meager savings, she bought a small plot in the village. She complains about the KCCA (Kampala Capital City Authority) tariffs. "This lady Jennifer Musisi [KCCA executive director] has tortured us for so long, and they arrest us, demand money from us for all sorts of taxes, and threaten to take us to prison." The little money that Zaina makes is eaten up in rent and KCCA taxes. She's weighing her options: "If I don't succeed here in the city, I will go back and dig on my land."[42]

Finally, every single one of the people interviewed expressed hope that when they die, they will be "returned home" and buried in the village on their ancestral land. As thirty-year-old Elizabeth, a vegetable vendor originally from Kasese, explained, this is "because here in the city we are just visitors."[43] Behind Elizabeth's statement is the belief that her "real home," the place of her true dwelling, is the village. The village is these migrants' *butaka*, for that is where their umbilical cord is buried, and thus where they belong as sons and daughters of the "soil."[44] Lawino is right. The roots of identity and belonging in Africa "reach deep into the soil." To the extent that modernity, development, and progress in

Africa require Africans being uprooted from the "soil," many will continue to experience a life apart from the village as alienating. In this case, the modern African finds herself both literally and metaphorically in a slum, in a "zone of exile," where she feels she has no choice but to "escape" from the soil (village), to which she nevertheless continues to have deep connection and attachment.

Land Conflicts and Land Reforms

In 2006, a report for the Danish Ministry of Foreign Affairs, conducted by the Danish Institute for International Studies, was already pointing to the growing cases of land conflicts in Africa. Land conflicts, the report noted, were not only intensifying, but becoming more widespread.[45] The situation has only become worse in recent years, with disputes over land drastically increasing in number and violence. These conflicts are influenced by a complex and interrelated web of causes.[46] In a recent op-ed piece in the *Daily Monitor*, the prime minister of Buganda Kingdom, Peter Mayiga, identified at least six factors that contribute to the rising tide of land conflicts in Uganda: (1) weaknesses in the police force that hinder timely investigation and evidence gathering; (2) the inefficiency and corruption of the court system in handling the cases; (3) population growth; (4) decreasing soil fertility so that families need bigger plots of land to grow food; (5) the inefficiency and confusion in all the country's land registries (the 1995 Constitution recognizes four types of land tenure systems: Mailo land, freehold land tenure, leasehold, and customary tenure); and finally (6) corruption and political interference.[47]

No need to engage here in an extended discussion of these and other contributors to the rise in land conflicts. Many excellent sources give detailed attention to the causes of these disputes.[48] My intention is to highlight the rather modern understanding of land as a "commodity" and as an "economic asset" that undergirds much of the discussion regarding land conflict. The op-ed by Prime Minister Mayiga confirms that land is increasingly a rare and precious commodity in Africa. Land, he points out, has become "the most important [economic] asset in most parts of the world that people can *own*" (emphasis mine).[49] This modern conception of land explains the emphasis on land "ownership" and land "rights" that dominates the discussion of land reforms in Africa and the focus on the legal and juridical adjustments necessary to make land tenure more amenable for economic development. Reflecting this emphasis on land as commodity, a number of African countries have recently embarked on changing their land policies as well as land legislation, greatly encouraged, and often heavily subsidized, by the international donor community and the Bretton Woods institutions the International Monetary Fund (IMF) and the World Bank. The case of Uganda's reform is particularly helpful in understanding what drives much of the debate on land reform in Africa.

There was no single land tenure system in precolonial Uganda. Systems of customary land tenure varied from one region to another. During the colonial era, the British, while keeping in place many of the customary land tenure systems, also introduced three types of land tenure that were previously unknown: (a) Mailo land, (b) freehold, and (c) leasehold.[50] British colonialists believed that communal land ownership impeded individual enterprise and economic development and introduced freehold and leasehold tenure to encourage individual land tenure. The 1975 Land Reform Decree enacted by Idi Amin decreed that all land in Uganda be vested in the state in trust for the people to facilitate its use for economic and social development. It declared all land in Uganda public land to be administered by the Uganda Land Commission. The 1995 Constitution nullified Amin's 1975 Land Act and recognized the four types of land tenure systems (Mailo, freehold, leasehold, and customary) that the British had left in place. The Constitution Commission did, however, recommend that customary ownership of land be gradually phased out, not radically, but by "encouragement," so as to cultivate greater "economic development and agricultural modernisation."[51] Thus the 1998 Land Act (set up to operationalize the 1995 Constitution) identified "reducing poverty" and "promoting the land market" as two key objectives behind its land reform, the others being promoting security of tenure to all citizens and reducing conflict. The logic behind individual ownership as a boost for economic development was that title certificates would enable holders to obtain credit from banks and would increase the economic value of their land through ease of transferability.

The 2016 Land Commission of Inquiry is part of the ongoing effort of land reform in Uganda.[52] The mandate of the commission is to "inquire into the effectiveness of Law, Policies and Processes of land Acquisition, Land Administration, Land Management and Land Registration in Uganda" and to propose reforms for improving their efficiency and effectiveness.[53] The mandate of the commission makes obvious an underlying assumption, namely that land conflicts arise primarily from "unregulated land economics and interests," resulting in competing claims of "ownership."[54] This assumption explains the commission's focus on the technical and legal aspects to streamline and make transparent the processes for land acquisition, titling, and administration.

But by assuming an essentially economic view of the land, the commission, just like the majority of modern land reforms, misses a crucial cultural and spiritual dimension of land. For as Professor Mwambutsya Ndebesa of Makerere University notes, land conflicts in Uganda arise not only out of multiple ownership but also out of multiple meanings.[55] According to Ndebesa, there is a difference between the definition of land and the meaning of land. Ndebesa's observation is similar to one made by Betty Okot, a Ugandan sociologist, lecturing on education for sustainability at London South Bank University: "Where I come from, land means more than real estate. It isn't just a slice of earth, which can be farmed, inherited, built on, sold or bought. In most of Uganda, land equates to history, heritage, identity, belonging, rights and relationships. It creates social security and helps define social, cultural, religious values and beliefs systems. However, when these collide with the idea of commoditising land, the people who live on and work the land suffer."[56]

If one takes both Ndebesa's and Okot's insights seriously, then land conflicts are not simply conflicts around competing claims of ownership. They reflect a growing sense of powerlessness and insecurity as people feel that not only their livelihood but also their sense of identity is threatened, and not simply by "unregulated land economics and interests" but by an economic vision that considers land merely as an economic entity.[57] It is telling that one of the triggers in the Apaa land conflict was the unofficial claim that huge tracts of land in Apaa had been assigned to an "investor" to plant sugarcane and build a modern sugar factory.[58] Thus what we witness in Apaa, and in many other cases of land conflict across

Africa, is a clash between the forces of the free market, let loose in the interest of development, and a people's cultural and spiritual connection to the land. Okot reminds us that this phenomenon has happened in other places and times:

> This is not just about land laws and land rights. What is happening now in Uganda is similar to what happened in England between the 14th and 18th centuries when enclosures, a massive land grab by the ruling class, drove small farmers off land they had tilled for centuries and turned them into low-waged labourers on what was once their land. Not only did they lose their heritage and culture constructed around land, but their landlessness meant they were disposed to supply the cheap labor needed at the nascent stages of the industrial revolution.[59]

The overall conclusion we must draw from the discussion here is that modern land reforms in Africa are not a solution to land conflicts; rather, they serve as triggers and sources of the conflicts. If the land conflicts are intractable, as often seems to be the case, it is partly due to that in-between location in which the majority of Africans now find themselves—operating within, and at times oscillating between, two registers of meaning. One register views land merely as an economic commodity (and thus as easily exchangeable for a sum of money); the other is a register of deep attachment to a piece of land, which ensures one's sense of identity and belonging.

An Economics of Eating the Land

A 2017 Global Nutrition Report caught me off guard: over 30 percent of households in Africa face food insecurity, and over sixty million children in Africa under the age of five face a series of nutrition-related challenges, including malnutrition.[60] This cannot be true, I thought. Africa is blessed with vast expanses of rich soil—more than six hundred million hectares of uncultivated arable land (more than 60 percent of the world's total)! If only half of that were to be utilized, Africa could not only attain food security but easily become a major food supplier to the rest of the world. Why has this not happened? We are instead faced with incredible statistics that show a worsening food situation in Africa. While the number of hungry people in the world declined from about a billion to approximately 795 million between 1990 and 2016, the number of "undernourished" or hungry people in Africa increased from about 182 million to around 233 million, according to the UN Food and Agriculture Organization (FAO).[61] What is going on?

Arguably, the factors contributing to the worsening food crisis in Africa are many and interconnected. But while observers typically blame higher population growth, natural calamities, and conflicts for hunger on the continent, economic and development policy is a significant factor. For instance, the international sovereign debt crises of the 1980s forced many African countries to sign on to the stabilization and structural adjustment programs (SAPs) of the Bretton Woods institutions. One casualty of SAPs was agricultural productivity, for "African countries were told that they need not invest in agriculture as imports would be cheaper. Tragically, while Africa deindustrialized thanks to the SAPs, food security also suffered."[62]

SAPs are simply a more recent iteration of the model of economics that has shaped modern Africa. This "top to bottom" model focuses on development, structural change, and growth as measured by GDP and other indicators. It not only is externally driven but serves the interests of a narrow base of economic and political elite, while neglecting the genuine interests of the majority of African men and women. This is what partly explains the irony of the finding in the 2016 World Bank Report that while the GDPs of many African countries have grown, the number of people living in extreme poverty has also grown substantially since 1990![63] The World Bank Report also finds that the majority of Africa's poor—particularly women, the youth, and rural populations—continue to feel excluded and to suffer from the consequences of successive programs of "development." The priority of "cash" crops over "food" crops is just one example of the marginalization of the everyday needs of Africans by policies focused on economic growth and development.

Even more catastrophic for Africa is the way in which modern development economics contributes to many of the continent's ecological woes by encouraging an exploitative and extractive relationship to nature in general and to land in particular. The roots of this outlook are traceable to the colonial view of Africa as a continent whose rich natural resources should be exploited. This is the vision that propelled the European scramble for Africa and shaped the colonial economics and policies of development on the continent. Whether it was through the mining industry, the development of cash crops, or the policies of what came to be known as "developmental deforestation," colonial economics was largely driven by the logic of extraction and exploitation of Africa's natural resources. The same attitude drives much of postcolonial economics as African governments in collaboration with multinational companies undertake oil and mineral exploration, unregulated logging, and the clearing of forests for cash crop development.

What is remarkable are the ways in which the vision of Africa as a resource for exploitation and its attendant extractive economics have come to be reproduced in the daily patterns of ordinary Africans. Consider the desperation of "artisan miners" in the Congo, women and children who search for riches in disease-ridden mud pits, mines, and mercury-tainted rivers. Or consider the indiscriminate cutting down of trees for charcoal, the digging out of marshes for clay and sand to make bricks, or the stripping of land of any natural vegetation.

Underlying these extractive and ecologically destructive practices by ordinary Africans is not only a desperate search for income but also an implicit assumption that the natural resources are there for the taking. We witness in these practices therefore a new scramble for Africa, where nature is considered primarily a resource waiting to be exploited and not so much as a living organism that has to be tended and cared for. If, as Maathai notes, in the past the tree was not only "a source of food, medicine, and building material but a place of healing, consolation, and connection with other human beings and with the divine," within the logic of modern development economics now "that tree is only as valuable as the amount of money that can be obtained for the products that can be made from it."[64] The irony is that an economics built on greed and extraction not only underwrites desperation and an exploitative relation to the earth but transforms a rich continent like Africa into one of poverty, hunger, and malnutrition. The more Africa's natural resources and environment come under the logic of "development," the more the continent, the earliest habitat of man, becomes increasingly uninhabitable.

What would it take to reinvent this odd modernity? What would a new economic vision—an "integral ecology," as Pope Francis describes it (*LS* 139), that fights poverty, protects nature, and restores human dignity—look like in Africa? Pope Francis points to the need for "spiritual conversion," and Lawino appeals to Ocol to "return home" to rediscover the wisdom of "our people" whose roots reach deep into the soil. Are there any experiments in this spirituality of deep connection and belonging to the land that could testify to the possibility of new modernity in Africa? Yes, the Songhai Center in Benin is such a model.

Godfrey Nzamujo and the Songhai Center at Porto Novo

"Africa stands up" is the slogan of the Songhai Center in the West African city of Porto Novo in the Republic of Benin. It was founded in 1985 by Fr. Godfrey Nzamujo to address the triple challenges of poverty, food insecurity, and unemployment in rural communities. The mission of Songhai Center is to train young entrepreneurs who will then replicate the Songhai model starting in their village communities. The graduates contribute to the sustainable development of their home communities "by creating jobs and thus preventing the rural exodus; by ensuring food self-sufficiency of the region and contributing to the well-being of the people." To date Songhai Center has trained over two thousand young people in sustainable and organic farming, value chain practices, and business creation skills, and 1,200 of these have gone on to create sustainable farms in their village communities.

The Songhai model is an integrated farming system that mimics the way nature works. According to the "dance of nature," everything is interconnected and nothing goes to waste. Thus crop production, livestock, and aquaculture form an integrated production system, where the waste from one area is used to feed other areas. This system of integrated farming produces a microeconomy, and thus a model that could easily be replicated throughout village communities in Africa.

What makes Songhai unique, and in what ways is it a reversal of the catastrophic convergence of development economics, poverty, and environment degradation in Africa? Four elements are the heart of Songhai's effort to reinvent Africa's problematic modernity: a clear diagnosis of the trap of poverty in Africa, the need for a new mindset, the dance of nature, and participation in the fragility (suffering) of nature.

A New Mindset

The story of Songhai Center goes back to the 1983–85 famine in Ethiopia that led to the death of over four hundred thousand people. Born in Kano, Nigeria, Fr. Godfrey Nzamujo, who had earned doctorate degrees in electronics, microbiology, and development science, was lecturing at the University of California, Irvine. As Professor Nzamujo watched images of emaciated African children on TV he felt a sense of shame and anger. The images were reinforcing the standard image of Africa as a "hopeless" continent of bloody wars, famine, and poverty, and of its people as helpless victims begging for a handout. Africa need not be like that, Nzamujo protested. For in his mind there was the memory of the great civilizations in Africa's history, like the West African empire of Songhai in the fifteenth century, which had attracted scientists, scholars, students, and merchants from far and near and had built cities like Timbuktu, a prestigious center of learning. In Songhai, agriculture and livestock grew, leading to a vibrant hide and skin industry. Historical Songhai reflected virtues of vision, courage, creativity, accomplishment, and, thus, pride in Africa. What went wrong, Nzamujo wondered, to bring Africans to the point where they seemed unable to feed themselves?

Africa's problem, Nzamujo surmised, is the "trap of poverty" in which the modern continent seems to be caught. That trap, which Nzamujo also calls the "logic of poverty," is the "incapacity to effectively harness the opportunities before us." While empires like Songhai confirm that this capacity was available in Africa's past, Africans have largely lost it, and as a result, "We have succumbed to the logic of poverty." Thus Africa suffers from the persistent problems of unemployment, poverty, famine, and environmental degradation, all manifestations of this faulty modern logic.[65]

Underlying the "trap of poverty," Nzamujo notes, is a mindset characterized, among other things, by three interrelated patterns. The first is extraversion: "We always look for outside solutions." No doubt this mindset is connected to a belief that many Africans have come to internalize: that "nothing good comes out of Africa." The second pattern is the colonization of the African mind whereby Africans "respond to Africa's problems using other people's experience, categories, and solutions." The third mind pattern is a slavish mimicry of Western habits of artificial consumption.[66] Nzamujo keeps returning to the image of Songhai to highlight the modernity of the "logic of poverty." In this connection, he, like Mazrui, claims that one of the unique "achievements" of modern European colonialism in the nineteenth and twentieth centuries was to convince Africans of their inferiority.[67] For Nzamujo the logic of poverty is a "mindset," but it is one perpetuated through forms of development economics, which have only succeeded in creating mass unemployment and establishing systems that work for less than 10 percent of the population. The effect has been the "erosion of dignity" and the destruction of "Africa's internal capacities to meet the challenges before her."[68]

What is needed is a new mindset that can shape a New African society. Nzamujo returns to the need for this new way of thinking in a number of his talks and describes it using various terms. He refers to it as "a new way of looking at ourselves, the world and others" and "another way of placing ourselves in the world."[69] He also describes it as a "vision" and a "methodology" to "help Africa not only raise its head, but live in dignity and pride." And he calls it a "paradigm shift" from extraversion to indigeneity, which is about "Africa learning to harness her internal capacities and local knowledge." For, as he argues, no society has ever developed without learning how to harness its internal capacities to meet the challenges before it. While talk of a "paradigm shift" and a "mindset" might sound too cerebral, for Nzamujo, it is a simple thing that begins with, and happens through, working with the land and changing the way we grow food. "God has given us everything we need right here," he notes. Not only will working the land stem the problem of rural-urban exodus, it "will recreate the villages as viable social economic units" and thus help create a new African society.

Reinventing African Economics from the Ground Up

Even though his ideas were not so clearly formulated in 1983 as Nzamujo watched the images of starving and emaciated African bodies from Ethiopia, they influenced his decision to resign from his faculty position at the University of California, Irvine, and return to Africa to set up Songhai Center. For a highly educated African priest (three PhDs) who was also a professor of engineering and microbiology at a prestigious American university to return to rural Africa to work with land defied both the cultural expectation (America as the destination) and the logic of the "ladder of economic development." It is perhaps not surprising that his home community in Nigeria thought his PhDs were fake and his project was just another scheme to bilk unsuspecting Nigerians. A group of Dominican sisters in neighboring, and much poorer, Benin did, however, embrace him and his vision and introduced him to officials in the Benin government, who assigned him a polluted piece of land, the site of a failed government development project, in Porto Novo, where he began to set up his Songhai Center. In Okot's *Song of Lawino*, Lawino appeals to her educated husband, Ocol, to "return home" and to embrace the village patterns of life whose "roots go deep into the soil." This is what Nzamujo literally did.

Working with five youths he picked up from the street and with Salim, a young Muslim who was on the wrong side of the law and whom the Dominican sisters had taken in for rehabilitation, Nzamujo started to work the polluted land, pulling up weeds, planting nitrogen-fixing plants on it, and gradually setting up other crops, livestock production units, and fish ponds. The early years were full of challenges, Nzamujo recalls. The container of tools he had shipped from California never made it to Benin, he had not been accepted in his home country of Nigeria, and (he jokes) the land the Benin government had given him was so polluted that "even weeds had trouble growing on it." But a deep sense of mission kept him going: "I really felt called to be here." Nzamujo also talks about the many gifts of those early years: the sisters, the five street kids, Salim, and others "who believed in me and worked alongside me." Beyond these there was also "the grace of God's providence." Whenever he felt ready to give up, he remembers, "God always brought unexpected gifts, exactly when I needed them, whether in terms of fresh ideas, new people or financial resources."

From one hectare of land, the Songhai Center in Porto Novo now covers a sprawling twenty-two hectares and serves as headquarters to three other Songhai Centers that have been created in Benin. When I visited the Porto Novo center in the summer of 2016, an army of about three hundred young people were working and training in various sectors: an integrated farm, on which crops, livestock, and fish were raised; a technology park, where simple farm machinery was produced; an industrial park, where water processing, palm oil extraction, and the production and packaging of fruit juice, snacks, and soap were under way; and different service units, such as restaurants, lodging, an Internet café, and a market.

As Nzamujo led the tour of the impressive center and its equally impressive and efficient sectors and production units, he kept repeating "the simple logic" that underlies the Songhai model, which is that everything is connected. Therefore, at the heart of the Songhai model is an integrated system of crops, livestock, and aquaculture, where waste from one unit becomes food for another unit (figure 5.1). This is the "primary production," which is supported by the secondary production of technology, processing, and manufacturing and the tertiary level of services, such as the market, restaurants, and lodging (see figure 5.2).

Figure 5.1. Songhai's integrated production system.

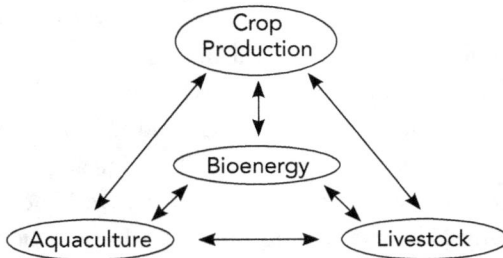

Figure 5.2. Songhai levels of production.

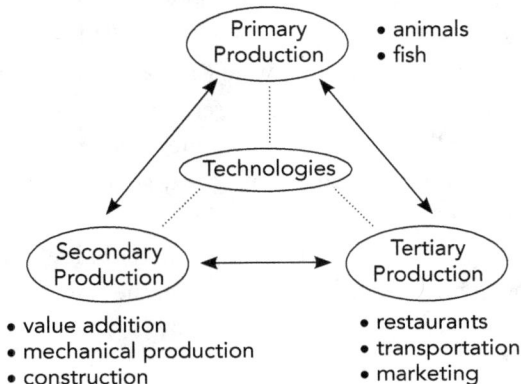

In the end what one is able to see at Songhai is a vibrant "micro-economy" generated by the primary production of an integrated farming system. Nzamujo's hope is that this microeconomy can be replicated throughout Africa and thus can turn villages, which as we have seen within Africa's unique modernity are coded "hopeless," into viable economic and social units. In 2008, the UN recognized Songhai Center as a Regional Centre of Excellence, and with the support of the United Nations Development Program (UNDP), Songhai Centers have been set up in fifteen African countries. All of this confirms the potential that Songhai has to reinvent Africa's economy literally from the ground up. In this model, rather than being the antithesis of economic development, the village becomes the heartbeat of a new African society.

A Dominican "Spirituality": The Dance of Nature

A spirituality underlies Nzamujo's work at Songhai Center. It is at the same time an invitation—to imitate nature, or to "enter into the dance of nature." "Do not fight nature,"[70] Nzamujo advises. Dance with nature and let nature do the work for you. For Nzamujo, the spirituality has two interrelated dimensions, a theological and a scientific one, reflecting his identity as a Dominican priest and as a scientist. First, let's consider the theological dimension. Nzamujo understands his work with Songhai Center as an extension of his calling as a Dominican priest. As a young man, Nzamujo had joined seminaries in his native Nigeria and later in Chicago to study to become a diocesan priest. He was, however, disillusioned by the Cartesian-Thomistic synthesis of his philosophical and theological education. "I rebelled," he says. The clear-cut opposition between inner and outer, sacred and mundane, spiritual and material, here and there, put him off. "That is not me," he said. "I was much more at home with the native African and Asian (Taoism) spiritualities where all things belong together." These stress a sense of harmony and a mystical, rather than an intellectual, approach to life. These native spiritualities are less about dissecting and analyzing reality as an object out there than about entering the mystery of being. Thomas Aquinas, Nzamujo explained, was himself to come to this insight (later in life) through a mystical experience, which led him to look back at the systematic elucidation of his earlier work and see it as rubbish.[71] "The unfortunate thing is that Thomists have largely missed this Thomistic mystical revelation. They spend their lives writing tomes on Aquinas's system, which Aquinas himself in a moment of mystical clarity had repudiated as straw."

It was the appreciation for the "mystical" connection with reality that drew Nzamujo to the Dominicans, especially to the French Dominicans—Yves Congar, Marie-Dominique Chenue, and Louis-Joseph Lebret, who had all played a key role at the Second Vatican Council and whose writings he started to read. Not only did Nzamujo find their works edifying, he found their ecumenicism, openness to reality in all its dimensions, pastoral praxis, and overall attempt to bring Christian faith into dialogue with different aspects of modernity quite striking.[72] For Nzamujo, they radiated the Dominican vision of reality as mystery to be embraced. The founder of the Dominicans, also known as the Order of Preachers, Fr. Dominic, had encouraged his friars to be both contemplative in study and mystical in their spirituality as a way to enter the mystery of reality and grasp its fullness. The charism of the Dominicans is to break down this grasped fullness of reality and communicate it to others through simple digestible sermons. Thus their name Ordo Praedicatorum, or order of preachers.

This is what Nzamujo is doing at Songhai, he tells me: "My work here is a form of contemplation, and a prayer. Prayer is not bubbling of words, but prayer is contemplation, and as the Dominicans say, contemplation is entering into the mystery of reality." Nzamujo also refers to Songhai as a "sermon" because "all we are trying to do is to 'contemplate' the dance of nature" and to "imitate the way nature works." A well-prepared and delivered sermon, Dominic had told his friars, has the power not only to "explain" the mystery but to "invite" and encourage the hearer to enter into its full reality. Like that good sermon, the training at Songhai does more than explain to the students the interconnectedness of nature: it immerses them in its full practical, ecological, and economic implications.

Second, Nzamujo sees great affinity between his being a Dominican and his scientific background, in particular, his appreciation of quantum physics. The latter, he notes, "allows you to enter into the mystery of being and see the interconnected nature of reality. The work of the scientist is to get inside this mystery of reality, grasp it, and exploit its connectivity to advance human flourishing." In the same way that Nzamujo rebelled against the Thomistic-Cartesian synthesis of his seminary formation, he rebelled against the dominant technocratic paradigm of Newtonian science, but he "fell in love with quantum physics." According to Newtonian science, atoms constitute the ultimate indivisible unit of matter. Where quantum physics goes beyond this classic view is to analyze the elementary particles that make up the atom in terms of energy waves (quantum = wave). Whereas classical physics conceives atoms as isolated particles of matter, the particles of quantum physics never exist in isolation but are always related to one another. The energy field is the result of this ongoing web of relationships. Thus what is new about Einstein's relative quantum theory is its claim that every phenomenon is a quantum reality, within which energy and mass are convertible. Energy can become matter and matter can become energy. The overall implications are that whereas classical mechanics is so much about an external force acting on matter—using the laws of motion and gravitation formulated by Newton—quantum mechanics is essentially about the ability to convert energy into matter and matter into energy within a given quantum reality. This is what Nzamujo found exciting about quantum physics and what helped bridge his spiritual and theological passion (as a Dominican priest), on the one hand, and his love for science and his work in the lab, on the other. Accordingly, Nzamujo does not see any dichotomy between nature and science, between creation care and scientific production, between agriculture and technological innovation. Rather, the organic farm, the technological park, and the service industry are interconnected and support each other in an ongoing dance of innovative experimentation. The scientific innovativeness at Songhai, far from being an attempt to "subdue" or "tame" nature, is just another dimension of the invitation to "enter into the dance of nature" and an example of harnessing the interconnectedness within nature to advance the flourishing of both the human community and nature herself.

The Passion of Songhai

Entering the dance of nature reveals another crucial dimension of the mystery of reality—yet human beings are an integral part of the universe and not a "master" who stands apart from the cosmic "we." Within that cosmic reality, everything belongs in an interconnected web of relationships. This means that light and darkness, as well as life and death, belong together. This, Nzamujo tells me, is the "mystery" that Paul talks about when he declares, "We always carry around in our body the death of Jesus, so that the life of Jesus may also be revealed in our body" (2 Cor. 4:10). Nzamujo adds that it was a mystical experience that led Paul to this realization—the Damascus event, in which Paul was thrown off his horse (Nzamujo describes the horse as Paul's "Cartesian righteousness") and was blinded. The irony is, it was only by being blinded that he was able to "see" in a new way. This is the "mysterion" that Paul writes about, which had been hidden but now came to be "revealed" in Christ, pointing to a new creation, a new way of seeing the world and locating oneself within it. For Paul, the "mysterion" encompasses "all things" and is thus the principle of reality, or the cosmic principle. In essence, the whole of creation is "groaning" as if in one great act of childbirth, waiting/longing for the full realization of the new creation (Rom. 8:8). Before Paul, Jesus had tried to communicate this insight to his disciples, who found it hard to accept that "the son of man had to suffer" (Matt. 16: 22). Jesus had already grasped it. He had already entered the mystery and had come to realize that there is no life without death: "unless the grain of wheat fall on the ground and die" (John 12:24).

Nzamujo became quite excited about explicating this theological dimension of reality as a mystery and relating it to science. Quantum physics, he notes, "reveals the same insight, namely that particles die many times and they are generated into new life forms." If Einstein was able to come to that insight, Nzamujo notes, it was because his quantum theory of relativity, unlike the Descartes-Bacon-Newtonian mechanistic science of "control and domination," was grounded in mysticism. The latter, Nzamujo observes, is what allows us to embrace the mystery of life and death in nature and in our own lives. In creation, he explains, birth and death, decay and renewal, belong together; light leads to darkness and darkness leads to light. We ourselves are part of this cycle of death and resurrection. The more we become connected with the earth, the more we discover that death leads to life, and, just like the rest of creation, we discover that we are dying every day and being resurrected.

In 2011, Nzamujo experienced this mystery of death and resurrection in an intimate way when he was diagnosed with cancer. I asked him about this experience, which he had described as a "critical turning point" that allowed him to become "even more creative, more inclusive, and to be fully engaged in the future of Songhai."[73]

"The sin of the world," he told me, "is to run away from pain and death. . . . We are afraid to change; that is what brings pain and suffering." However, if we let go and accept suffering and embrace our death, then we are released. We become fully alive, as we become reconnected to the earth's "fragile fertility": "The acceptance of my fragility has on the contrary re-energized me and reconnected me in an incredible way to myself, to the GOD in me, and to others. The power of the resurrection can only be accessed from our freedom to die. The experience of our fragility or our limitedness becomes a pathway to a fuller life. The near-death experience well lived opens a new way of living, a gift from God. One can perhaps speak of a fertile fragility."[74]

A Confluence

Attending to four crucial elements at the heart of Nzamujo's effort to reinvent Africa's problematic modernity helps us bring this chapter to conclusion.

First, at the heart of Nzamujo's Songhai Center is a spirituality. Pope Francis noted that there can be no "integral ecology" in Africa as elsewhere without a necessary "spiritual conversion"—without, in other words, a spirituality that "cultivates ecological citizenship" (*LS* 211). This conversion cultivates (an agricultural metaphor!) a sense of "belonging" to the earth and humanity's unique place in this cosmic we. It is this spirituality that makes Songhai a unique and promising experiment of integral ecology, one that is able to respond to both the cry of the earth and the cry of the poor in Africa. What is obvious is that even though Nzamujo comes to this spirituality by way of a theological (Dominican) and scientific (quantum) journey, the spirituality has much in common with the African (native) spiritualities that encourage a mystical approach to nature, a view of nature as at once sacred and mundane, respect and listening to nature, and an appreciation of work as the collaboration between humans and nature.

Second, Songhai is about a mindset. In calling for ecological conversion, Pope Francis rightly noted that the challenges of ecological degradation, pollution, the depletion of natural resources, and poverty cannot be solved by mere technical adjustment. They require "a distinctive way of looking at things, a way of thinking" (*LS* 111). Nzamujo rightly attributes the problems of poverty, food insecurity, and ecological degradation in Africa to a mindset—the logic of poverty. Similarly, for a new future to take shape in Africa a new mindset is required, "a new way of looking at ourselves, the world, and others" and "another way of placing ourselves in the world." If at the heart of Africa's unique modernity is a lie that encourages Africans to believe that "nothing good comes out of Africa"—thus underwriting patterns of extraversion, colonialism, and a lifestyle of slavish mimicry—Nzamujo invokes the historical accomplishments of the Songhai Empire to disprove the lie. Moreover, he seeks to recreate the same revolutionary thinking, discipline, and innovativeness of this historical memory at Porto Novo in Benin, thereby reinventing a sense of pride in what it means to be African. The broader lesson from his attempt is that there can be no true ecological renewal in Africa or elsewhere without a corresponding restoration of human dignity to the poor. A true ecological conversion, as Pope Francis notes, requires an anthropological reassessment.

Third, Songhai is a "return" to the soil. In Okot's *Song of Lawino*, Lawino appeals to her educated husband not to uproot the pumpkin but to "return home" and rediscover the ways of our people whose roots "go deep into the soil." As noted, this is what Nzamujo has done both literally and metaphorically. But Nzamujo's return is not merely a return to a pristine, subsistence mode of living on and off the land. Rather, it is a return to a sense of belonging and citizenship with the earth and an invitation to enter "the dance of nature" and discover from within it the web of relationships and possibilities that advance the flourishing of both the earth and the human community.

Fourth, Songhai is a new synthesis. What Nzamujo's story illumines is that the return is a new synthesis, which overcomes the standard binary of "either-or," tradition or modernity, backwardness or progress, village or city, spirituality or technology, nature or science, past or future. What we see at Songhai is the invention of a new modernity, one that is not built on the sacrifice (rejection) of Africa but grounded deep in the African soil. This soil is in itself a mystery, within which one discovers that "everything is connected." The integration of science and technology with the skills of crop, animal, and fish farming is at once a reflection and an enhancement of this interconnectedness of reality.

Throughout this chapter we have located Africa's ecological crisis within what we have been describing as Africa's unique modernity—a catastrophic convergence of development economics, poverty, and ecological degradation. Pope Francis reminded us that the cry of the earth and the cry of the poor belong together. We are not faced with two separate crises, one environmental and the other social. And a true ecological approach is always a social approach. Nzamujo's Songhai Center not only confirms this insight, it helps to highlight why and how an ecological approach is always also an economic approach. Peace scholars insist on the need for an intersectional approach (an approach that recognizes the confluence of multiple factors, such as historical, social, political, gender) in understanding and addressing issues of violence. This is particularly true in relation to ecological violence. What makes Nzamujo's Songhai Center a unique experiment is not only its implicit theoretical critique of Africa's modernity in its multiple dimensions but the center's appeal as a demonstration of an alternative confluence of spirituality, science, economics, and creation care. In this case Songhai Center offers both the argument and evidence of a "return" to the land, which becomes the basis of an integral ecology that is able to fight poverty, protect creation, and restore human dignity to the poor in Africa.

The Logic of the Cross

The logic of the Gospel is a logic not of power, but of the cross. . . .
The only response to the excess of evil is the excess of love.
—Archbishop Emmanuel Kataliko, pastoral letter, 2000

In *Who Are My People?* I have grappled with two questions that were
asked in the wake of the 1994 Rwanda Genocide: "Why do you Africans
always kill your own people?" and "Is the blood of tribalism deeper than
the waters of baptism?" Sorting through the complex relationship between identity, violence, and Christianity in Africa behind the two questions has led me through a vast terrain of scholarly inquiry. I have
engaged not only scholars on issues of identity and violence but also
grassroots communities and activists in various countries in Africa.
While there is no all-encompassing way to summarize the rich and numerous conclusions this study has raised, I will touch on the most
important.

Throughout the book, I have tracked the widespread and recurrent
patterns of violence in Africa. In chapter 5, I described, following Rob
Nixon, Africa's ecological crisis as a form of "slow violence." While this
is obviously true in relation to ecology in Africa, it is also true in relation
to other spheres of life in Africa, where violence remains largely imperceptible, undetected, and untreated. What this study has highlighted is
that once slow violence becomes systemic, it moves through the social
body and like a cancer eats the body from within until it erupts into the

kind of direct, explicit violence we witnessed in the 1994 Rwanda Genocide and in the 2013 religious war in CAR. While the study has been obviously interested in accounting for ("making thinkable") the explicit manifestations of "ethnic," "religious," and "ecological" violence, it has increasingly pointed to the imaginary within which these incidents of explicit violence grow and fester and out of which they eventually erupt. More specifically, I have been interested in the processes through which an imagination of violence has come to shape and drive Africa's modern institutions. That process has largely to do with a story through which Africa is at once rejected ("nothing good out of Africa") and projected as the beneficiary of the European project of civilization, pacification, and development. Not only has this story given rise to a crisis, which we have been describing, following Wole Soyinka, as the "crisis of Africa's emergence into modernity," it in turn helps to shape a unique modernity in which Africa tumbles along as a perpetually disabled, deficient, and violent continent. Herein lies the root of Africa's slow violence.

I have also throughout this study been interested in the political nature of violence. While I have paid specific attention to ethnic, religious, and ecological violence respectively, I have made it clear that I consider these, not as three distinct, separable forms of violence, but as faces of the same complex reality of violence within Africa's unique modernity. Initially, I had thought of adding a chapter on political violence, and thus of organizing the book around four manifestations of violence. It soon became clear, however, that I did not need a separate treatment of political violence for two reasons. First, it became clear that all the faces of violence I was looking at are political at least in the sense that they are all connected to and radiated through the political and economic institutions of modern Africa. In my previous work *The Sacrifice of Africa*, I referred to the African nation-state as the "successor institution" to colonial regimes that stands within the same story and thus perpetuates the colonial imagination, reproducing the crisis of Africa's rejection even as it purportedly, not unlike its colonial predecessor, claims to "save," "pacify," and "develop" Africa. Second, including a separate treatment of political violence would be confusing since I was working with a more comprehensive notion of politics, not merely as the exercise of state power and the balancing of special interests, but as an "ordering of bodies in space and time."[1] Within this broad understanding, ethnic, religious, and ecological forms of violence reflect a particular account and thus ordering of African bodies, which grows out of and reflects Africa's political modernity. This is also why, within this broad understanding, Christian faith does not simply have political implications; rather, Christian faith is politics. Christian faith is an account of, and thus is, an ordering of bodies.

Who Are My People? is a book of stories and a book about stories. It is a book about my story, the story of modern Africa, the story of Christianity in Africa, and the stories of African men and women caught at the intersection of the modern and Christian stories of Africa. The book's stories are not anecdotal. There are methodological, metaphysical, moral, and epistemological claims connected to these stories.[2] In terms of methodology, I have not only used a narrative style of writing (weaving my own and other stories as part of the argument), I have employed "theological portraiture" (a unique blend of analysis and ethnography) as a method of investigation. Behind this use of a narrative methodology is a metaphysical claim that reality is constituted by and through stories. This is what makes "story" inescapable, for stories not only shape identity but structure reality, including the way bodies are ordered in space and time (politics). Connected with this metaphysical claim is an essential moral dimension: stories do kill, but stories can also heal and save. While a key goal of *Who Are My People?* has been to illumine the power of stories and their effects, I have not tried to pursue a "neutral" investigation. Instead, impelled by an epistemological conviction that the truth of a story is judged by the reality it creates and the lives it shapes, I have been interested in showing the possibility, indeed the reality, of an alternative—a nonviolent—"Africa," one shaped by the story of God's self-sacrificing love.

Who Are My People? is also a book about suffering. The 1994 genocide and Kurian's question "Why do you Africans kill your own people?" reveal the depth of violence and suffering on the African continent. In less than a hundred days almost a million Rwandans were killed by fellow Rwandans, neighbors killing neighbors, Christians killing Christians. We have depicted Rwanda, following Mamdani, as a "metaphor" for postcolonial Africa. To do so is to grasp the devaluation and wanton sacrificing of African lives, which we have traced through the ethnic, religious, and ecological violence of Africa's modernity. However, what has become clear through the different portraits of Christian activists studied here—Barankitse, Mvukiyehe, Fr. Anthony, Kinvi, Nzamujo, and others—is that healing from the wounds of Africa's violence, and overall healing from "the burden of Africa's history," involves another form of suffering—another form of violence, "the violence of love," which the activists discover in the story of God's self-sacrificing love. For these men and women, embracing the story of God's love not only heals their own woundedness but allows them to embrace the reality of suffering, which, as Jean Baptiste described, "is at the heart of human identity." Ironically, embracing this "mystery" of suffering is what liberates them and allows them to invent new communities and practices through which they seek to heal, restore, and renew God's love for other victims of violence. Herein lie both the irony and radical transformation of Africa's suffering: from the sacrificing of Africa to the true Sacrifice (*sacra facere*: making sacred) of Africa, from the sacrificing of others to self-sacrificing service, from a love of violence to "the violence of love." To capture this transformation, which is the very essence of hope, requires a theological language—"the cross," which is able to account for its odd logic and display its concrete possibilities in a world marked by violence.

Tracing the logic of God's self-sacrificing love in the life and agency of the portraits we studied is what landed us in the deep waters of spirituality. When one thinks of Africa's challenges, the challenge of violence in particular, one is tempted to immediately think about policy, ethical, and structural adjustment recommendations required to address these challenges. *Who Are My People?* has not been primarily about these, which may be frustrating to those schooled in this type of prescriptive social ethics. Others might even accuse me of evading the task of "Christian social responsibility" by not offering recommendations to help make Africa more peaceful and more democratic. Here I have instead engaged a more basic—but by far more critical—issue: the foundations of Africa's modernity. I have sought to understand these foundations that make violence an ever-recurrent pattern of social life in Africa and have sought to reimagine, and thus "reinvent," Africa. That task has pointed to the role of stories, and accordingly to the mythical and spiritual foundations of a society. Remarkably, all the Christian activists portrayed in *Who Are My People?*, in speaking about their agency, describe it less in terms of a

"program" than as a "simple" message or a "spirituality." For them, however, spirituality is not a free-floating, private, or inner reality discon-
nected from the material processes of everyday life. In fact, the "simple"
message opens up a rich variety of alternatives and a range of practical
and social possibilities. This is what their spirituality is about, which is
also the true sense of Christian spirituality as politics. The late archbishop of Bukavu Emmanuel Kataliko invoked this politics of spirituality, and its apparently contradictory logic of "simplicity" and "excess,"
when in 2000, at the height of war in the Congo, he wrote a pastoral
letter from Butembo, where he had been exiled by the military generals
controlling Eastern Congo, to his Christians in Bukavu. In the pastoral
letter, he reminds them that "the logic of the Gospel is a logic not of
power, but of the cross." In *Who Are My People?* I have traced the logic
of this simple message—spirituality—of God's self-sacrificing love in the
midst of Africa's ethnic, religious, and ecological violence and have displayed the rich forms of praxis it generates. In the end, this simple message is the response to the questions of why Africans kill each other, and
of whether the blood of tribalism is deeper than the waters of baptism.
For, as the former archbishop of Bukavu wrote in his 1999 Christmas
message, "The only response to the excess of evil is the excess of love."[3]

Finally, *Who Are My People?* has been an extended reflection on the
nature of identity in general, African identity in particular, and more specifically African Christian identity—what it means to be an African and
a Christian. I have engaged this issue not merely speculatively: rather,
I have reflected on my own identity as an African and as a Christian.
Having come to the conclusion that identity is not a *thing* we possess,
or an attribute grounded in some enduring metaphysical essence or
biological, cultural, or spiritual oneness, but a journey shaped by a story
and a shared sense of belonging, I felt compelled to offer my own story
as a lens to illuminate the gifts and challenges, the limits and possibilities
of the journey of Christian identity. What continues to amaze me is how
the journey has taken someone like me—from the remote village of
Malube (in Uganda)—to the heart of American intellectual life (Duke,
and now Notre Dame). This is a journey that neither my parents nor
I could have predicted or anticipated—yet another confirmation that
identity (who we are or who we become) always remains beyond one's

control, and thus is to be received as a gift. And now that I find myself as an academic, I try to live into what it means to be a professor and a scholar at an American university and to participate in dynamics of local life here in South Bend, which as Taiye Selasi reminds us, involves participating in daily rhythms of rituals, relationships, and restrictions.[4] Among other things, this means not only cultivating, discovering, and nurturing rich friendships but also learning to deal with people I disagree with or whose political and religious views I do not necessarily ascribe to. These are my people. Not all of them are Americans, or Catholics, or Christians.

But just because the journey has taken me from Malube to Notre Dame does not mean that I cease to be someone who grew up in Malube, or the son of my parents, who themselves grew up in Rwanda. These things continue to be part of me and to influence how I live into my identity as an American professor, how I do my scholarship and the kinds of issues I attend to in my scholarship. For this reason, it is perhaps not surprising that most of my scholarship has been focused around the reality of violence on the African continent—as an attempt to deal with, on an intellectual level, the philosophical, theological, and missiological issues raised by the Rwanda Genocide.[5] Being a professor at an elite American university (the likes of Duke and Notre Dame) provides distinct resources and a unique platform from which to do this, not least the time and opportunity to do research, engage with other scholars, and explore theoretical frameworks. I take this work seriously. For as Appiah noted, this theoretical work can contribute, even though slowly and marginally, to the "disruption" of the entrenched notions (e.g., of "race" and "tribe") and standard accounts and regimes of knowledge, so as to allow for a re-imagining of the world ("Africa") in fresh ways. But important and (even impressive) and necessary as this *theoretical* work might be, it is not sufficient to deal with the wounds of the world—with the realities of violence, poverty, and other vulnerabilities that affect "my people"—the people of Malube, where I grew up; Uganda, the country of my birth; or Africa, the continent of my origin. For again, as Appiah reminded us, "Every time I read another report in the newspapers of African disaster—a famine in Ethiopia, a war in Namibia, ethnic conflict in Burundi—I wonder how much good it does to correct the theories with which these evils are bound up; the solution is food, or mediation, or some other more material, more practical step."[6]

Being keenly aware of this, I have been fortunate to find myself, over the years, engaging these material realities of Africa—food, water, education, mediation—even more than I had anticipated. And I do not do it alone, but with colleagues, students, and friends that I have been lucky to have along the way. Accordingly, for a number of years, I have led journeys to Uganda and Rwanda, which I call "Pilgrimages of Pain and Hope." On these pilgrimages I invite my students, colleagues, parishioners, and friends from the United States and from around the world to "come and see" Africa—with the hope that those on these pilgrimages will not only come to know "Africa" differently but become emotionally bound up with the places and people they visit. Out of one such pilgrimage emerged Share the Blessings, a not-for-profit organization that supports education and water needs in Uganda. In 2006, as part of the work of the Duke Center for Reconciliation (see chapter 2), Chris Rice and I invited a group of Christian leaders from the Africa Great Lakes Region and shared with them a theological vision of reconciliation, offering them an opportunity to share their stories of pain and hope in that journey. That initiative has turned into an annual Institute for Christian Reconciliation gathering that brings together over 150 leaders from Eastern Africa and beyond for a week to learn and share their stories and experience of reconciliation. Since 2012, I have been working with young people in the rural diocese of Luweero to address the challenges of food insecurity, deforestation, and poverty in the rural communities through the Bethany Land Institute, an organization that I cofounded with two Ugandan priest classmates.[7]

Moving back and forth between my work in the academy and my work "on the ground" and discovering rich connections between these two worlds that are often kept apart has been a precious gift that has helped me cope with the stresses of the American academy, while at the same time enriching my scholarship and deepening my practical engagement.[8] For example, in and through my work with Bethany Land Institute I came to a better understanding of the deep interconnectedness between the different forms of violence explored here: ethnic, religious, ecological. For as Pope Francis notes in *Laudato Si'*, "The cry of the earth and the cry of the poor go hand in hand"—and these cries of violence arise out of the same spiritual crisis, which is a crisis of belonging, or the lack thereof. At the same time, in this work with the youth on land, I am trying to nurture spirituality and attempting a similar work of caring, tending, and mending the wound of violence, as I have learned through my research from the likes of Nzamujo, Barankitse, Mvukiyehe, and Kinvi. The hope is that through this work, not only will the immediate needs of food security, ecological repair, and economic well-being of rural communities be met, but a new sense of dignity and belonging will be nurtured, one grounded in a renewed appreciation of God's love that extends to all, especially the poor, the weak, the suffering, and the vulnerable.

I briefly highlight this practical work because it helps to confirm that the "me" that I am is not simply one identity but multiple identities. I belong not to one but to multiple, at times overlapping, communities of belonging and shared concerns. But this is true of everyone else. How these communities are connected, how one is able to move back and forth through these multiple identities, and how one is able to "negotiate" the limits, challenges, and possibilities of these identities constitute a unique journey that can only be narrated. From a Christian point of view, telling the story of one's journey, which is to say narrating one's identity, will have to assume or at least be cognizant of the bigger drama of what God is doing in the world, within which one's particular story is located. In terms of my own narrative this concretely means that even though at any given time I may describe myself using any one of the identities I bear, as a Catholic priest, a professor, a pilgrim, a Ugandan, an African, or an American, given the sense of journey as well as the fact of multiple belongings, I am never fully any one of those identities but always remain a "sort of"—a sort of scholar, a sort of practitioner, a sort of African, a sort of Catholic, a sort of American. I have come to see that this Mestizo condition is part of God's design, a gift of God's ongoing work of reconciliation through which God is determined to reverse the story of the Tower of Babel by shaping communities of a "new we" across divides. Christians self-consciously understand their lives to be part of this divine drama. However, since God is God of all, not only Christians but indeed the whole of creation is part of this drama and so eagerly waits for the full realization of a new humanity and a new creation. Even as we wait, the invitation is to invent and foster communities of a "new we" that are both the vanguard and the foretaste of that new creation. At any rate, this invitation and journey toward a "new we," and this ever-expanding hori-zon of "my people," constitute the response to the two questions that have been at the heart of this investigation: "Why do you Africans kill your own people?" and "Is the blood of tribalism deeper than the waters of baptism?" But that is also why there might be no better way to con-clude this reflection than by sharing this last sermon I preached at Duke Divinity School on the story of Ruth in the Old Testament, which cap-tures the gist of what I have tried to say here in *Who Are My People?*

A New We—on Being
Some Kind of Catholic

A Sermon

Godson Chapel, Duke Divinity School
November 13, 2012
Readings: Ruth 1:15–19; 3:1–5; 4:13–17

It was a cold winter morning in January 2001 when I arrived here at Duke Divinity School. Willie Jennings, by then senior associate dean for academic affairs, welcomed me and showed me my office. I did not know what I was doing, and even less did my bishop, Cardinal Wamala, know when he allowed me to come for two years as a visiting professor. There were a number of things to figure out. One thing I could not get over—still am not able to get over—was the promiscuous range of denominations I encountered here at Duke Divinity School. In my mind, there were only two categories of Christians: Catholics and Protestants. But here I was now confronted not only with Methodists, Lutherans, Presbyterians, Episcopalians, and Baptists (in so many shapes and forms) but denominational and nondenominational Evangelicals, Free Church, AME, affiliated as well as nonaffiliated, as well as those still figuring out what they were. If I was having trouble getting a sense of this denominational landscape, my students were having an even greater challenge figuring me out. They were not only straining to understand my thick

African accent, they were not sure what to make of the theological eccentricities I represented.

You see, a number of my students simply assumed, for reasons that are still not clear to me, that I was Baptist. They could not understand the heavy emphasis I was placing on the Eucharist. I remember in this one course, it was on "the faces of Jesus in Africa," I was explaining how in Africa faith is not simply a matter of belief, and the soul and the afterlife, it is about cabbages, goats, millet, sickness, and health. I was also trying to explain that in many places in Africa Christians worship, not inside a sanctuary, a beautiful sanctuary like this, but under a tree. It is here, under a tree, they listen to the word of God and celebrate the Eucharist. I must have carried on about the significance of celebrating the Eucharist and how it is the Eucharist that makes the church. This chap in the front row was looking at me with what seemed to be a mixture of interest and pity, but the more I talked the more the expression turned into a big question mark on his face. Finally, when I paused, he asked, "Are you some kind of Catholic?"

Some kind of Catholic? I replied that I was not simply "some kind of Catholic," I was a Roman Catholic priest. "I see," he said.

Over the years, as I have thought about this student's question, I have come to realize this has been the most precious gift for me living and working here among non-Catholics: how I have indeed become "some kind of Catholic." And now as I look back on my life—a Ugandan, son of immigrant parents from Rwanda; an African who has been living here in the US for the last twelve years; a Catholic among non-Catholics—I realize a clear pattern, namely that God has kept pushing me beyond "my people," beyond "my home," to a place where I am no longer sure who my people are and where my home is.

But I have also come to believe that this is what God is determined to do with each one of us. Regardless of the particular details of our biography, God is committed to stretch, expand, in fact confuse our sense of who "my people" are, so as to make us *some kind of* Catholic, *some kind of* Methodist, *some kind of* Lutheran, *some kind of* black person, *some kind of* white person, *some kind of* American, *some kind of* African.

For it is this *some kind of* identity that allows us to catch a glimpse of and live into the new future, into a "new we" which God is determined to create in our midst through unlikely friendships. Just as the case of Ruth and Naomi.

Naomi, an Israelite woman, during famine goes with her family to live in the country of Moab. Her two sons marry Moabite women. When Naomi's husband and her two sons die, Naomi decides to return to her hometown, Bethlehem. Her daughters-in-law wish to come with her, but Naomi tells them: I am an old woman; I do not have any more sons to give you. Go back each to your own mother's house, to your own people. Orpah, one of the daughters-in-law, returns to Moab, but Ruth, the other daughter-in-law, insists on coming with Naomi. She pleads with her mother-in-law: "Do not press me to leave you or to turn back from following you. Where you go, I will go; where you lodge, I will lodge; your people shall be my people and your God my God. Where you die, I will die. There I will be buried. May the Lord do thus and so to me and more as well if even death parts me from you" (Ruth 1:16–17).

And so Naomi returns to Bethlehem together with her daughter-in-law Ruth. Here she helps Ruth not only find work but a husband, Boaz, who happens to be Naomi's relative. Ruth and Boaz conceive, and Ruth gives birth to a son, Obed, the father of Jesse, the father of David.

But Obed is not simply *a kind of* Israelite—he is a Moabite-Israelite. This is a hyphen that was never supposed to happen. For the Moabites and Israelites were bitter enemies. The Israelites not only hated but despised the Moabites. They believed that the Moabites originated from the act of incest between Lot and his older daughter (Gen. 19:30–38). According to the Israelites, the Moabites were cursed "to the tenth generation"—which is to say, forever. Therefore, according to Deuteronomy, "No Ammonites or Moabites or any of their descendants may enter the assembly of the Lord, even down to the tenth generation" (Deut. 23:3).

The hostility was mutual. The Moabites not only refused to give Israel hospitable reception, their king, Balak, hired Balaam to curse Israel. Never mind that God turned the curse into a blessing (Num. 23).

What irony! For Obed is not only *a kind of* Israelite, an Israelite-Moabite, he is the father of Jesse, the father of David. David, Israel's hero, is the descendant of this union—this Mestizo—between Israel and her bitter enemy! The story of Ruth is meant to remind Israel of this, especially in those moments when Israel might wish to conveniently "hate" and therefore have nothing to do with the Moabites—and might invoke her sacred text to confirm that "no Moabites or their descendants may enter the assembly of the Lord, even to the tenth generation" (Deut. 23:3).

The fact that Jesus himself is descended from David means that the Messiah is also *a kind of* Jew. This is the reason that Matthew, the most Jewish of all the Gospel writers, addressing a predominantly Jewish audience, makes sure his audience does not forget this. And so, at the very beginning of his proclamation of the Good News, Matthew includes Ruth (as one of the four Old Testament women—"strange" women who do not quite belong)—in the genealogy of Jesus. Ruth is the grandmother of David, the great-great-grandfather of Jesus.

Matthew's intention is also to make sure that we too do not forget. Not only Israel but all of us who are grafted into this story—and who therefore become children and friends of God—are drawn into this drama of God, who is determined to create a new future in which, as the letter of James reminds us, "He chose to give us birth through the word of truth, that we might be a kind of first fruits of all he created" (James 1:18).

There are a number of things that make Ruth and Naomi's story such a beautiful story, including its happy ending: Naomi holding Ruth's son, Obed, the grandfather of David. Something also of the intimacy of Naomi and Ruth is striking. The two women not only support each other, they plot and conspire and play Boaz, leading to the fruitful marriage of Ruth and Boaz. In this connection, a number of euphemisms (see, e.g., chapter 3: Ruth and Boaz at the threshing floor, particularly all reference to Boaz's "foot"), make this a beautiful love story.

However, even most significant, what makes this a powerful story of friendship is the way it is built up around food and eating. It is famine that drives Naomi and her husband into Moabite territory, looking for food. When Ruth and Naomi return to Bethlehem, it happened to be harvest time. The first preoccupation of the women on their return is to find food. And so Ruth tells Naomi: "Let me go and glean ears of grain in the field of anyone who will permit me" (2:2). It happens to be the field of Boaz, who not only allows her to glean but invites her to eat with him. She eats and has her fill and even asks for a doggie bag! At the end of the day, Ruth takes back home to Naomi not only the barley she has gleaned but a doggie bag, with leftovers from her lunch with Boaz.

Their friendship is built around food and eating. I am reminded of the Rwandan proverb "Unless you hear the mouth eating, you cannot hear the mouth crying." Eating matters, and who we eat with matters a lot. For it is in learning to eat with strangers and those who are different from us that we become part of God's "new we." This is the lesson that Peter had to learn, first in a dream, and in reality when he entered the house of Cornelius, a Roman centurion. It was only through Peter (an Israelite) and Cornelius (a Roman centurion) eating together that Peter came to discover that "in truth, God has no favorites" (Acts 10:34).

But of course this put Peter into a lot of trouble. And sometimes he hesitated and wanted to turn back. Paul had to challenge him. By eating with Cornelius, Peter had "betrayed" his own people. Just like Naomi and Ruth, Peter had become *a kind of* Jew, whose loyalty had become suspect.

On my first pilgrimage to Burundi in 2008, we met a young man, Melance Ntahompagaze. Burundi is a very small country—south of Rwanda. It is a very beautiful country and also a predominantly Christian country. However, with the long history of ethnic hatred between Hutu and Tutsi, the blood of tribalism tends to run deeper than the waters of baptism. The social history of Burundi is a history of ethnic killings back and forth. In 1993 there was a massacre at Kibimbi, not too far from Giteega: a Hutu mob rounded up Tutsi students and teachers from the Friends (Quaker) school, along with some neighbors, and crammed them into a gas station, and set the gas station on fire. Over 120 people were killed. Melance together with a few others survived the smoke and heat and crawled out of the smoldering ruins.

At first Melance did not know what to do. Most of his friends were dead. With time he got together with a few other young people, some Hutu and some Tutsi, and they organized themselves into a peace team—committed to live as friends. They work together in fields, celebrate weddings and other events, and go into the villages and on hillsides, inviting both Hutu and Tutsi to a new life of friendship and fellowship. With time a number of other peace teams have been formed. And an organization, MiParec (Ministry of Reconciliation under the Cross), supports their work.

To be a Burundian is to be either Hutu or Tutsi—which means to see each other as bitter enemies. And yet here is a Ntahompagaze. His name means, "I have nowhere to stand"—*a kind of* Burundian—living true to his name.

"It has not been easy," Melance told us. "Most of the times we are suspected by both communities. But the peace teams have also been a source of friendships." Working together in the fields growing crops, celebrating feast days and weddings as well other opportunities of eating together, keep Ntahompagaze and his friends going. We visited a new-lywed couple, Hutu and Tutsi, who could not stop talking about the cele-bration they had had at their wedding. If Ntahompagaze and his friends take every opportunity for Hutu and Tutsi to eat together, they are a sign, *a kind of first fruits of* a new future in Burundi.

If practices like growing crops and eating together—as well as wor-ship (as a vision of reconciliation through the cross)—build up their friendship, they also form Melance and his friends into patterns of pa-tience and courage necessary for the demands that living a life of that *kind of* requires.

On the same visit to Burundi in 2008, we went to Buta, a Catholic high school, where we heard the story of another *kind of first fruits* of a new creation, of a new future in Burundi.[1] It happened in the fall of 1997. Shortly before dawn, a militia group, headed by a fierce woman com-mander, attacked the seminary; they ordered the high school students to separate, Hutu on one side, and Tutsi on the other. Three times the order was given, but the students refused to separate. So the commander ordered the rebels to open fire. The students fell, and others tried to es-cape. In all, forty students were killed. The rector heard the gunshots from his house and crawled under his bed. One of the students who had been wounded ran to the rector's and called for the rector to open the door for him. When the rector opened the door, the boy dashed in-side the small house. Gasping for breath, he told the rector: "Father, we have won. They told us to separate and we refused. We have won!" And he collapsed and died!

"We have won!" What a strange victory! As we heard the story told to us by Fr. Zacharie Bukuru, who was the rector then, as we stood in the cemetery with the neat rows of forty graves and looked at the "Martyrs of Unity" mural with the painting of the young seminarian martyrs holding palms in their hands, as we drove back to Bujumbura that evening, the words of the seminarian, "We have won," kept ringing in my ears.

This is therefore what through my own journey I have come to see and understand. God is determined not only to stretch but to confuse the sense of "who is my people" so as to create, even here and now, a new future in our midst. And the way that God does this is first through his odd friendship with us: "He came to dwell among us." God became human—*a kind of* God! This Odd God who became our friend invites —nay, pushes us—into strange places and friendships, friendships that are not supposed to be. Through these odd friendships, and only through them, can we get a glimpse of God's exciting new future, as well as a sense of what it means, in the midst of so much tribalism and divisions that wreck our world, to say together with those students in Burundi, "We have won."

Figure A.1. "We have won!" mural at Buta Seminary, Burundi.

NOTES

Introduction

1. Martin, "Rwanda," 1–2.
2. Mamdani, *When Victims Become Killers*, ix.
3. This I take to be the main thrust behind Gifford's *Christianity, Development*.
4. Soyinka, *Of Africa*, 48. See more in chapter 1.
5. Rob Nixon coined this phrase in his book by the title, *Slow Violence*. See more in chapter 5.
6. See Katongole, *Born from Lament*, 33–38.
7. Lawrence-Lightfoot and Davis, *Art and Science*, xv.
8. English, "Critical Appraisal," 22.

Chapter 1. On Being an African

1. For more on my scholarly journey, see Katongole, "African Theological Reimagination."
2. Chabal and Daloz, *Africa Works*. For a more extended discussion of this book, see Katongole, *Sacrifice of Africa*, 60.
3. See Katongole, *Sacrifice of Africa*, especially 64–86 in relation to B. Anderson, *Imagined Communities*, and Cavanaugh, *Theo-Political Imagination*.
4. In his 1998 Harvard Lectures, Chinua Achebe raises similar concerns about the word *tribe* in reference to the Igbo. See his *Home and Exile*, especially 4–5.
5. Louis de Lacger, *Ruanda*, quoted in Gourevitch, *We Wish to Inform You*, 55. See Gourevitch's discussion of this work in *We Wish to Inform You*, 54–55.
6. For a helpful introduction to European views on "race" during the Enlightenment and how they were connected to Europeans' growing perception of themselves as a superior race, see Eze, *Race and the Enlightenment*.

7. Mudimbe, *Tales of Faith*, 169–70.

8. This is the broad argument that Mudimbe develops in *Idea of Africa*.

9. Hegel, *Philosophy of History*, 91.

10. For a helpful and comprehensive introduction to and discussion of Mudimbe and his work, see Brenner, "Reading Mudimbe."

11. Mbembe, *On the Postcolony*, 1.

12. Said, *Orientalism*, especially 49–72.

13. See Emmanuel Katongole, *Beyond Universal Reason*. On how I discovered Hauerwas, and how as a student of philosophy I had come to study the work of a theologian, see Katongole, "Hauerwasian Hooks."

14. For more, see Katongole, "Christianity, Tribalism."

15. *Foreign Policy*, "Prospect." Annan quoted in *Q-News*, "Mazrui."

16. Mazrui, "Re-invention of Africa," 69.

17. Ibid., 71.

18. Ibid., 75.

19. Ibid.

20. Ibid., 74.

21. Ndlovu-Gatsheni, "Ali A. Mazrui," 216.

22. Soyinka, *Of Africa*, 27.

23. Ibid., 45.

24. Ibid., 48; see also 99.

25. Ibid., 48.

26. My interest here is not a critical assessment of Mazrui's work, which on the whole I find rich (and thus helpful) on diagnosis but not so helpful when it comes to constructive proposals for a way forward. Others, like Jane Conrad, have criticized his work as shallow at times and missing "an integrated approach of the external and internal forces which created and help to perpetrate the 'paradoxes.'" See Conrad, "African Condition," 187.

27. For a similar point regarding the ambiguities of race as a delineation of African identity, see Adibe, "Africa without Africans," 16–25.

28. More recently, in *Lies That Bind*, Appiah takes up this claim by examining the "essentialist" lies that are at the core of each of the five bases of modern identity: creed, country, class, color, and culture.

29. Appiah, *In My Father's House*, 176.

30. Ibid., 155.

31. Ibid., 179.

32. Ibid.

33. Appiah, *Lies That Bind*, xvi.

34. Serequeberhan, "Reflections," 116.

35. Appiah, *In My Father's House*, 177, 180. Coming from a different angle, Adibe argues for an African identity based on the rejection of essentialism. Citing Mammo Muchie, he notes, "There is no such thing as an essential African character that has been frozen from time immemorial. Africa has always lived in his-

tory and through history. Its identity must be expressed through the rejection of racism, ethnicity, parochialism, exclusivity and barbarism. . . . Thus an African identity must posit an inclusive, non-essentialist and emancipatory goals [sic]." See Adibe, "Africa without Africans," 22.

36. Although he does not explicitly say so in *In My Father's House*, in *In Lies That Bind*, Appiah says outright that identities are held together by narratives (199). This is an important point that confirms both Mudimbe and Mazrui's views earlier of "Africa" and "African identity" as an imagination. And of course the fact that they are an "imagination" does not mean that therefore they are not real. They are the realest thing imaginable!

37. *Lies That Bind*, xvi.

38. Appiah, *In My Father's House*, 180.

39. Ibid.

40. Ibid., x.

41. Ibid., ix.

42. Ibid., x.

43. Towa, "Propositions sur l'identite culturelle," *Presence Africaine* 109 (1979): 82–91, esp. 84.

44. Appiah, *In My Father's House*, 179.

45. Ibid.

46. Ibid., ix.

Chapter 2. On Being an African Christian

1. For more on my parents' story, see Katongole, *Mirror to the Church*, 14–22.

2. Quoted in J. Martin, "Rwanda," 1–2.

3. Bediako, *Christianity in Africa*, 256.

4. Asamoah-Gyadu, "Bediako of Africa," 5.

5. Bediako, *Christianity in Africa*, 256. Bediako refers to Hastings, *African Christianity*, 50, and Fasholé-Luke, "Quest," 259–69.

6. The 1992 book is based on his dissertation of the same title for the University of Aberdeen in 1983. See Asamoah-Gyadu, "Bediako of Africa," 12.

7. While Tatian and Tertullian tended more to stress the discontinuity of Christianity with the existing culture, Justin and Clement stressed continuity with the pre-Christian past.

8. Bediako, *Christianity in Africa*, 331, 345.

9. Bediako's other writings portray a more nuanced position and at times seem to suggest discontinuity to be more important than continuity. See Wagenaar's helpful review "Theology, Identity."

10. Bediako, *Theology and Identity*, 36.

11. Mbiti, *African Religions and Philosophy*, 261.

12. Maluleke, "In Search," 218.

13. Bediako, *Theology and Identity*, 16.

14. Stinton, *Jesus of Africa*, 13. See also Bediako, "Understanding African Theology," 6–7.

15. Stinton, *Jesus of Africa*, 6.

16. Pobee, *Giving an Account*, 158. Pobee refers to his previous essay, "I Am First an African," 268–77.

17. Tarus and Lowery, "African Theologies," 307.

18. ALARM, *Restoring the Beauty*, 55.

19. In the debate between "inculturation" and "liberation," African women's concerns, overlooked for so long, now constitute a key locus for theology, and the work of Mercy Amba Oduyoye and other members of the Circle of African Women Theologians can rightly be seen as a dynamic and engaging form of second-generation liberation theology. See Oduyoye, "Reflections from a Third World Woman's Perspective." For a good introduction to the history, key voices, and major contributions of the Circle, see Fielder, *History of the Circle*.

20. Notice the growing list of scholarly works focusing on Christian identity in relation to the political issues of a specific country, such as Kamaara, "Towards Christian National Identity," and Tarus and Gathogo, "Conquering Africa's Second Devil," both responding to the 2007 postelection violence in Kenya.

21. Tarimo, "Ethnicity, Common Good."

22. Appiah, *Lies That Bind*, 67.

23. Bujo, "Enthusiast of African Theology," 16.

24. Lowery, *Identity and Ecclesiology*, 49.

25. Ibid.

26. Mudimbe often refers to his former teacher, the theologian Vincent Mulago, whose work Mudimbe respects and which demonstrates that "nothing blends so well as intellectual vigilance, anthropological knowledge, and existential participation in the studied area." See Mudimbe, *Parables and Fables*, 56. However, Mudimbe concludes that in the end, Mulago's project of "adaptation theology" fails because it "has recourse to the same controversial logical empiricism it wants to relativize." See Mudimbe, *Tales of Faith*, 89. The paradox lies in the fact that although Mulago and his like-minded colleagues wanted to invoke the "truths of place," that is local discourse, in developing their theological writings, their project was ultimately grounded in a "scientific" tradition that was external to the "place." See Brenner, "Reading Mudimbe."

27. See Lowery, *Identity and Ecclesiology*, 164.

28. Ferdinando, "Christian Identity," 139.

29. For more about this journey, see Katongole and Rice, *Reconciling All Things*, and Katongole, *Journey of Reconciliation*.

30. For a more extensive discussion of the gifts from the work of the Duke Center for Reconciliation, see Katongole, "How Reconciliation Saved My Scholarship."

31. Volf, *Exclusion and Embrace*, 37.

32. Ibid., 40.

33. Ibid., 38.

34. Ibid., 39.

35. Ibid., 45.

36. Ibid., 47.

37. Ibid., 48.

38. All direct quotations in this paragraph are from ibid., 49. Volf cites Campbell, *Paul's Gospel*, vi.

39. Niebuhr, *Christ and Culture*.

40. Volf, *Exclusion and Embrace*, 49.

41. The Spanish word *mestizo* was first used to describe the children of the violent encounter between European fathers and Amerindian mothers; neither European nor Indian, these children belonged to a new people, a people of mixed heritage. See definition accessed November 30, 2019, www.dictionary.com /browse/mestizo.

42. Elizondo, *Future Is Mestizo*, 26.

43. Ibid., 67–86.

44. Ibid., 129.

45. Ibid.

46. Hatzfeld, *Machete Season*, 122–23.

47. Hauerwas and Willimon, *Resident Aliens*, 49.

48. Ibid., 57.

49. Ibid., 12.

50. The free Online Dictionary, accessed 2019, www.thefreedictionary.com /colony.

51. Uzukwu, *Listening Church*, 67.

52. Walls, "Gospel as Prisoner," 21.

53. Ibid., 22.

54. Ibid., 25.

55. See, e.g., Bevans, *Mission and Culture*.

56. Ibid., 27.

57. Walls, "Ephesian Moment."

58. Ibid., 76.

59. Ibid., 78.

60. Sibomana, *Hope for Rwanda*, 131–32.

Chapter 3. Ethnic Violence and the Reinvention of Identity

1. Most accounts put the Christian population of Rwanda prior to the genocide between 85 and 90 percent. See, e.g., Rittner, Roth, and Whitworth, *Genocide in Rwanda*, xi; Longman, *Christianity and Genocide*, 4. See also Katongole, "Christianity, Tribalism," 67–68.

2. For some of these cases, see Katongole, *Mirror to the Church*, especially 9–26. More recently, in 2017, the pope issued an apology for the Rwanda Genocide. In an audience with Paul Kagame, the Rwandan president, Pope Francis acknowledged that some Catholic priests and nuns had "succumbed to hatred and violence" by participating in the genocide. Asking for forgiveness on behalf of the church, the pope noted the extent to which the "sins and failings of the church and its members" had "disfigured the face" of Catholicism. See Wooden, "Pope Apologizes." A year earlier, the Rwanda Catholic bishops had apologized for "all the wrongs the church committed" during the genocide. See Associated Press, "Catholic Church."

3. The direct quote and the information in this paragraph are drawn from Rwamasirabo's account in Chris Heuertz's "'God Is Innocent'" and in my pilgrimage notes from July 2013 and July 2015.

4. Every time I have stood in the demolished church, now turned into a mass grave, I have imagined (or felt I heard) those buried under the church crying out, not unlike the victims in the book of Revelation, "How long, Sovereign Lord, holy and true, until you judge the inhabitants of the earth and avenge our blood?" (Rev. 6:10).

5. For my previous reflections on this issue of identities, see Katongole, *Mirror to the Church*, "Christianity, Tribalism," and *Sacrifice of Africa*, 74–81.

6. Gourevitch, *We Wish to Inform You*, 55.

7. Mamdani, *When Victims Become Killers*, 22.

8. Ibid., 57–58.

9. Ibid., xi.

10. Appiah, *In My Father's House*, 179.

11. Sankara, *Thomas Sankara Speaks*, 144: "You cannot carry out fundamental change without a certain amount of madness. In this case, it comes from nonconformity, the courage to turn your back on the old formulas, the courage to invent the future. We must dare to invent the future."

12. Ibid.

13. For my earlier reflections on this story as exemplifying the kind of courage Christians need if they are to resist the madness of tribalism, see Katongole, *Mirror to the Church*, 149–52, and "Threatened with Resurrection."

14. Fr. Jean Baptiste Mvukiyehe, interview by author, January 7, 2017, Entebbe.

15. Ibid.

16. The following conversation and direct quotes are from Fr. Jean Baptiste Mvukiyehe, interview by author, January 22, 2018, on drive from Kigali to Ruhango, Rwanda.

17. All direct quotes above are from ibid.

18. The Pallottines were founded in Rome in 1835 by an Italian priest, Vincent Pallotti (1795–1850). The Pallottines were born from his visionary desire to unite the factions in the church and to encourage lay apostolic activity.

19. Unless otherwise stated, the information on Ruhango is based on Jean Baptiste, interview by author, January 22, 2018.

20. Specioza (not real name), one of the original members of the Charismatic group at Ruhango, interview by author, January 22, 2018, Ruhango.

21. Jean Baptiste, interview, January 2018.

22. Jean Paul, interview by author, January 22, 2018, Ruhango.

23. Ibid.

24. The following relating of Jean Baptiste's story is drawn from my interview with him, January 22, 2018.

25. All direct quotes above are from ibid.

26. Carney, "Generation after Genocide," 803.

27. Filipek, "Path of Hope."

28. For a fuller description of the Divine Mercy shrine at Kabuga that situates it within the circle of the church's liturgical year, see Seah, "Reconciliation after Betrayal."

29. Jean Baptiste, interview, January 22, 2018.

30. The following conversation and direct quotes are from my conversation with Fr. Anthony at the Emmanuel Community Center, January 22, 2018, Kigali.

31. From my notes as a participant observer, January 19, 2018, Kigali.

32. Øystein Rakkenes, interview by author, January 20, 2018, Oasis of Peace center, Kigali.

33. Katongole, *Sacrifice of Africa*, 178.

34. I give a fuller treatment of Maggy's story in *Sacrifice of Africa* and in *Born from Lament*. Unless otherwise stated, the direct quotations are from Katongole, *Sacrifice of Africa*, 166–92.

35. Katongole, *Born from Lament*, 276–77.

36. Katongole, *Sacrifice of Africa*, 181.

37. Maggy Barankitse, interview by author, April 10, 2017, Notre Dame.

38. Jean Baptiste, interview, January 7, 2017.

39. Romero, homily, November 27, 1977, in *Violence of Love*, 12.

We have never preached violence,
except the violence of love,
which left Christ nailed to a cross,
the violence that we must each do to ourselves
to overcome our selfishness
and such cruel inequalities among us.
The violence we preach is not the violence of the sword,
the violence of hatred.
It is the violence of love,
of brotherhood,
the violence that wills to beat weapons
into sickles for work.

40. Marguerite Barankitse, testimony at Together in Hope event, Malmö, Sweden, October 31, 2016.

41. Rakkenes, interview by author, January 20, 2018.

Chapter 4. Religious Violence and the Reinvention of Politics

1. United Nations Development Programme, "Human Development Index," table 1 in *Human Development Report 2020*, http://hdr.undp.org/en /composite/HDI.

2. Council on Foreign Relations, "Global Conflict Tracker," accessed November 30, 2019, www.cfr.org/interactive/global-conflict-tracker/conflict /violence-central-african-republic.

3. Smith, "CAR's History," 18.

4. Lombard and Carayannis, "Making Sense of CAR," 3.

5. See Wrong, *It's Our Turn to Eat*.

6. Lombard and Carayannis, "Making Sense of CAR," 5.

7. Carayannis and Lombard, "Concluding Note," 325.

8. Ibid., 325–26.

9. The following information, including direct quotes, is based on Fr. Soh Keugne Nouthak Jules, interview by author, February 2, 2018, Bangui.

10. Smith, "CAR's History," 17.

11. Dalby, "Multifaceted Business," 135.

12. Jean Pierre Meme, interview by author, March 5, 2018, Bangui.

13. Alex Gumba, interview by author, March 3, 2018, Bangui.

14. Lombard, "Autonomous Zone Conundrum," 144.

15. Ibid.

16. Ibid., 144, 143.

17. Ibid., 149.

18. Ibid., 147.

19. Bridget, interview by author, March 3, 2018, Bangui.

20. Imam Yacoub, interview by author, March 4, 2018, Bangui.

21. Kilembe, "Local Dynamics," 100.

22. Marchal, "Being Rich, Being Poor," 57.

23. Ashforth, *Witchcraft, Violence*, 127.

24. Ibid. See also Chabal and Daloz, *Africa Works*, and Peter Geschiere's *Modernity of Witchcraft*.

25. Student leader, interview by author, March 5, 2018, Bangui.

26. Barwendé Médard Sané, interview by author, March 4, 2018, Bangui.

27. Poko (former militia member), interview by author, March 7, 2018.

28. Fr. Joseph, secretary-general of Bishops' Conference, interview by author, March 8, 2018.

29. Louise, interview by author, March 4, 2018, Bangui.

30. Jonathan, interview by author, March 4, 2018, Bangui.

31. Imam Omar Kobine Layama, interview by author, March 8, 2018, Bangui.

32. Fideli Modat, interview by author, March 4, 2018, Bangui.

33. Quotes in this paragraph all from Barwendé, interview.

34. Quotes in this paragraph from Fr. Joseph, interview.

35. Barwendé, interview.

36. Sankara, *Thomas Sankara Speaks*, 144.

37. Fr. Bernard Kinvi, interviews by author, January 6 and 7, 2017, Entebbe, Uganda.

38. For a short history of the Camillian order, see Camillian Religious, "A Short History of the Order," accessed June 5, 2021, www.camilliani.org/en/a-short-history-of-the-order/. For a more comprehensive history, see Bartholomaus, *Camille de Lellis*.

39. A related sense of "locality" as the key to identity and reality is found in Taiye Selasi's 2014 TED Talk "Don't Ask Where I'm From, Ask Where I'm a Local." Here Selasi suggests replacing the language of nationality with the language of locality, because in her argument all experience is local, and nations are "fictions." The experience of being local, according to Selasi, is shaped around three Rs: Rituals, Relationships, and Restrictions. These relationships, rather than country of origin, define an individual, making it possible for one to be local in more than one place, in a way that nationality does not.

40. In telling the story of his father, Kinvi remembers especially his father's faith (his example and encouragement to the young Kinvi to go to mass and say his prayers at home) but especially his hospitality. How he was always inviting people, travelers, strangers into the house. "We had a small house, but there were always people, some relatives but others who dad invited to stay with us." Fr. Kinvi, interview by author, March 7, 2018, Bossemptele.

41. J. Anderson, "Mission."

42. See Pope Francis, "Big Heart": "The thing the church needs most today is the ability to heal wounds and to warm the hearts of the faithful; it needs nearness, proximity. I see the church as a field hospital after battle." Pope Francis spoke similarly in a General Audience to Arab Speaking Pilgrims on August 9, 2017: "Therefore, the primary and fundamental mission of the Church is to be a 'field hospital,' a place of healing, mercy and forgiveness, and to be the source of hope for all suffering, the desperate, the poor, the sinners, and the discarded." Lubov, "Church."

Chapter 5. Ecological Violence and the Reinvention of Land

1. Ten years ago, through a nonprofit organization called Share the Blessings (www.share-the-blessings.org/), I helped to raise funds for a borehole for the village.

2. Davis, *Planet of Slums*, 1.

3. Ibid., 19.

4. Muggah and Kilcullen, "These Are Africa's Fastest-Growing Cities."

5. According to estimates by UN-Habitat, two hundred million people in sub-Saharan Africa were living in slums in 2010, or 61.7 percent of the region's urban population. Racelma, "Towards African Cities."

6. Davis, *Planet of Slums*, 19.

7. Fleshman, "Saving Africa's Forests."

8. Josephat, "Deforestation In Uganda."

9. See, e.g., Horning, *Politics of Deforestation*.

10. See various news stories on "Buduuda landslides."

11. Parenti, *Tropic of Chaos*, 5. According to Parenti, the effects of this convergence are particularly evident in what he describes as the "tropic of chaos," "a belt of economically and politically battered postcolonial states girding the planet's mid-latitudes. . . . The societies in this belt are also heavily dependent on agriculture and fishing, thus very vulnerable to shifts in weather patterns. The region was also on the front line of the Cold War and of neoliberal economic restructuring. As a result in this belt we find clustered most of the failed and semi-failed states of the developing world" (9). Parenti's analysis extends beyond Africa to include Asia and Latin America and offers revealing insights into the relation between politics, global development economics, climate change, and violence in select African countries.

12. According to *Slow Violence* author Rob Nixon, slow violence, unlike violence that is episodic, bounded, and dramatic, refers to "calamities that are slow and long lasting, calamities that patiently dispense their devastation while remaining outside our flickering attention spans" (6).

13. See, e.g., Hendrix and Glaser, "Trends and Triggers"; Suliman, *Ecology, Politics*. See also Parenti, *Tropic of Chaos*.

14. O'Brien, *Violence of Climate Change*, 4.

15. That is why, even though on the whole I find Parenti's *Tropic of Chaos* highly insightful in its analysis of the violence of climate change as the new "geography" of violence, his recommendations for technical, political, and economic adaptation still fall short of the need to transform our relationship with the earth. In this case, Parenti's recommendations are still framed from within the "technocratic paradigm" of modern capitalism. From within this paradigm the best recommendation for a way forward seems to be to "decarbonize our economy" (12). While doing so could go a long way in slowing down the rate of global warming, it does not address the forms of alienation (between humans and the earth, individual and community, and us and God) that are the root of the modern ecological crisis.

16. Pope Francis, *Laudato Si'*, para. 15. Hereafter cited parenthetically in the text as *LS* followed by the paragraph number.

17. Boff, *Cry of the Earth*, 123.

18. Ibid.

19. Ibid.

20. Ibid., 125. Boff cites Archibold, "Pemasky en Kuna Yala," 37, and Potiguara, *Terra é a mãe*.

21. Mires, *Discurso de la naturaleza*, 105–11, quoted in Boff, *Cry of the Earth*, 125.

22. Boff, *Cry of the Earth*, 126.

23. Ibid., 127.

24. Maathai, *Replenishing the Earth*, 79.

25. Mbiti, *African Religions and Philosophy*, 1.

26. Maathai, *Replenishing the Earth*, 101.

27. Magesa, "African Spirituality," 122.

28. For this notion, see Danson Sylvester Kabyana, "Okot p'Bitek's Diagnostic Poetics." By "diagnostic poetics" Kabyana means the "use of poetry to probe into postindependence realities with the aim of discovering the ailment of Africa that prevents Africa from achieving a cultural revolution" (18). In his reading of *Song of Lawino and Song of Ocol*, Kabyana particularly attends to the metaphors of health and sickness, through which Lawino views Ocol's bombastic arrogance and rejection of African traditional ways of life.

29. p'Bitek, *Song of Lawino and Song of Ocol*, 118. Subsequent citations to this work by page number are from this edition and are given parenthetically in the text.

30. McKibben, *Eaarth*, 163.

31. Sachs, *End of Poverty*, 35–36.

32. Davis, *Planet of Slums*, 201.

33. Davidson, *Black Man's Burden*, 42.

34. Davis, *Planet of Slums*, 201.

35. Robert, interview by author, August 5, 2018, Kampala. All quotes and descriptions in the paragraph are drawn from this interview.

36. Apollo, interview by author, August 5, 2018, Kampala. All quotes and descriptions in the paragraph are drawn from this interview.

37. Shifah, interview by author, August 6, 2018, Kampala. All quotes and descriptions in the paragraph are drawn from this interview.

38. Davis, *Planet of Slums*, 19.

39. Joseph, interview by author, August 5, 2018, Kampala. All quotes and descriptions in the paragraph are drawn from this interview.

40. Robert, interview.

41. Sam, interview by author, August 6, 2018, Kampala.

42. Zaina, interview by author, August 6, 2018, Kampala.

43. Elizabeth, interview by author, August 5, 2018, Kampala.

44. The practice of burying the umbilical cord of a newly born child in the soil, a ritual widely practiced by many African communities, inextricably ties the individual to a place—to the earth—in the same way as that umbilical cord joined

the mother and child. The joining of the individual to the earth makes the earth, or the soil, the new "mother," ensuring one a sense of security and nourishment, as well as a sense of identity and of belonging to the human community, both of those present now and of those gone before (the ancestors), and to the earth community.

45. Lund, Odgaard, and Sjaastad, "Land Rights."

46. Lund, Odgaard, and Sjaastad, "Land Rights," for instance, highlighted market development and population growth as important factors, as well as other interrelated factors like increased competition between different land utilization patterns (e.g., cultivation, pastoralism, hunting and gathering, conservation).

47. Mayiga, "Reasons."

48. See, e.g., Elias Bongmba, "Land and Authority," on the conflict in his native region of Wimbun (Cameroon), part of the Contending Modernities series. The December 2017 issue (60, no. 3) of *African Studies Review* dedicated an entire forum to "Land Disputes and Displacement in Postcolonial Africa" (Fratkin and Redding, "Land Disputes"). See the various essays in this volume and resources cited. For a more focused study that connects land conflict to ethnicity in Uganda, see Ssentongo, "Spaces for Pluralism."

49. Mayiga, "Reasons."

50. See Mugambwa, "Comparative Analysis," 40–54.

51. Ibid.

52. Headed by Lady Justice Catherine Bamugemereire of the Uganda High Court, the commission was also a response to the widespread incidents of corruption in the land office and growing cases of land disputes and conflicts, some of them attracting nationwide attention, e.g., the Apaa land conflict that divided the Acholi and Madi communities in northern Uganda. On the latter, see, for instance, the short film produced by the Refuge Law Project and the Advisory Consortium on Conflict Sensitivity, "'Shoot Us All Down': The Lakang and Apaa Land Conflict," www.youtube.com/watch?v=2IJUP4xuHp8.

53. Judiciary of the Republic of Uganda, "Land Inquiry Commission Sworn-In."

54. Refugee Law Project, "Border or Ownership Question."

55. Ndebesa, "Understanding the Meaning."

56. Okot, "Uganda."

57. Refuge Law Project, "Border or Ownership Question."

58. On the Apaa land conflict, see Refugee Law Project and Advisory Consortium, "'Shoot Us All Down.'"

59. Okot, "Uganda."

60. Development Initiatives, *Global Nutrition Report 2017.*

61. Chowdhury, "Hunger in Africa."

62. Ibid.

63. World Bank, "While Poverty in Africa Has Declined."

64. Maathai, *Replenishing the Earth*, 79, 86.

65. Nzamujo, "Using Agriculture."
66. Nzamujo, interview by author, July 5–6, 2016, Porto Novo.
67. See chapter 1 above.
68. Nzamujo, interview.
69. Nzamujo, "Songhai," 117.
70. Nzamujo, interview.
71. Nzamujo seems to be referring to an incident in the life of Thomas Aquinas. On the feast of St. Nicholas in 1273, Aquinas was celebrating mass when he received a revelation that so affected him that he wrote and dictated no more, leaving his great work the *Summa Theologiae* unfinished. To Brother Reginald's (his secretary and friend) expostulations, he replied, "The end of my labors has come. All that I have written appears to be as so much straw after the things that have been revealed to me." When later asked by Reginald to return to writing, Aquinas said, "I can write no more. I have seen things that make my writings like straw" (Mihi videtur ut palea). Chesterton, *Saint Thomas Aquinas*, 115–16.
72. Nzamujo, interview. Nzamujo's indebtedness to Louis-Joseph Lebret becomes especially evident when you consider Nzamujo's observation that "Lebret was one of the first to attempt to intuitively combine 'humanism' and 'economics,' efficiency in productions and the values of civilization. While at Shongai we claim that the real measure of wealth is the human being, it is adding worth to all that takes an individual beyond caricatures, which oppose 'being' and 'having' or 'doing.' For us in Songhai, it is important to see the human being as a bird—the eagle—which flies with two wings, the economic and the social, for both go together. The economy nourishes society, and society nourishes the economy, the human being in the center" (Nzamujo, "Songhai," 45–46). Lebret's key influence in introducing the notion of "integral human development" within the Catholic social tradition has been widely recognized. As Keleher notes: "The first place we see the phrase 'integral human development' is in Pope Paul VI's very influential 1967 encyclical *Populorum Progresio*, or the *Development of Peoples*. But much of the thought found in this encyclical, and therefore the conceptual foundations of integral human development, can be traced back even earlier to the work of French economist, social activist and Dominican priest Louis-Joseph Lebret. Lebret's work with sea fisheries in France in the 1930s and decades of work in grass roots mobilization in Latin America, led him to the realization that the traditional economic schemes that focus only on growth and wealth accumulation were inadequate to address human needs. In response, Lebret introduced the significant idea of human economy, which goes beyond the mere 'integration of the human element into the social sciences' to be 'an economy whose very functioning . . . would be favourable to human development' which offers 'the greatest possible number of people, a fully human life.' Lebret's understanding of a fully human life was grounded in human dignity and involves cultural, economic, political, social and spiritual dimensions." See Keleher, "Development of Every Person," 29.

73. Nzamujo, "Songhai," 8.

74. Ibid.

Conclusion

1. Cavanaugh, "Church in the Streets," 385.

2. For a more extended reflection on the methodological, metaphysical, moral, and epistemological claims behind my use of "story," see Katongole, *Journey of Reconciliation*, Introduction, xvii–xxii.

3. Emmanuel Kataliko, Christmas message, 1999, quoted in Katongole, *Born from Lament*, 125–26.

4. Selasi, "Do Not Ask Me."

5. See Katongole, "African Theological Imagination." In this regard, the reader will detect numerous connections especially between *The Sacrifice of Africa* (2011), *Born from Lament* (2017), and *Who Are My People?* In fact, as my friend Stan Ilo has suggested, the three form a trilogy of Faith (*The Sacrifice*), Hope (*Born from Lament*), and Love (*Who Are My People?*).

6. Appiah, *In My Father's House*, 179.

7. See their website at www.bethanylandinstitute.org.

8. For more on this, see "How Reconciliation Saved My Scholarship."

Afterword

1. A different event from the one narrated earlier in chapter 3, which took place at St. Joseph's School in Rwanda.

BIBLIOGRAPHY

Achebe, Chinua. *Home and Exile*. New York: Penguin Books, 2001.

Adibe, Jideofor. "Africa without Africans." In *Who Is an African? Identity, Citizenship and the Making of the Africa-Nation*, edited by Jideofor Adibe, 16–28. London: Adonis and Abbey, 2009.

ALARM (African Leadership and Reconciliation Ministries). *Restoring the Beauty and Blessing of Ethnic Diversity*. Nairobi: Africa International University, Nairobi Evangelical Graduate School of Theology, 2010.

Anderson, Benedict. *Imagined Communities: Reflections on the Origin and Spread of Nationalism*. London: Verso, 1983.

Anderson, Jon Lee. "The Mission: A Last Defense against Genocide." *New Yorker*, October 20, 2014. www.newyorker.com/magazine/2014/10/20/mission-3.

Appiah, Anthony. *In My Father's House: Africa in the Philosophy of Culture*. New York: Oxford University Press, 1992.

———. *The Lies That Bind: Rethinking Identity, Creed, Country, Color, Class, Culture*. New York: Liveright, 2018.

Archibold, Guillermo. "Pemasky en Kuna Yala: Protegiendo a la Madre Tierra . . . y a sus hijos." In *Hacia una Centroamérica verde: Seis casos de conservación integrada*, edited by Stanley Heckadon Moreno et al., 37–52. San José, Costa Rica: Departamento Ecuménico de Investigaciones, 1993.

Asamoah-Gyadu, J. Kwabena. "Bediako of Africa: A Late 20th Century Outstanding Theologian and Teacher." *Mission Studies* 26 (2009): 5–16.

Ashforth, Adam. *Witchcraft, Violence and Democracy in South Africa*. Chicago: University of Chicago Press, 2004.

Associated Press. "Catholic Church in Rwanda Apologizes for Role in 1994 Genocide." Vatican Radio, November 22, 2016. http://en.radiovaticana.va/news/2016/11/22/catholic_church_in_rwanda_apologises_for_role_in_genocide/1273928.

Barankitse, Marguerite. Testimony at Together in Hope event, Malmo, Sweden, October 31, 2016. www.facebook.com/lutheranworld/videos/16214435648 22945/?hc_ref=ARSPHM3dlPQ3MNjUT8RHA9L579E3PxL_KuZ5X vBCswsO8s9yCEoukrToE-Thm9wp0.

Bartholomäus, Lore. *Camille de Lellis: Serviteur des malades*. Strasbourg: Éditions du Signe, 1995.

Bediako, Kwame. *Christianity in Africa: The Renewal of a Non-Western Religion*. Edinburgh: Edinburgh University Press, 1997.

———. *Theology and Identity: The Impact of Culture upon Christian Thought in the Second Century and in Modern Africa*. Oxford: Regnum, 1992.

———. "Understanding African Theology in the 20th Century." *Bulletin for Contextual Theology in Southern Africa and Africa* 3, no. 2 (June 1996): 1–11.

Bevans, Stephen B., ed. *Mission and Culture: The Louis J. Luzbetak Lectures*. Maryknoll, NY: Orbis, 2012.

Boff, Leonardo. *Cry of the Earth, Cry of the Poor*. Maryknoll, NY: Orbis, 1997.

Bongmba, Elias. "Land and Authority in Postcolonial Cameroon." Contending Modernities, May 8, 2017. https://contendingmodernities.nd.edu/field-notes/land-authority-postcolonial-cameroon/.

Brenner, Louis. "Reading Mudimbe as a Historian." *Journal of African Cultural Studies* 17, no. 1 (2006): 67–80. www.tandfonline.com/doi/full/10.1080/0090988052000344657?src=recsys.

Bujo, Bénézet. "An Enthusiast of African Theology." In *African Theology in the Twenty-First Century: The Contribution of the Pioneers*, edited by Bénézet Bujo, vol. 1, 16–38. Nairobi: Paulines, 2011.

Campbell, William S. *Paul's Gospel in an Intercultural Context: Jew and Gentile in the Letter to the Romans*. New York: Peter Lang, 1991.

Carayannis, Tatiana, and Louisa Lombard. "A Concluding Note on the Failure and Future of Peacebuilding in CAR." In *Making Sense of the Central African Republic*, edited by Tatiana Carayannis and Louisa Lombard, 319–41. London: Zed Books, 2015.

———, eds. *Making Sense of the Central African Republic*. London: Zed Books, 2015.

Carney, J. J. "A Generation after Genocide: Catholic Reconciliation in Rwanda." *Theological Studies* 76, no. 4 (2015): 785–812.

Cavanaugh, William T. "The Church in the Streets: Eucharist and Politics." *Modern Theology* 30, no. 2 (2014): 384–402.

———. *Theo-Political Imagination: Discovering the Liturgy as a Political Act in an Age of Global Consumerism*. Edinburgh: T&T Clark, 2002.

Chabal, Patrick, and Jean-Pascal Daloz. *Africa Works: Disorder as Political Instrument*. London: International African Institute in association with Indiana University Press, 1999.

Chesterton, G. K. *Saint Thomas Aquinas*. New York: Doubleday, 1956.

Chowdhury, Anis. "Hunger in Africa, Land of Plenty." Share the World's Resources website, October 18, 2017. www.sharing.org/information-centre/articles/hunger-africa-land-plenty.

Conrad, Jane. "The African Condition: A Political Diagnosis by Ali A. Mazrui." *Canadian Journal of African Studies / Revue Canadienne des Études Africaines* 16, no. 1 (1982): 186–88.

Dalby, Ned. "A Multifaceted Business: Diamonds in the Central African Republic." In *Making Sense of the Central African Republic*, edited by Tatiana Carayannis and Louisa Lombard, 123–41. London: Zed Books, 2015.

Davidson, Basil. *Black Man's Burden: Africa and the Curse of the Nation-State*. New York: Three Rivers Press, 1992.

Davis, Mike. *Planet of Slums*. New York: Verso, 2006.

Development Initiatives. *Global Nutrition Report 2017: Nourishing the SDGs*. Bristol: Development Initiatives, 2017.

Dusengumuremyi, Jean d'Amour. *No Greater Love: Testimonies on the Life and Death of Felicitas Niyetegeka*. Lake Oswego, OR: Dignity Press, 2015.

Elizondo, Virgilio. *The Future Is Mestizo: Life Where Cultures Meet*. Boulder: University Press of Colorado, 2000.

English, Fenwick W. "A Critical Appraisal of Sara Lawrence-Lightfoot's Portraiture as a Method of Educational Research." *Educational Researcher* 29, no. 7 (2000): 21–26.

Eze, Emmanuel C., ed. *Race and the Enlightenment: A Reader*. Oxford: Blackwell, 1996.

Fasholé-Luke, Edward W. "The Quest for an African Christian Theology." *Ecumenical Review* 27, no. 3 (1975): 259–69.

Ferdinando, Keith. "Christian Identity in the African Context: Reflections on Kwame Bediako's *Theology and Identity*." *Journal of the Evangelical Theological Society* 50, no. 1 (March 2007): 121–43.

Fielder, Rachel Nyangondwe. *A History of the Circle of Concerned African Women Theologians, 1989–2007*. Oxford: African Books Collective, 2017.

Filipek, Stanislas. "The Path of Hope for Rwanda." Society of the Catholic Apostolate, Asia Oceania, E-Bulletin #133, 2014, reposted from Pallottines, Society of the Catholic Apostolate, website, May 3, 2014.

Fleshman, Michael. "Saving Africa's Forests, the 'Lungs of the World.'" *Africa Renewal*, January 2008. www.un.org/africarenewal/magazine/january-2008 /saving-africa's-forests-'lungs-world'.

Foreign Policy. "The Prospect/FP Top 100 Public Intellectuals." October 14, 2005. https://foreignpolicy.com/2005/10/14/the-prospectfp-top-100-public -intellectuals/.

Fraiture, Pierre-Philippe. *V. Y. Mudimbe: Undisciplined Africanism*. Liverpool: Liverpool University Press, 2013.

Fratkin, Elliot, and Sean Redding, eds. "Land Disputes and Displacement in Postconflict Africa." Special issue, *African Studies Review* 60, no. 3 (December 2017).

Geschiere, Peter. *The Modernity of Witchcraft: Politics and the Occult in Postcolonial Africa*. Charlottesville: University Press of Virginia, 1997.

Gifford, Paul. *Christianity, Development and Modernity in Africa*. New York: Oxford University Press, 2016.

Gourevitch, Philip. *We Wish to Inform You That Tomorrow We Will Be Killed with Our Families: Stories from Rwanda*. New York: Farrar, Straus and Giroux, 1998.

Grosfoguel, Ramon. "The Epistemic Decolonial Turn." *Cultural Studies* 21, nos. 2–3 (2007): 211–33.

Hastings, Adrian. *African Christianity: An Essay in Interpretation*. London: Geoffrey Chapman, 1976.

Hatzfeld, Jean. *Machete Season: The Killers in Rwanda Speak*. New York: Farrar, Straus and Giroux, 2005.

Hauerwas, Stanley, and William H. Willimon. *Resident Aliens: Life in the Christian Colony*. Nashville, TN: Abingdon Press, 1989.

Hebblethwaite, Peter. "In Rwanda, 'Blood Is Thicker Than Water—Even the Water of Baptism.'" *National Catholic Reporter*, June 3, 1994.

Hegel, Georg Wilhelm Friedrich. *The Philosophy of History*. Translated by J. Sibree. New York: Dover, 1956.

Hendrix, Cullen S., and Sarah M. Glaser. "Trends and Triggers: Climate, Climate Change, and Civil Conflict in Sub-Saharan Africa." *Political Geography* 26, no. 6 (2007): 695–71.

Heuertz, Chris. "'God Is Innocent': Rwamasirabo on the Genocide in the Church at Nyange, Rwanda." *Red Letter Christians*, August 7, 2013. www.redletterchristians.org/god-is-innocent-rwamasirabo-on-the-genocide-in-the-church-at-nyange-rwanda/.

Horning, Nadia Rabesahala. *The Politics of Deforestation in Africa: Madagascar, Tanzania, and Uganda*. Cham, Switzerland: Spring International, 2018.

Josephat, Musasizi. "Deforestation in Uganda: Population Increase, Forest Loss and Climate Change." *Environmental Risk Assessment and Remediation* 2, no. 2 (2018): 46–50. www.alliedacademies.org/articles/deforestation-in-uganda-population-increase-forests-loss-and-climate-change-10008.html.

Judiciary of the Republic of Uganda. "The Land Inquiry Commission Sworn-In." Judiciary of the Republic of Uganda website, February 22, 2017. http://judiciary.go.ug/data/news/298/359/The%20Land%20Inquiry%20Commission%20Sworn-in.html.

Kabyana, Danson Sylvester. "Okot p'Bitek's Diagnostic Poetics and the Quest for an African Revolution in *Song of Lawino and Song of Ocol*." In *Decolonisation Pathways: Postcoloniality, Globalization, and African Development*, edited by Jimmy Spire Ssentongo, 17–47. Kampala: Center for African Studies, Uganda Martyrs University, 2018.

Kamaara, Eunice. "Towards Christian National Identity in Africa: A Historical Perspective to the Challenge of Ethnicity to the Church in Kenya." *Studies in World Christianity* 16, no. 2 (2010): 126–44.

Katongole, Emmanuel M. "African Theological Reimagination through Stories: How My Mind Has (Not) Changed." In *Faith in Action*, vol. 3, *Reimagining the Mission of the Church in Education, Politics, and Servant Leadership in Africa*, edited by Stan Chu Ilo, Nora K. Nonterah, Ikenna U. Okafor, Justin Clemency Nabushawo, and Idara Out, 39–57. Nairobi: Paulines, 2020.

———. *Beyond Universal Reason: The Relation between Religion and Ethics in the Work of Stanley Hauerwas*. Notre Dame, IN: University of Notre Dame Press, 2000.

———. *Born from Lament: The Theology and Politics of Hope in Africa*. Grand Rapids, MI: Eerdmans, 2017.

———. "Christianity, Tribalism and the Rwanda Genocide: A Catholic Reassessment of Christian Social Responsibility." In *A Future for Africa: Critical Essays in Christian Social Imagination*, edited by Emmanuel Katongole, 95–117. Scranton, PA: University of Scranton Press, 2005.

———. "Hauerwasian Hooks and the Christian Social Imagination." In *God, Truth, and Witness: Essays in Conversation with Stanley Hauerwas*, edited by Greg Jones, Reinhard Hütter, and C. Rosalee Velloso Ewell. Grand Rapids, MI: Brazos, 2005. Reprinted in *A Future for Africa: Critical Essays in Christian Social Imagination*, by Emmanuel Katongole, chap. 10 (Scranton, PA: University of Scranton Press, 2005).

———. "How Reconciliation Saved My Scholarship." In *Public Intellectuals and the Common Good: Christian Living for Human Flourishing*, edited by Todd C. Ream, Jerry Pattengale, and Christopher J. Devers, chap. 6. Downers Grove, IL: InterVarsity Press, 2021.

———. *The Journey of Reconciliation: Groaning for a New Creation in Africa*. Maryknoll, NY: Orbis, 2017.

———. *Mirror to the Church: Resurrecting Faith after Genocide in Rwanda*. With Jonathan Wilson-Hartgrove. Grand Rapids, MI: Zondervan, 2009.

———. *The Sacrifice of Africa: A Political Theology for Africa*. Grand Rapids, MI: William B. Eerdmans, 2011.

———. "Threatened with Resurrection." In *The Journey of Reconciliation: Groaning for a New Creation in Africa*, 104–12. Maryknoll, NY: Orbis, 2017.

Katongole, Emmanuel, and Chris Rice. *Reconciling All Things: A Christian Vision for Justice, Peace and Healing*. Westmount, IL: InterVarsity Press, 2008.

Keleher, Lori. "Development of Every Person and of the Whole Person." In *Routledge Handbook of Development Ethics*, edited by Jay Drydyk and Lori Keleher, 29–34. New York: Routledge, 2018.

Kilembe, Faouzi. "Local Dynamics in the PK5 District of Bangui." In *Making Sense of the Central African Republic*, edited by Tatiana Carayannis and Louisa Lombard, 76–101. London: Zed Books, 2015.

Lacger, Louis de. *Ruanda*. Rwanda: Kabgayi, 1959.

Lawrence-Lightfoot, Sara, and Jessica Hoffman Davis. *The Art and Science of Portraiture*. San Francisco: Jossey-Bass, 1997.

Lombard, Louisa. "The Autonomous Zone Conundrum: Armed Conservation and Rebellion in North-Eastern CAR." In *Making Sense of the Central African Republic*, edited by Tatiana Carayannis and Louisa Lombard, 142–65. London: Zed Books, 2015.

Lombard, Louisa, and Tatiana Carayannis. "Making Sense of CAR: An Introduction." In *Making Sense of the Central African Republic*, edited by Tatiana Carayannis and Louisa Lombard, 1–16. London: Zed Books, 2015.

Longman, Timothy. *Christianity and Genocide in Rwanda*. African Studies 112. New York: Cambridge University Press, 2010.

Lowery, Stephanie A. *Identity and Ecclesiology: Their Relationship among Select African Theologians*. Eugene, OR: Pickwick, 2017.

Lubov, Deborah Castellano. "'Church Is to Be Field Hospital,' Pope Reminds Pilgrims from Middle East, Egypt, Holy Land." *Zenit*, August 9, 2017. https://zenit.org/articles/church-is-to-be-field-hospital-pope-reminds -middle-east-pilgrims/.

Lund, Christian, Rie Odgaard, and Espen Sjaastad. "Land Rights and Land Conflicts in Africa: A Review of Issues and Experiences." Report for the Danish Ministry of Foreign Affairs, coordinated by Danish Institute for International Studies. https://pure.diis.dk/ws/files/68278/Land_rights_and _land_conflicts_in_Africa_a_review_of_issues_and_experiences.pdf.

Maathai, Wangari. *Replenishing the Earth: Spiritual Values for Healing Ourselves and the World*. New York: Doubleday, 2010.

Magesa, Laurenti. "African Spirituality and the Environment: Some Principles, Theses, and Orientations." *Hekima Review* 53 (2005): 119–28.

Maluleke, Tinyiko S. "Identity and Integrity in African Theology: A Critical Analysis." *Religion and Theology* 8, no. 1 (2001): 26–41.

———. "In Search of the True Character of African Christian Identity: A Review of the Theology of Kwame Bediako." *Missionalia* 25, no. 2 (1997): 210–19.

Mamdani, Mahmood. *When Victims Become Killers: Colonialism, Nativism, and the Genocide in Rwanda*. Princeton, NJ: Princeton University Press, 2002.

Marchal, Roland. "Being Rich, Being Poor: Wealth and Fear in the Central African Republic." In *Making Sense of the Central African Republic*, edited by Tatiana Carayannis and Louisa Lombard, 53–75. London: Zed Books, 2015.

Martin, James. *This Our Exile: A Spiritual Journey with the Refugees of East Africa*. Maryknoll, NY: Orbis, 2011.

Martin, John. "Rwanda: Why?" *Transformation* 12, no. 2 (1995): 1–3.

Mayiga, Charles Peter. "Reasons Land Conflicts Are Rampant in Uganda." *Daily Monitor*, June 26, 2017. www.monitor.co.ug/OpEd/Commentary/Reasons

-land-conflicts-are-rampant-in-Uganda/689364-3988562-7njo8uz/index
.html.

Mazrui, Ali. "The Re-invention of Africa: Edward Said, V. Y. Mudimbe, and Beyond." *Research in African Literatures* 36, no. 3 (2005): 68–82.

Mbeki, Thabo. "I Am an African." Speech to the African National Congress in
Cape Town on May 8, 1996, on the occasion of the passing of the new Constitution of South Africa. www.youtube.com/watch?v=dCeLwTITRoQ.
Transcript at https://web.archive.org/web/20141018182833/http://www
.anc.org.za/show.php?id=4322.

Mbembe, Achille. *On the Postcolony*. Johannesburg: Wits University Press, 2015.

Mbiti, John S. *African Religions and Philosophy*. Oxford: Heinemann, 1969.

McKibben, Bill. *Eaarth: Making Life on a Tough New Planet*. New York: Times
Books, 2010

Mires, Fernando. *El discurso de la naturaleza: Ecología y política en América Latina*.
San José, Costa Rica: Departamento Ecuménico de Investigaciones, 1990.

Muchie, Mammo. "Many into One Africa, One into Many Africans." *African
Renaissance* 1, no. 2 (2004): 24–30.

Mudimbe, V. Y. *The Idea of Africa*. Bloomington: Indiana University Press, 1995.

———. *The Invention of Africa: Gnosis, Philosophy, and the Order of Knowledge*.
Bloomington: Indiana University Press, 1988.

———. *Parables and Fables: Exegesis, Textuality, and Politics in Central Africa*.
Madison: University of Wisconsin Press, 1991.

———. *Tales of Faith: Religion as Political Performance in Central Africa*. London:
Athlone Press, 1997.

Mugambwa, J. "A Comparative Analysis of Land Tenure Law Reform in Uganda
and Papua New Guinea." *Journal of South Pacific Law* 11, no. 1 (2007):
39–55.

Muggah, Robert, and David Kilcullen. "These Are Africa's Fastest-Growing
Cities—and They'll Make or Break the Continent." World Economic
Forum, May 4, 2016. www.weforum.org/agenda/2016/05/africa-biggest
-cities-fragility/.

Ndebesa, Mwambutsya. "Understanding the Meaning of Land." Comment in
The Independent, August 3, 2017. www.independent.co.ug/comment-under
standing-meaning-land/.

Ndlovu-Gatsheni, Sabelo J. "Ali A. Mazrui on the Invention of Africa and Postcolonial Predicaments: 'My Life Is One Long Debate.'" *Third World Quar-
terly* 36, no. 2 (2015): 205–22.

———. "'My Life Is One Long Debate': Ali A. Mazrui on the Invention of Africa and Postcolonial Predicaments." Public lecture presented at the University of the Free State, Bloemfontein, South Africa, October 30, 2014.
www.ufs.ac.za/docs/librariesprovider20/centre-for-africa-studies-docu
ments/all-documents/mazrui-lecture-2032-eng.pdf?sfvrsn=f836fb21_0.

Niebuhr, Richard. *Christ and Culture*. New York: Harper and Row, 1975.

Nixon, Rob. *Slow Violence and the Environmentalism of the Poor*. Cambridge, MA: Harvard University Press, 2011.

Nzamujo, Godfrey. "Songhai: Africa, It Is Our Time Now." Unpublished translation of Godfrey Nzamujo, *Songhaï: L'Afrique maintenant!* (Paris: Éditions du Cerf, 2016).

———. "Using Agriculture to Challenge Africa's Triple Threat." TEDx Ikoyi Talk. www.youtube.com/watch?v=Caw2htKiT0I.

O'Brien, Kevin. *The Violence of Climate Change: Lessons of Resistance from Nonviolent Activists*. Washington, DC: Georgetown University Press, 2017.

Oduyoye, Mercy Amba. "Reflections from a Third World Woman's Perspective: Women's Experience and Liberation Theologies." In *Irruption of the Third World: Challenge to Theology*, edited by V. Fabella and S. Torres, 246–55. Maryknoll, NY: Orbis Books.

Okot, Betty. "Uganda: Breaking the Links between the Land and the People." International Institute for Environment and Development, March 11, 2013. www.iied.org/uganda-breaking-links-between-land-people.

Parenti, Christian. *Tropic of Chaos: Climate Change and the New Geography of Violence*. New York: Nation Books, 2011.

p'Bitek, Okot. *Song of Lawino and Song of Ocol*. Oxford: Heinemann, 1984.

Pobee, John Samuel. *Giving Account of Faith and Hope in Africa*. Eugene, OR: Wipf and Stock, 2017.

———. "I Am First an African and Second a Christian." *Indian Missiological Review* 10, no. 3 (1989): 268–77.

Pope Francis. "A Big Heart Open to God: An Interview with Pope Francis." Interview by Antonio Spadaro. *America Magazine*, September 30, 2013. www.americamagazine.org/faith/2013/09/30/big-heart-open-god-interview-pope-francis.

———. *Laudato Si': On Care for Our Common Home*. Vatican City: Libreria Editrice Vaticana, 2015.

Potiguara, Eliane. *A terra é a mãe do Indio*. Rio de Janeiro: Grumin, 1989.

Prioul, Christian. *Entre Oubangui et Chari vers 1890*. Vol. 6. Paris: Societé d'ethnologie, 1981.

Prunier, Gerard. *The Rwanda Crisis: History of a Genocide, 1959–1994*. Kampala: Fountain, 1995.

Q-News. 2000. "Mazrui: The Tributes." No. 321 (July): 24–25.

Racelma, Kaci. "Towards African Cities without Slums." *Africa Renewal*, April 2012. www.un.org/africarenewal/magazine/april-2012/towards-african-cities-without-slums.

Refugee Law Project. "Border or Ownership Question: The APAA Land Dispute." Refugee Law Project, Situation Brief, September 9, 2012. www.refugeelawproject.org/files/ACCS_activity_briefs/The_Amuru_and_Adjumani_land_dispute.pdf.

Refugee Law Project and Advisory Consortium on Conflict Sensitivity. "'Shoot Us All Down': The Lakang and Apaa Land Conflict." 2011. www.youtube .com/watch?v=2IJUP4xuHp8.

Rittner, Carol, John K. Roth, and Wendy Whitworth, eds. *Genocide in Rwanda: Complicity of the Churches?* St. Paul, MN: Paragon House, 2004.

Romero, Oscar. *Violence of Love.* Compiled and translated by James R. Brockman. Maryknoll, NY: Orbis, 2004.

Sachs, Jeffrey D. *The End of Poverty.* New York: Penguin, 2006.

Said, Edward W. *Orientalism.* New York: Pantheon, 1978.

Sankara, Thomas. *Thomas Sankara Speaks: The Burkina Faso Revolution, 1983– 1987.* New York: Pathfinder Books, 1988.

Schreiter, Robert J., ed. *The Faces of Jesus in Africa.* Maryknoll, NY: Orbis, 1991.

Seah, Audrey. "Reconciliation after Betrayal and Violence: Lessons from the Church in Post-genocide Rwanda." *Liturgy* 34, no. 1 (2019): 48–57. www .tandfonline.com/doi/full/10.1080/0458063X.2019.1559618.

Selasi, Taiye. "Don't Ask Where I'm From, Ask Where I'm a Local." TED Talk, 2014. https://video.search.yahoo.com/search/video?fr=mcafee&p=taye +selasi+ted+talk#id=1&vid=22a1c8f2b954d6b4bf25d4566f4f654e&action =view.

Serequebarhan, Tsenay. "Reflections on 'In My Father's House.'" *Research in African Literatures* 27, no. 1 (1996): 110–18.

Shorter, Alyward. *Christianity and the African Imagination: After the African Synod. Resources for Inculturation.* Nairobi: Paulines, 1999.

Sibomana, André. *Hope for Rwanda: Conversations with Laure Guilbert and Hervé Deguine.* Eugene, OR: Wipf and Stock, 1999.

Smith, Stephen W. "CAR's History: The Past of a Tense Present." In *Making Sense of the Central African Republic,* edited by Tatiana Carayannis and Louisa Lombard, 17–52. London: Zed Books, 2015.

———. "The Elite's Road to Riches in a Poor Country." In *Making Sense of the Central African Republic,* edited by Tatiana Carayannis and Louisa Lombard, 102–22. London: Zed Books, 2015.

Soyinka, Wole. *Of Africa.* New Haven, CT: Yale University Press, 2012.

Ssentongo, Jimmy Spire. "Spaces for Pluralism in 'Ethnically Sensitive' Communities in Uganda: The Case of the Kibaale District." PhD diss., University of Humanistic Studies, Utrecht, 2015.

Stinton, Diane B. *Jesus of Africa: Voices of Contemporary African Christology.* Maryknoll, NY: Orbis, 2004.

Suliman, Mohamed. *Ecology, Politics and Violent Conflict.* London: Zed; Development and Peace Foundation; Institute for African Alternatives, 1999.

Tarimo, Aquiline. "Ethnicity, Common Good and the Church in Contemporary Africa." *Africa Tomorrow* 1, no. 2 (July 2000): 153–80.

Tarus, David K., and Julius Gathogo. "Conquering Africa's Second Devil: Ecclesiastical Role in Combating Ethnic Bigotry." *Online Journal of African Affairs* 5 (2016): 8–15.

Tarus, David K., and Stephanie Lowery. "African Theologies of Identity and Community: The Contributions of John Mbiti, Jesse Mugambi, Vincent Mulago, and Kwame Bediako." *Open Theology* 3 (2017): 305–20.

Towa, Marcien. "Propositions sur l'identite culturelle." *Presence Africaine* 109 (1979): 82–91.

Uzukwu, Elochukwu E. *A Listening Church: Autonomy and Communion in African Churches*. Eugene, OR: Wipf and Stock, 2006.

Volf, Miroslav. *Exclusion and Embrace: A Theological Exploration of Identity, Otherness, and Reconciliation*. Nashville, TN: Abingdon, 1996.

———. "Soft Difference: Theological Reflections on the Relation between Church and Culture in 1 Peter." *Ex Auditu* 10 (1994): 15–30.

Wagenaar, Hinne. "Theology, Identity and the Pre-Christian Past." *International Review of Mission* 88, no. 351 (1999): 364.

Walls, Andrew. "The Ephesian Moment." In *The Cross-Cultural Process in Christian History: Studies in the Transmission and Appropriation of Faith*, 72–81. Maryknoll, NY: Orbis, 2002.

———. "The Gospel as Prisoner and Liberator of Culture." In *New Directions in Mission and Evangelization*, vol. 3, *Faith and Culture*, edited by James A. Scherer and Stephen B. Bevans, 17–28. Maryknoll, NY: Orbis, 1999.

Wooden, Cindy. "Pope Apologizes for Catholics' Participation in Rwanda Genocide." *National Catholic Reporter*, March 20, 2017. www.ncronline.org /blogs/francis-chronicles/pope-apologizes-catholics-participation-rwanda -genocide.

World Bank. "While Poverty in Africa Has Declined, Number of Poor Has Increased." 2016 Report. www.worldbank.org/en/region/afr/publication /poverty-rising-africa-poverty-report.

Wrong, Michela. *It's Our Turn to Eat: The Story of a Kenyan Whistle-Blower*. New York: HarperCollins, 2008.

INDEX

The letter *t* following a page number denotes a table; the letter f indicates a figure.

Abrahamic revolution, 52, 54–55, 63
adaptation theology, 192n26
Adibe, Jideofor, 190n35
Africa: attitude to nature, 134, 141;
    cartography of, 20; Christianity
    in, 41, 174–75; colonial era,
    19–20, 21; crisis of belonging, 3,
    135, 141–42, 143; ecological crisis,
    6, 131–36, 158, 170, 171–72, 173,
    198n12; economic development,
    136, 158; etymology, 19; external
    conceptualization of, 19–20, 21;
    food insecurity, 156–57; GDPs,
    157; hunger in, 157; ideological
    mindset, 146; as "imagined"
    reality, 16, 17, 20, 23; interaction
    of civilizations in, 19, 21, 23,
    25–26; Islamization of, 20;
    modernity, 2, 3, 21–22, 135, 142,
    148, 152–53, 169, 170, 172, 174;
    nation-states, 13, 172, 198n11;
    native spiritualities, 139, 141;
    natural resources, 158; pilgrim-
    ages to, 177; postcolonial
    condition, 21–23; poverty, 148,
    149, 157, 160; religions, 19, 39;

rituals, 199n44; scholarship,
    15–16; slums, 132, 133, 198n5;
    tariffs, 152; urban population,
    133, 149; values of communality
    and solidarity, 12; violence, 3,
    12–13, 73, 171, 173–74, 176; in
    Western imagination, 12, 16, 17,
    19, 42–43, 160–61; as zone of
    exile, 147, 153
African Christian identity: as a
    journey, 5; material basis for, 40;
    perception of, 46; problem of, 31,
    40, 175; in relation to other iden-
    tities, 5; as spiritual identity, 39
African identity: basis of, 26–27; vs.
    Christian identity, 1–2, 3–4,
    36–37, 45–46; ethnicity and, 25;
    evolution of, 41–42; as founda-
    tion of new modernity, 23–24; as
    imagination, 191n36; material
    realities and, 29–30; meaning of,
    13–14, 15, 30; multiplicity of,
    27–28; myth of racial unity and,
    24–25; as "natural" identity,
    42–43; pragmatic conception of,
    27; rejection of essentialism,

213

African identity (*cont.*)
190n35; studies of, 5, 14–15, 29,
38–39; theological approach to,
30–31, 37–38; tribe and, 14, 25;
Western perception of, 27
Africans, The: A Triple Heritage (TV
series), 18, 20
African solidarity, 27
African theology, 41, 42, 45
Amazon peoples, 139, 140
Amin, Idi, 154
Anderson, Benedict, 13
Annan, Kofi, 18
anthropocentricism, 137
anti-balaka violence, 111, 114, 116–17
Apaa land conflict, 200n52
Appiah, Fr. Anthony, 5, 176; on
"burden of ethnicity," 85, 87;
Christian activities, 174; critique
of racial unity, 24–25; on ideas of
race and tribe, 73; *In My Father's
House*, 24, 25, 26, 27–28, 30,
191n36; *The Lies That Bind*, 26,
27, 190n28, 191n36; polyglot
identity, 26; on Rwanda Genocide, 96; on spirituality, 85; story
of personal healing, 84–85, 86,
90, 95, 174; study of African identity, 15, 24–30; view of
Christianity, 45
Ashforth, Adam, 113, 114, 116

Bahnson, Fred, 138
Bamugemereire, Catherine, 200n52
Bangui, 103, 107–8, 110
Barankitse, Maggy: adopted children
of, 91; awards of, 90; exile in
Rwanda, 88–89, 90; influence of,
126, 178; invention of "new we,"
93, 95; on lies of ethnicity, 92;
Maison Shalom and, 88, 92–94;

memories of massacre, 91–92, 93;
Oasis of Peace and, 6, 88, 90;
reinvention of love, 90, 92, 94,
96, 174; reputation of, 90–91;
story of compassion, 89–90
Bayart, François, 103
Bediako, Kwame, 37–38, 39, 40, 46,
56
belonging, crisis of, 3, 135, 141–42, 143
Benin, 159, 162
Berry, Wendell, 138
Bethany Land Institute, 177
Boaz (biblical character), 183, 184
body of Christ, 53
Boff, Leonardo, 140, 142; *Cry of the
Earth, Cry of the Poor*, 139, 141
Boganda, Barthélemy, 105, 120
Bokassa, Jean-Bédel, 100–101
Bossemptele: mission and hospital at,
124, 125, 127, 128; Séléka violence
in, 124
Bozizé, François: military coup of,
101t, 111–12; presidency, 103, 105,
107
Bridget (Catholic lay leader), 109,
110–11, 112, 120
Bugesera district, 82, 84
Bujo, Bénézet, 45
Bukuru, Fr. Zacharie, 186
burden of ethnicity, 85, 87
burden of identity, 87, 90
Burkina Faso, 122
Burundi: Belgian rule, 91; Catholic
schools, 186–87; ethnic politics,
91, 92, 94, 176; formation of new
community in, 185–87; independence of, 91; Maison Shalom in,
95; religions of, 185; violence in,
73, 90, 91, 185
Buta Seminary, 186–87; "We have
won!" mural at, 187f

Camillians, 124, 125

Camillus de Lellis, Saint, 125, 126

Carayannis, Tatiana, 103, 106

Catholic Church: as an activity and a "moment," 59; care for the sick and poor, 125, 128–29; as Christ's body, 62; as community, 44, 54, 58, 63; complacency of, 49; as a field hospital, 129–30, 197n42; institutional weakness of, 120, 121–22; mission of, 58, 63, 130; as "a new clan," 45, 46, 63, 130; peacebuilding efforts, 119–20; prophetic role of, 123–24

Cavanaugh, William, 13

Center for Reconciliation of the Merciful Jesus, 83

Central African Republic (CAR): abandoned population, 106–9, 127; abuse of power in, 107; anti-balaka militias, 99–100, 109, 110–11, 116–17; autochthony in, 127–28; autonomous zone, 108; Catholic Church in, 105, 119–20; Christian population of, 119–20; colonial mentality of, 110, 112; concessionary companies, 100; disarmament policy, 106; displaced persons, 100; economy, 109, 110, 112–13; foreign interests in, 105–6; French colonization of, 100; future of, 121, 122; highway robbers, 116; history of, 100; humanitarian assistance to, 118–19; leadership crisis, 105, 107, 108, 119; magical faith in, 114–15, 116; map of, 102f; microdynamics of society, 104; militia groups, 106, 117; Muslim population, 109, 110, 111, 112–13, 127–28; National Council for Nonviolence, 111;
National Council for Youth, 114; national language, 109; natural resources, 99, 113; neighboring countries, 102f, 103; political development, 101, 103–6, 120, 128; Pope Francis's visit to, 120; post-independence history, 101t; religious war, 6, 100, 103, 111–12, 172; rural areas, 108–9; Séléka rebels, 99, 107–8, 109, 110, 112, 115–16; sense of insecurity, 113–14, 116–17, 129; Siriri group, 116; state building, 113; UN forces in, 105, 106; violence in, 104, 110–11, 113–17, 120–21; work ethics, 110; youth in, 114

Chabal, Patrick, 13

Chad, 103

Charismatic Renewal Movement, 84

Chenue, Marie-Dominique, 165

Christian faith, 52, 173

Christian identity: vs. African identity, 1–2, 3–4, 31, 36–37, 45–46; complexity of, 38, 182; culture and, 54–55, 63; dialectic of departure and belonging, 52, 53; dynamics of, 53–54; formation of, 38, 40, 50–51; Galilean Principle and, 55; in Greco-Roman Empire, 56; impact on violence, 3–4; Incarnation and, 55; as a journey, 5, 37, 44–45, 46, 55, 58, 60, 63, 175–76; material nature of, 40; as "Mestizo," 55–57; natural identity and, 40, 41–45, 46; reality of the church and, 61; relation to other identities, 40, 46; as spiritual identity, 37

Christianity: act of coming together in, 60–62; act of eating together in, 62, 185; in Africa, 1, 2–3, 182;

Christianity (*cont.*)
    denominations of, 181–82; dis-
    continuity of, 191n7; formation
    of, 38, 40; new form of com-
    munity, 4, 178–79; politics and,
    44; social role of, 35; two dif-
    ferent lifestyles, 60; as a verb, 45
Christian life: as a journey, 47, 51; as
    response to violence, 51–52
Christian theology, 3
Circle of African Women Theolo-
    gians, 192n19
cities, 151, 152
civilization, 142, 144–45
Clement of Alexandria, Saint, 191n7
climate change, 135–36, 138, 171–72,
    198n12, 198n15
colony, 58
compassion, 87–88
Congar, Yves, 165
Congo, 158, 175
Conrad, Jane, 190n26
Contending Modernities Research
    Project, 4, 7, 18
Cornelius (biblical character), 185
Creation, biblical account of, 137
cross, 53
cultural churches, 59

Dacko, David, 101t, 105, 106
Dalby, Ned, 106
Daloz, Jean-Pascal, 13
dance of nature, 159, 164, 165, 166–67,
    169
David (biblical character), 183–84
Davidson, Basil, 148
Davis, Mike: *Planet of Slums*, 132–33
deforestation, 133–34
Democratic Republic of Congo
    (DRC), 103

Derby, Idriss, 103
diagnostic poetics, 199n28
Djotodia, Michel, 99, 120
Dominicans, 164, 165
Duke University's Center for
    Reconciliation, 49

ecological violence, 6, 131, 134
economic development, ladder of,
    146–47
Elizondo, Virgilio, 5, 55, 56, 57
Emmanuel Community, 84, 85, 86, 96
Ephesian Moment, 59–60, 61, 62, 63
erosion of dignity, 161
eschatology, 126
Etchegaray, Roger, Cardinal, 1, 36
Ethiopia famine of 1983–85, 160, 161
ethnic identity, 25, 37, 44, 73–74, 75,
    96
ethnicity, 6, 43, 44, 73, 88, 95
ethnic violence, 69–70, 73, 96
ethnographic research, 7
Eucharist, 182

Fanon, Frantz, 117
Ferdinando, Keith, 46
Filipek, Fr. Stanislas, 82–83
food insecurity, 156, 157
Francis, Pope, 93; on account of
    Creation, 137; apology for the
    Rwanda Genocide, 194n2; call
    for spiritual conversion, 138–39;
    on ecological crisis, 138, 159, 168,
    169, 170, 177; on human rela-
    tionship with nature, 137–38;
    Laudato Si' encyclical, 135, 136,
    177; on mission of the Church,
    130, 197n42; opening of Jubilee
    Year of Mercy, 105; visit to the
    CAR, 120

French Equatorial Africa (AEF), 100, 109

Front Patriotique le Progres (FPP), 107

Galilean Principle, 55
Ganda people, 70
Genocide Convention, 12
Gentile Christians, 60, 61–62
Global Nutrition Report (2017), 156
God's love: invention of, 4, 63–64, 90, 92, 93, 94, 96; to the poor, the sick, and the vulnerable, 130; story of, 6, 92, 96, 97, 173, 174
Gospel, 57, 59–60, 175
Guerekoyame-Gbangou, Nicolas, 119
Gumba, Abel, 106
Gumba, Alex, 106–7, 108, 120, 127

Hamitic mythology, 17–18
Harnack, Adolf von, 39
Hauerwas, Stanley: on Christian life, 58, 63; on church, 58; influence of, 57; narrative methodology of, 28; *Resident Aliens*, 58; theological work of, 17, 31, 57–58
healing: as gift and mission, 84–85; in God's suffering, 95; of memories, 85; redemptive spaces for, 94; spirituality and, 87
Hegel, Georg Wilhelm Friedrich, 16, 17
Heilig Geest College, 11
Hellenistic society, 60
human economy, 201n72
Hutu people, 14, 18; identity of, 69–70, 71–72, 91, 96; marginalization of, 70; vs. Tutsi, 70, 71

identity: burden of, 87, 90; citizenship and, 48; complexity of, 1–2; confused, 56; country of residence and, 47–48; cultural, 53–54, 70–71; discovering of true, 97; ethnicity and, 73; narrative role in, 191n36; nature of, 26, 175; place of birth and, 47; political, 69, 70–71; reinvention of, 94; religion and, 3, 47, 48, 49–50, 123; social division and, 27; *some kind of*, 182, 183; violence and, 3; as zero-sum game, 69
Igbo people, 70
Incarnation, 55
indigenizing principle, 59
indigenous peoples: attitude to nature, 140; celebration and dancing, 140; experience of God, 140–41; mysticism of, 140; progress and, 142–43, 144–45, 146; sense of belonging, 143; spirituality of, 139; wisdom of, 139–40
Institute for Christian Reconciliation, 177
integral ecology, 159, 168, 170
integral human development, 201n72
Interfaith Platform (IFP), 119, 121
Israelites, 183
Ivory Coast, ethnic violence in, 73

Jackson, Wes, 138
Jennings, Willie, 181
Jesse (biblical character), 183
Jesus: in Africa, faces of, 41; identity of, 41, 184; self-sacrifice of, 53
Jewish Christians, 60, 61–62
Jewish society, 60
John Paul II, Pope, 81

Jones, Greg, 50
Josephat, Musasizi, 133
Jubilee Year of Mercy, 105
Justin, Saint, 191n7

Kabuga district: healing ministry in,
    83–84, 94; shrine of Divine
    Mercy in, 83, 195n28
Kabyana, Danson Sylvester, 199n28
Kagame, Paul, 194n2
Kampala (city), and slums, 132, 149
Kataliko, Emmanuel, 175
KCCA (Kampala Capital City
    Authority), 152
Keleher, Lori, 201n72
Kembe, Stanislaus, 120
Kenya, ethnic violence in, 73
Kigali, and community center for
    Burundian refugees, 88
Kinvi, Fr. Bernard, 6, 178; account of
    violence, 124; awards of, 124, 127;
    background of, 124; father of,
    197n40; influence of, 128; local
    engagement, 127–28; loss of
    family members, 125–26; pastoral
    work in Bossemptele, 124–26,
    127, 128–29; politics of love, 129,
    130; spiritual formation, 126–27
Kobine Layama, Omar, 119
Kolingba, André, 101t
Kolingmba, 105
Komezubutwari Nyange (student
    organization), 76

Lacger, Louis de, 14, 70
land: economic value of, 153–54, 156;
    legislation, 154; people's attach-
    ment to, 155, 156; tenure system,
    154
land conflicts, 153, 155–56, 200n52

land reforms, 154–55, 156
landslides, 134, 135
Laudato Si' encyclical letter, 135,
    136, 177
Lawrence-Lightfoot, Sara, 7
Layama, Omar Kobine, 119
Lebret, Louis-Joseph, 165, 201n72
liberation theology, 192n19
"local" theology, 46
logic of poverty, 169
Lombard, Louisa, 103, 106, 108
love: as antidote to violence, 4–5, 6;
    celebration of, 89; vs. hatred, 89;
    identity and, 89; modernity and,
    148; politics of, 129, 130; spaces
    of redemptive and suffering,
    94–95; as true identity, 92. See
    also God's love; violence of love
Lowery, Stephanie, 43
Lumumba, Patrice, 122

Maathai, Wangari, 141, 158
Magesa, Laurenti, 142
Maison Shalom: children of, 94;
    establishment of, 88; expansion
    of, 92–94; graduation celebration
    at, 88–90, 95; headquarters, 94;
    spirituality of, 96–97; suppression
    of operations of, 95
Making Sense of the Central African
    Republic (Carayannis and
    Lombard), 106
Mali Empire, 19
Malube village, 131–32
Mamdani, Mahmood, 70–71, 72, 73,
    173; When Victims Become Killers,
    117
Mandela, Nelson, 122
Marchal, Roland, 113
Mayiga, Peter, 153

Mazrui, Ali: on African identity, 5, 14, 191n36; conceptualization of Africa, 19–24; critique of, 190n26; reputation of, 18; works of, 18, 21

Mbiti, John, 141

Mbiti, Quoting, 39

McKibben, Bill, 138

Médard Sané, Fr. Barwendé, 121, 129; on magical faith, 115; on new kind of imagination, 123; on problem of violence, 117; on prophetic role of the church, 123–24; social activity of, 111, 119; on "tiredness" of youth population, 114–15

Mestizo identity, 56, 57, 193n41

Ministry of Reconciliation under the Cross (MiParec), 185

Moabites, 183, 184

Modat, Fideli, 120

Mother Earth, 140

Mtingo, Francis, 114, 115, 117

Muchie, Mammo, 190n35

Mudimbe, Valentin, 14, 15–16; The Invention of Africa, 15, 23, 24

Mudimbe, Valery, 5, 46, 191n36, 192n26

Mulago, Vincent, 45, 46, 87, 192n26

Musekura, Célestin, 44

Musisi, Jennifer, 152

Mvukiyehe, Fr. Jean Baptiste: background of, 75, 81; ecclesiastical career of, 77, 80; education of, 75; memory of genocide, 74–76, 77, 80, 81; on "miracle" of Ruhango, 77–78; on reconciliation, 76; story of personal healing, 80, 81, 84, 86–87, 90, 95, 174

Naomi (biblical character): friendship with Ruth, 184–85; story of, 183, 184

Nateete slum, 132–33, 149, 151

nationality, vs. locality, 197n39

natural identity, 40, 41–45, 46, 50

nature, spiritual meaning of, 141

Ndadaye, Melchior, 91

Ndebesa, Mwambutsya, 155

Newtonian science, 166

"new we," invention of communities of, 93, 95, 178–79, 182

Niebuhr, Richard, 54

Nixon, Rob, 171, 198n12

Nkurunziza, Deusdedit R. K., 88, 95

Ntahompagaze, Melance, 185, 186

Ntarama church killings, 68

Nyamata church massacre, 67–68, 74, 96

Nyange church massacre, 68–69, 74, 96

Nyange St. Joseph's School killings, 74, 75–76

Nyarubuye church killings, 68

Nzamujo, Godfrey: career path, 161–62; on dance with nature, 164; Dominican background of, 164–65; economic views of, 201n72; education of, 162, 164; illness of, 168; influence of, 178; on life of Thomas Aquinas, 201n71; on logic of poverty, 169; on Newtonian science, 166; return to Africa, 162; on sin of the world, 168; on theological dimension of reality, 167; view of quantum physics, 166; work at Songhai Center, 6–7, 159, 160, 162–64, 165

Nzapalainga, Dieudonne, Cardinal, 119, 120

Oasis of Peace Center, 6, 88, 90
Obed (biblical character), 183, 184
Oduyoye, Mercy Amba, 192n19
Okot, Betty, 155, 156
Orpah (biblical character), 183

Pallotti, Vincent, 194n18
Pallottine missionary, 77, 79, 80, 81, 84, 194n18
Parenti, Christian, 198n11, 198n15
Patassé, Ange-Félix, 101t, 103, 105
Paul the Apostle, Saint, 52–53, 60, 61, 63, 90, 167, 185
Paul VI, Pope, and *Populorum Progresio* encyclical, 201n72
p'Bitek, Okot: *Song of Lawino and Song of Ocol*, 142–46, 148, 162, 169, 199n28
Peter the Apostle, Saint, 185
Pilgrimage of Pain and Hope to Uganda and Rwanda, 50
pilgrim principle, 59
Pobee, John Samuel, 42
postcolony, 22
poverty, trap of, 160–61
progress, idea of, 142

quantum physics, 166, 167

race/racism, 20, 24–25, 26
Rakkenes, Oystein, 90, 96
reconciliation, 49, 177
religion: ethnicity and, 53; violence and, 97
resident aliens, 58, 63
Restoring the Beauty and Blessing of Ethnic Diversity, 43

Rice, Chris, 49, 177
Romero: *Violence of Love*, 195n39
Romero, Oscar, 95, 97
Ruhango district: community at, 87; ministry of healing, 77–79, 80, 81, 82–83, 84, 94; refugees in, 82
Ruth (biblical character), 183–84, 185
Ruvunabagabo, Gerard, 79
Rwamasirabo, Aloys, 68
Rwanda: Christian population of, 193n1; colonial mythology, 71; ethnic division in, 70, 71–72, 85–86, 94; family life in, 33–34; Hutu-Tutsi divide, 34–35, 71, 72; identity politics, 69–70, 72, 85; reconciliation efforts, 76; refugees, 82; violence, 85–86
Rwanda Genocide: aftermath of, 62; Christianity and, 31, 36; clergy participation in, 68–69, 194n2; eyewitness accounts, 36; identity context, 5, 6, 56–57, 70, 171; international community and, 1, 12; killings in churches, 67–69, 194n4; memorials, 36; origin of, 14, 17; outbreak of, 11–12, 68, 82; political imagining of Rwanda and, 96; Pope apology for, 194n2; as postcolonial crisis, 3; Ruhango miracles, 77–79; theological issues raised by, 173, 176; violence of, 23, 29, 79, 172
Rwanda Patriotic Front (RPF), 75, 81, 82

Sachs, Jeff, 146, 147
Sacrifice of Africa, The (Katongole), 13, 22, 172
Said, Edward: *Orientalism*, 15, 17

Samba-Panza, Catherine, 100, 120
Sankara, Thomas, 74, 122
Schreiter, Robert: *The Faces of Jesus in Africa*, 41
Scrosoppi, Luigi, 126
Selasi, Taiye, 176, 197n39
Séléka movement: popular base of, 109, 110, 112; resistance to, 115–17; rise of, 103, 107–8; violence of, 110–11, 112, 115, 124
Seminarians of Buta, 126
Seromba, Athanase, 68, 69, 74, 96
Share the Blessings organization, 177
Sibomana, Father Andre, 62
slow violence, 134–35, 171, 198n12
slums, 132–33, 149–50, 198n5
Smith, Steven, 106
Soh Keugne Nouthak Jules, 104–5
Songhai Center: approach to wealth, 201n72; development of, 162; experiment of integral ecology, 168, 170; foundation of, 159; integrated production system, 163*f*; international recognition of, 164; as invention of a new modernity, 159–60, 170; microeconomy of, 164; mission of, 6–7, 159; new mindset of, 160–61, 169; as new synthesis, 169–70; "return" to the soil, 169; scientific innovativeness at, 166; as a "sermon," 165; spirituality of, 168; training program, 159, 162–63
Songhai Empire, 19, 160, 169
Song of Lawino and Song of Ocol (p'Bitek), 142–46, 148, 162, 169, 199n28
Soyinka, Wole, 21, 22, 172
spiritual insecurity, 113–14

spirituality: biblical sources of, 85; dimensions of, 164; healing and, 87; of native peoples, 139; as politics, 96–97, 175; vs. violence, 175
Stinton, Diane, 42; *Jesus of Africa*, 41
stories: of modernity, 2; power of, 95–96, 173, 178
structural adjustment programs (SAPs), 157
Sudan, 73, 103

Tarus, David Kirwa, 43
Tatian, 191n7
Tertullian, 191n7
theological portraiture, 7, 173
theology, 60
Thomas Aquinas, Saint, 164; *Summa Theologiae*, 201n71
Thomistic mystical revelation, 164–65
Timbuktu, 160
Touadéra, Faustin-Archange, 120
trees, symbolic meaning of, 158
tribal identity, 14, 25, 69–70
tribe/tribalism, 1, 3, 5, 6, 14, 26, 73
Tutsi people, 14, 18; vs. Hutu people, 70, 71; identity of, 69–70, 71–72, 91, 96
Twa people, 91

Uganda: deforestation, 133–34; economic opportunities, 34; everyday life, 131–32; land conflicts and reforms, 153, 154, 155–56, 200n52; landslides, 134, 135; slums, 132–33
UN Food and Agriculture Organization (FAO), 133
United Nations Development Program (UNDP), 164

United Nations Office for the Coordination of Humanitarian Affairs (OCHA), 118
Urbaniak, Fr. Stanislas, 77–78, 79, 82, 84, 86, 88, 96
urban life, 147, 150

village: backwardness of, 149–50; vs. city, 148–49; education in, 150–51; escape from, 151–52; hardship of life in, 150; identity, 152
violence: Christianity and, 2–3, 175; ecological forms of, 173, 198n15; identity and, 3, 69–70, 85–86;

love as antidote to, 4–5, 6; political, 172; resistance to, 2, 74; study of, 5–6; systemic, 171; tribalism and, 1, 3. *See also* slow violence
violence of love, 95, 97, 174, 195n39
Volf, Miroslav, 5, 52, 53, 54–55; *Exclusion and Embrace*, 51, 57

Walls, Andrew, 5, 59, 60
Wamala, Emmanuel, 181
Willimon, William H., 57, 58, 63
Wirzba, Norman, 138
World Bank Report (2016), 157
Wrong, Michele, 101

EMMANUEL KATONGOLE is professor of theology and peace studies at the Kroc Institute, Keough School of Global Affairs, and Department of Theology at the University of Notre Dame and Extraordinary Professor of Theology and Ecclesiology at the University of Stellenbosch in South Africa. He is author of several books, including *The Sacrifice of Africa: A Political Theology for Africa* and *Born from Lament: The Theology and Politics of Hope in Africa*.